Myra: October 1965

The police car drove westwards over the moors. It was late in the evening, and sunset had faded from the sky ahead. The clouds were grey on grey and raced with the cold northern wind over rough green scrub, tearing the coarse little bushes and ruffling the pools of standing water. There was nothing to block its path on these thirty-five miles of the East Lancs Road. The prison out there in the darkness lay low on the land.

From time to time, another vehicle came out of the black. The westernmost boundary of Manchester was left far behind. Then the car turned right and headed north on the final approach to Risley Remand Centre.

Inside sat three men and a woman. Under her white-blonde, firmly set hair, she had strong, boxy features and heavy-lidded eyes. She was smartly dressed in court shoes and a pencil skirt.

The car's lamps lit up a thirty-foot razor-topped fence – the prison's outermost perimeter. At its base were more spirals of wire. The structure loomed as the ground dropped lower. The car halted so that guards could identify the prisoner. The first gates opened and the car drove forward into what seemed like the bottom of a well, bricked in but open to the darkness above. The moor-facing gate shut behind with a clang.

***

The little round headlamps, lost in the open air, threw their dazzle on an inner gateway. The engine note swelled in the tight bright space. The second gate opened. The car chugged through to the compound inside, and stopped.

The front-seat passenger alighted. He walked round to the back right-hand door and assisted as the prisoner climbed out. A waiting officer in a navy skirt and jacket led her the fifteen-yard walk towards Risley's first locked door. The prisoner's shiny heels tap-tapped their way out of the world.

In the hallway, the glare from the broad flat lights overhead made her blink after night on the moors. Everything here was still new, for Risley had been open just a year. It wasn't long since the prisoner herself had been re-housed in the clearance of Gorton's slums, and moved with her boyfriend and elderly mother to a smart modern council place in Hattersley, just outside Manchester.

She was led down a passageway and into a carpeted office where she waited at a counter. On her right were shelves of toiletries for prisoners to purchase with their earnings: baby lotion, dandruff shampoo, toothpaste. There wasn't much space. The walls closed in.

The prisoner's hands were unchained. She was given a small towel, a bar of carbolic soap and a uniform dress which was bright, acidic orange. Told to remove all her clothes, she did so, and was handed a rough blue dressing gown. There was form-filling too, but as she was the only arrival, it only took moments to record her name, the date and the time. Joined by more officers now, she was led to a room filled with cages. Had she arrived in a vanload with others, she'd now be placed inside one, to wait while those ahead of her were processed. The cages were low and made out of wire, like chicken coops. Each woman sat with no space to change position, cross her legs, stretch her arms or stand. The wait could take hours. But she was alone and the officers marched her straight through.

The next room she entered was a bathroom, tiled, low-ceilinged and cold. It held a metal tub and stank of carbolic. In the tub was a couple of inches of water. The prisoner was ordered to bathe. While she knelt in the water, her set blonde hair was washed with soap. She dried herself on the thin towel. She put on the orange prison dress and rubbed at her scratchy, tar-scented tangle of hair.

In the next room, she saw the doctor. A black metal chair faced stirrups that hung from the ceiling. The doctor hoisted her legs into position, checked her pubic and head hair for lice and swabbed her internally to test for sexually transmitted disease. Her anus and vagina were checked for contraband items. Now she was ready for admission.

It was the night of October 11th, 1965. Prisoner W/605 Myra Hindley was in Risley on remand.

***

Other preparations for Hindley's arrival had also been made. News of her coming was known in the women's wing.

The newspapers were full of a murder in a council house in Manchester. It was four days since Hindley's boyfriend, Ian Brady, had been arrested. Not much was yet known to the public. But inside, rumours spread quickly. The enquiry was widening. Police had begun to suspect this quiet young man of involvement in other disappearances – the disappearances of children.

The horrific details of the Moors murders would soon be revealed to the world. But in prison there's trade: in tobacco, in drugs, in drink and information. Already, word had reached Risley that Hindley had committed crimes that were beyond comprehension.

***

Nicky Nicholls, aged twenty, was on remand in the women's wing charged with a minor offence – trying to break into a cotton mill in Bradford. She'd been caught before she managed to do it. She was a newcomer, but because she was quiet and polite, she had quickly become a trustee. This meant she was thought unlikely to cause trouble. Trustees performed tasks around the prison: painting, tidying, cooking. It gave them release from their cells, where everyone else spent twenty-three hours each day.

Nicky was fetched with another trustee. An unexpected task was explained to them. In twenty minutes' time, a new prisoner would arrive, to be placed in an isolation cell. The prisoner had not yet been convicted and her cell would be fitted with a lamp, a carpet and curtains.

The women's wing was never silent at night. Prisoners cried out in the dark. But now, the place was electric with menace. Behind locked doors, voices rose as Nicky walked along the upper landing. Rage sparked from woman to woman – the first yells rang out. Raw, tight faces stared from cells' wired grills.

On the empty cell's threshold were a small folded rug with a fringe, a green lamp and plain white curtains with hooks to be fitted to the bars on the window. The trustees picked them up and entered the cell. Nicky nearly dropped the heavy lamp because her fingers were trembling. "Take care," said the screw in the doorway. She fumbled her end as the two trustees rolled out the rug, stepping around in the tiny space to make sure it was down straight on the floor. She couldn't reach to hang up the curtains; the taller girl stretched and hooked them into place.

Now the cell was ready, but the two trustees had not been quick enough. As the screw in the doorway nodded that they were done, Nicky heard the clatter of keys. The gate to the wing was being unlocked. The connecting door opened. Then there was a deafening howl.

The sound that greeted Hindley's arrival might have burst the roof off Risley. Women screamed and bayed, and crashed their metal mugs on the tables in their cells. Out of a frenzy of hammering and smashing, a rhythm began, like a heartbeat which seemed to come from the walls.

Evil bitch! We'll kill you, bitch! Like you killed that kid! We'll get in there and we'll kill you! We'll kill you slowly, bitch!

Nicky had to walk into the sound. She approached the cell door, stepped out and turned to her right.

The prisoner was here, flanked by six officers almost in step. Hindley was taller than her guards and as she rose and dipped with her footfalls, her head and shoulders were plainly in view.

Nicky stood inches from the face that would gaze from front pages all over the world. She saw the heavy jaw and wide cheekbones, a long pale brow, full lips and sleepy eyes below a mess of wet and sticky blonde hair. Hindley gazed through her, impassive. Though close enough to touch, she was nowhere at all. Hindley was just twenty-three years old. Nicky met her empty stare. For a second, she looked into the dark.

Then she made it back down the landing and reached the staircase. Hindley's cell door slammed shut. That sound was met by redoubled bouts of shrieking. A screw opened Nicky's cell. Outside, the pandemonium increased. The whole wing was shaking. The terror that had been unleashed made Nicky tremble so much that she couldn't stand up. She crouched to the ground and covered her face.

But the noise wouldn't stop.

Maybe the prisoner had brought with her some demented spirit from the moors that could not cease to call on destruction. Or perhaps the despair and rage and fear of Risley itself had found its voice. On and on it went. The women were screaming, sometimes in speech, at other times without using words. The lights were put out but the sound was worse in the darkness. No one knew how to make it end.

At 2am, the order was given to hose the prisoners down.

Male officers from the men's side of the prison fetched the hose-pipe up. It was sandy beige canvas, with a nozzle that linked up to standpipes in the prison walls. The lights were switched on. The officers worked fast, eager to stop the intolerable noise.

When the tap was turned, the force of the jet was so great it took two to control it, with a third man back at the wall and a fourth standing by to unlock each cell door in turn. The door man threw the first cell open. The hose twisted into life, coming close to jerking itself from the operators' hands.

Quickly the men found a competent routine. In went the water with a roar, aimed straight at the cell's far wall so that splashback sprayed everything around. Then the hose turned directly on the prisoners, bitterly cold and hard enough to knock an adult down. In seconds, everything was drenched – clothing, bedding, pictures pinned to the walls. The prisoners lay still on the floor or curled on their beds. Once hosed, they were silent.

Each cell was doused, including the trustees' cells. Nicky too was soaked by the hose. She welcomed it.

Already in her young life, she was no stranger to horror. But in Hindley's eyes she saw something worse than hurting or pain. She saw a woman far away from her fellow human beings – so far that all suffering, theirs and her own, had ceased to have meaning. Hindley was lost in a place where there was only nothingness. In that moment, Nicky felt its terror.

Now she sat on the floor with her back to the wall, knees drawn up and arms curled tightly around her head. The scouring stream whipped over her, removing the air of Hindley's cell from her lungs. It washed the touch of the lamp – which the torturer's hand would reach for – from her fingers and the fibres of its rug from her feet. It cleansed all contact between them.

The landings and stairways were rivers. The only sound that remained was cold droplets on metal. The men packed their hoses and left. The sky lightened. It was dawn, October 12th, 1965.

Chapter One

I dreamed I could
breathe underwater

Each day, I come home from school by myself. This time is just for me and my grandfather. We have a secret. We do things together that only he and I know about.

Grandfather sits in his chair by the hearth. First he looks over his shoulder to make certain no one is there. Everyone's at work, and my grandmother's out fetching food. Shopping, cooking and washing take all of her time.

He stands me right between his knees. His breath stinks. I see sweat in the cracks around his mouth. His pores are all blackened with coal dust. He takes one more sharp-shouldered glance at the room behind, then he puts my hand on the front of his trousers.

On the sideboard, I can see a green and gold tin. The whole time I stand there, I stare at the tin. 'Biscuits', it says, in slippery gold writing like treacle. There's a long smooth swish from the final 's' looping back the whole way to end in a curly round blob. I let my eyes drift through the letters again and again, the big bouncy 'b' and the little curvy 's', then a 'c' that you think will close tightly but opens its mouth for the low loopy 'u' and then the 'i' that comes next, until all of the word that's left pours into its fine swirling tail. 'Biscuits... Biscuits...' I stare and stare. I learn the word so well that I never once spell it wrong.

My grandfather puffs. When he touches me, his calloused palms are like blades. The calluses nick at my skin and sometimes I think he might cut me. If I don't do what he wants, he pulls at my wrist in a pinch-tight grip to make

7

my hand jerk faster.

At the end, grey beads of moisture fly from his face. Saliva flicks from his dry open lips with their wrinkly tags of flesh. Then he makes a mess on my hands.

And after that, he's always angry with me. He gets up from his chair and paces to the big white sink by the kitchen window. He stoops to look outside, leaning his weight on the edge. At these times, I know that anything I do will disgust him. He can barely look at my face.

"You're not a proper child, you," he says to me. His voice is bitter. "You're a bad girl. Dirty. If you were a proper child, I wouldn't have to do it."

***

The rag-and-bone man came down Fletcher Road on his cart. He had yellow balloons for the children who gave him their rags. I really wanted a balloon.

"Do we have any rags, Gran?"

"You're wearin' 'em, duck," she said.

Stoke-on-Trent was black with smoke from the potteries. Fumes swirled up from the furnaces all day long, as though a sorcerer was stirring his potions. All around hung the smell of burning chalk. The pottery dust on the soles of our shoes left trails of footprints like talcum powder.

I used to go and play on the slag heaps. They looked like black boils on giants – some of them a hundred feet high. The slag heaps were made out of mining waste and rubble from bombed-out houses. That's why they were so slippery and loose. They'd even move about beneath your feet as you climbed them. There were small streams flowing through, and sometimes you'd get wet feet as you clambered up high. The grown-ups would tell us that they weren't safe and forbid us from going there to play.

I lived with my grandparents. When I was born, I was left in a shoebox outside Stoke City football ground, which was just around the corner. A label on the shoebox gave the address and my birth certificate was tucked into the bottom.

Our house was cherry-black brick with a shabby green door, just like all the rest of the street. The lavvy was out round the back and there was a cold water tap in the kitchen. Gaslights made the indoors look as dusty and smudgy as it did outside. Fletcher Road was a long straight street and that's where we all played. We rolled marbles and chased each other along the backs – long flagstone lanes behind our rows of small, dark, narrow houses.

The war had ended the year I was born, but rationing hadn't ended at the same time, and there was never enough. We were short of bread and vegetables, butter and sugar. Gran counted out all the ration coupons at the kitchen table, and when you got paid on a Friday, you handed your earnings straight to her, so that she could keep us all fed. Everyone in the family worked. It was the same in all the other families I knew. Not all the men had come back from the fighting, so the girls and mothers spent long, hard days in the potteries too, or working down the Mich. That was our name for the Michelin factory, where they made tyres. There was always lots of work around - a filthy old grind it was, but plenty to be had if you went out and looked. That's what we did, all of us, as soon as we turned fourteen and left school.

We didn't feed pets in Fletcher Road, or have pets at all. There was just the one reason for an animal to be around, and that was to keep down rats. That's how our dogs and cats fed themselves. We'd eat the scraps of meat that butchers would sell by the bag, a penny a time to use in stews. 'Lobby', my grandmother called it, a great big pot of whatever-it-was – mostly gristle, as often as not. The pot was put down on the table and everyone piled in for themselves. I didn't get much because I was the smallest.

But we did have a dog, though he fed himself too. I called him just 'Dog' and he was my friend. That made me worried about the meat in the pot. I knew that dogs disappeared sometimes, and I remembered a bulldog shot dead just outside our house. He must have eaten the poison they put out all over, to try to keep down the rats. A policeman chased me off before he shot the bulldog, to put him out of his misery. I ran away down the backs in terror.

Each Sunday we ate roast meat, then spun it out in slivers the rest of the week. Who knew where the joint had come from? I worried. What if – just what if? – the meat we were eating was dog, and my Dog was next on the menu?

So at weekends the two of us would go together to hide on the slag heaps near Fletcher Road. Dog and I would climb right to the top and sit there happily together. No one ever came looking for us. We would stare far away over Shelton Bar, out beyond Stoke to the rim of the sorcerer's bowl and the distant grey hills.

***

Our family's house was very full when I was a little girl. My grandmother Sarah had five sons and four daughters, my aunties and uncles. One of her daughters, Sylvia, my mother, had vanished, and nobody talked about her. My auntie June had died aged eight, before I was born, and the story was she ate rhubarb leaves which make you sick but shouldn't kill you. It had to be poison she ate on the leaves, everyone said. Uncle Mack had been killed in an accident, and Uncle Norman was serving at sea, as my grandfather had once done. Then in 1950, the Korean War began. My Uncle Vernon enlisted and went off to fight. Uncle Charlie and Uncle Dennis were miners. My aunties, Opal and Frieda, worked in the potteries.

Everyone's work was dirty. My grandfather, Edwin, was always dirty too; he'd retired from the navy now, but he picked coal from the slag heaps and brought it back home in a great big sack on the front of his bicycle. Then he sat down in his chair by the hearth to rest. His eyes were always glinting in his crusted, blackened face, and his hair was all scaly with dust.

Uncle Norman and Uncle Vernon would come home on leave from the army. I was always frightened when Uncle Vernon was there, because he was pale and tight-lipped and strange. I recognised the sound of his big army boots in the yard outside. When I heard him coming, I'd hide under the kitchen table with Dog, watching through bars made from chair legs until it was safe to come out.

When Uncle Vernon came home, he sometimes played the piano in the front room – Gran's room – and tapped his feet on the floor to keep time. That was the only time he would ever smile. I loved to listen to the music. Uncle Vernon brought presents from Korea: one was a long piece of silk which looked green, but under the light it would ripple and sheen in purple and blue until you didn't know what colour it really was. The silk was the softest thing I'd ever touched, softer than skin. He gave it to his sisters and they couldn't stop wrapping it around them, laughing and squealing with delight, imagining dresses that fell all the way to the floor. To me, my aunties looked like beautiful princesses. Vernon gave Gran a little ivory box for her special things, and she put her mother's wedding ring in it for safe-keeping.

Once Uncle Vernon told me that Sylvia, my mother, had a beautiful voice. When they were children he'd play the piano, he told me, and then she would sing. I loved to imagine my mother singing, but then Gran heard him and started to shush. She wouldn't let anyone talk to me about her. The radiogram on the front room mantelpiece only played the talking shows and always in Welsh, because my grandfather spoke it. He despised all the people in England, he said.

At night, my grandfather slept up at the back of the house on his own. My grandmother stayed downstairs at the front. The rest of us all shared the one other upstairs room: me and my aunties, Opal and Frieda, and as many brothers and uncles as were at home. We all slept together in one big double bed with itchy brown blankets. A thick army greatcoat would cover the last to arrive, or most often it covered the smallest. I lay underneath it and spied on the grown-ups through the buttonholes.

***

I thought my aunties were beautiful, and I loved them a lot.

Once Auntie Frieda saved up her factory wages to buy me a doll – pretty, shiny Lucy – who was almost too lovely to touch. Lucy had smooth hard skin and sparkly platinum hair springing out through a row of holes in her head. She wore a party dress with netting sewn stiffly into her skirt so it stood right out, and a wide smooth sash with a bow at the back. But after a while, big pieces of Lucy's hair fell out leaving just the holes. I felt sorry for her now that she wasn't so pretty, but I couldn't have loved her as much as I loved Dolly, my other doll. Dolly was made out of only cloth, and she slept every night under the big khaki army coat with me.

One day Auntie Frieda made my grandfather very angry by bleaching her long dark hair as brightly as Lucy's and putting on lipstick and rouge. As soon as he saw her, he flew into a rage.

"Get that muck off your face, you tart!" he bellowed.

"I will not!" she shouted back at him. My grandfather muttered and huffed, and blonde Auntie Frieda flounced straight through the front room and out by the big green door that we weren't allowed to use. She slammed it behind her so hard that the whole room shook. Grandfather's fist pounded down on the table in fury and a bottle of brown sauce flew right up in the air.

When Auntie Opal stepped out with her new young man, my grandmother sent me as tag-along. Courting couples in Stoke went walking in Trentham Park, to enjoy the fresh air by the lake. The two of them whispered and giggled all the way there. Then when we arrived, Opal said bossily, "Feed the ducks and don't move a step!" She gave me some bread in a paper bag, and off they went together. I had to wait a very long time on my own with the ducks, but I never told my gran what Auntie Opal had done.

When both of them got married and left the house in Fletcher Road to live with their husbands, I missed my aunties very much.

***

At five years old, I start school. I'm wearing a cut-down dress that used to belong to Auntie Frieda. My grandmother cuts my hair for school, straight round the edge of the pudding basin placed on the top of my head.

My school is Boothen Juniors, just at the end of our street. We sit in a great big room with rows of desks and white-tiled walls. Some of the girls have pretty bows tied in their hair, even though the ribbons are a little bit ragged. Their parents shine their shoes every day, even when the soles are worn almost through. I feel very strange and a little bit sad when I see those ribbons and their shiny shoes, almost as if I don't belong with those children at all. I feel like an outsider and I wonder what I did that was wrong, and why I'm not a proper child like them.

I don't like school at all. There's a very big space behind my chair and a door in the corner that's out of my sight. I'm scared when I sit with my back to the door. I don't like that great big gap with nobody watching who's coming in. So I keep turning round to keep watch. That makes it difficult for me to follow what the teacher is saying. He's called Mr Blacknor, and sometimes he slaps my head and tells me to pay attention in class. But I can't stop turning around.

After we've learned our letters by heart, we children of Boothen Juniors write down our names on a sheet of paper. I'm proud because I can write my own name. I don't write my proper one, though, because nobody ever uses that. I write the name I know, slowly and carefully in my very neatest letters.

"What does this say?"

"It says: Basterd. That's my name."

Mr Blacknor slaps me. I don't know what I've done wrong. I've even remembered I should start with a capital B.

***

Before she got married and went away from home, Auntie Opal used to cut herself sometimes. Nobody ever said anything about it.

Mostly the cuts weren't so bad. But once in the kitchen, Opal slashed her wrist very hard while I was there. The blade of the knife went in so deep that dark red blood spurted up from it. I could see how it pumped with the beat of her heart. The blood jet splashed as far as my face.

Opal moaned, and my grandmother sprang to her feet. She grabbed me by the shoulders and bundled me out into the yard between the washing line and the entrance to the coal hole. I stood there on my own in the sunshine, feeling very frightened. I kept trying to wipe Opal's blood away with my clothes, but mopping just made the mess a lot worse, and now I was covered in blood.

When I went back inside, her cuts had been bound up. The stain she had made on the floor and the table were both wiped away, and just a muddy brown mark remained. I couldn't understand what had happened or why – only that Auntie Opal's dark, pumping blood was never once mentioned again in my family. It felt like an awful secret we all had to keep. I didn't know why that was, but I kept our secret too.

***

On one magical day before Opal and Frieda were married, a circus parade came right through the streets of Stoke. We could never have paid to see the show, but instead the elephants came to see us, and walked right past our house. For once, we opened the green front door and stood there all in a row to watch them come. My aunties were giggling with excitement. Even my grandfather waited there, and looked towards the corner when we first heard the band.

At the front came the men who were blowing their trombones.

Then there were the clowns with bright paint on their faces, laughing and banging the children on the heads with balloons and pretending to push each other over. Next we saw the trapeze ladies, all in their sequins, and the jugglers throwing clubs in the air as they marched along. Then right at the back came two elephants with mountainous flanks.

Their skin was draped in delicate folds around their shoulders and bellies, as though they were covered in sheets of crepe paper. They wore bright jewelled discs on their foreheads above their long patient faces, and glittery straps beneath their great ears. And then, high on the back of the first great beast, her pink legs folded beneath her, arms aloft in a V with her wrists and her forearms all shiny and spangled, I saw the elephant lady.

I stood on the step with my grandmother's apron clutched against my face in awe. I stared and I stared. The elephant lady was the most magnificent sight I had seen in the whole of my life.

***

The best day of the week is Saturday. That's when I go walking with Dog. We climb up the slag heaps, so high that we can see over everything. Sometimes the dirt slides away from my feet when I'm scrambling up. I keep tight hold of the piece of string that makes a lead for Dog. He pulls me and I pull him and we make it right up to the top. He licks my nose when I sit down next to him.

I can see the roof of Boothen Juniors from here. I can see the roofs of thousands of little houses. The pottery chimneys stand like bottles of black medicine. Far, far away I can see the hills, much too far away for me to go.

***

One day at Boothen Juniors, I go back to the classroom after school. I've forgotten my book. I run like the wind down the passage. It's totally still. I think that the classroom will be empty already.

A tall girl with long hair in pigtails called Anne is standing by the teacher's chair. They're looking at a book together. Her head is bent far forwards. But Mr Blacknor isn't reading. He's staring at Anne as though she's said something wrong. His eyes are in sharp creases and his mouth's in an O. He looks as though he's just about to shout. I know what that look means. I freeze.

Mr Blacknor's hand is right up Anne's dress at the front. The hem of her skirt folds back on the bend of his elbow.

I know all about secrets. They are very important, just like the secret that I have with my grandfather. I act as if I haven't seen. I don't let the tapping of my feet stop. I pick up my book from the bench in the corner and scamper away.

Perhaps tall Anne with her round freckled face isn't a proper child either, even though she looks pretty to me.

***

I liked Miss Lester, the lady who taught our class sometimes. She showed us her book about the Great Barrier Reef.

She held it up and pointed at the pictures. When I looked, it seemed to me as if the Australian sun was rising over Boothen Juniors. The wondrous undersea kingdom glowed in its smooth shining pages. I slid from my seat and came closer to see and she told me to go and sit down. But after the lesson, she smiled at me and let me look again.

I saw great grey turtles with pebbly flippers which sailed like ships past the eye-popping reds and deep-jewelled blues and metallic hot yellows of the reef. Coral glowed in the long bright beams of sunlight shining underneath the sea. I saw every dazzling fantastical colour you could ever imagine.

At night, I started to dream about the blue-green world below the waves. Deep down there, I could ride on a turtle and breathe underwater, making my stately journey in radiance and light. The sun would always shine through the water and its rays lit up the golden, magical staircase to climb to the surface above.

Sometimes we read stories from the Bible in school. In my dreams I would muddle up the stories of Jesus and the stories of the turtles, who seemed kinder and bluer and wiser than anything. When I was a little girl, I longed for the beautiful turtles to sail me to heaven.

Chapter Two

My world is split in two

In the spring of 1951, when I was five years old, my whole world changed in a day. But nobody ever said why.

There was a knock at the green front door one morning. It was Saturday. Then I heard a voice I'd never heard before. Quite quickly there were other voices, raised – grandfather and grandmother, having a terrible argument.

Hiding underneath the kitchen table, I saw the visitor's feet first of all, in her black shiny shoes. Her high sharp heels rapped smartly on the floor. When I peeped up, there was a glamorous lady, dressed in a lilac jacket and skirt. Most beautiful of all was her coil of dark hair, swept up to the back of her head and tucked under a little black hat. Her lips were dark red and shiny like blood. She had rouge on her cheeks. I thought that must be why my grandfather was angry. He hated that muck. Perhaps that was why they were arguing.

But what was a posh lady doing here, where everything was dirty and everything was always the same? Gran looked very small alongside her, wearing her hairnet and her freshly starched apron for working in the kitchen.

"I've come to take her with me, Ma," the lady was saying very loudly, "and that's what I'm going to do. You can't be telling me what I can and can't do. She's mine and she comes with me!"

I didn't understand what they were arguing about. Then Gran reached beneath the table and grabbed me by the arm. She held on to me so tightly that it hurt. I tried to pull free, but then she lifted me out from between the chair legs.

"But Sylvia, you can't! You can't just take her away!"

"You watch me! She's coming to my house now, mine and Lionel's, and she'll live with us. What can you do with her here? My God, this place is a dump. It's a rat hole. And" – she looked over at my grandfather – "how's the big rat?"

Grandfather called the posh lady terrible names. He quickly grew hoarse. Gran squeezed her cold fingers tightly around the bones of my wrist.

"Nothing changes, does it?" the posh lady hissed. "I don't need to ask if anything's different – I know it's not! Probably the best thing to take her away, if you think about it."

She strode across the kitchen with her sharp, clicking steps. The square white sink by the window was piled high with dirty pots.

"It's a dump!" Her voice grew louder. "Get her things, Ma! If you won't, I will!"

I was starting to feel very frightened. Gran's voice was still soft and low.

"Syl, you shouldn't do this. She – she – Syl, lis –"

Then my grandfather was suddenly roaring.

"Get out of my house, you tart! Go back where you came from! You're not welcome in this house!"

"Don't worry, I won't be staying," said the lady. "I'll leave, but I'll take what's mine with me. Get her things! There'll be a train coming."

I remembered how my grandfather's shouting hadn't stopped Auntie Frieda from bleaching her hair and putting on rouge. It wasn't going to stop the posh lady either.

Gran let my arm go and vanished upstairs. It didn't take long to pack my two dresses. I was wearing my only pair of shoes. She brought me my coat and held out my clothes in a limp string bag.

"Is that the lot?" said the posh lady, looking at the bag. "My God, is that all?"

"Yes, Syl," said gran. "But you can't – Syl –"

"Are these things clean, Ma?"

"Yes, Syl."

"You're mine," the lady rapped out. "You're my daughter. I'm taking you to London to live with me."

The mantel clock started to strike. I liked the clock and always counted the chimes. Now I was too afraid to count. I didn't want to go away with her. I wanted to stay here with Dog, in the world that I knew.

My grandmother's features grew wobbly, with watery eyes and a trembling mouth. She looked as if her whole face was breaking apart. I'd never seen her look that way before. When she spoke, her voice was a waver.

"But Syl – she belongs –"

"I'm not taking nothing that's not mine to take, so you just shut your mouth," the posh lady told her. Gran flinched and half turned away. She rubbed at her eyes with the heel of her hand.

"Where's Dolly?" I whispered.

"Dolly?"

"Can I take my Dolly?"

"Her doll. Of course you can take Dolly," said Gran. She hurried back upstairs to fetch her. The posh lady didn't look at me while gran was gone. Instead she took two long strides to the kitchen window and ducked down her head to look outside, leaning on the edge of the big white sink. She did it the exact same way that my grandfather did.

Dolly was grubby and flat. She'd fallen off the big upstairs bed and been trodden on so many times, and squeezed on so many cold nights. I gripped her thin arm between my fingers.

"I won't be coming back here again. Good God, what a place it is." The posh lady poked my shoulder to make me walk towards the door. I had to let go of my grandmother's hand.

"*Sylvia!*" cried Gran – the loudest sound I'd ever heard her make. She lifted her hands to her tight white face and cupped them around her mouth. Her eyes were squeezed shut.

"Sylvia, you shouldn –"

The posh lady swung back on her heel, like a clockwork toy. I took the mantel clock apart once, and found the intricate brown and brass world that moved inside. I loved its little perfection, and always wanted to find out how things worked. It made me feel safe when I could see and understand. The clock was up on a very high shelf now, out of my reach.

"*Don't – you – Sylvia – me!* This is a stinking dump! I'm not coming back! She's not coming back either!"

Gran clutched me in a very tight hug then let me go. I felt her tears on my forehead. I'd never once imagined that my gran could ever cry. Then her arms fell back to her sides. My grandfather sat down at the table. He didn't say anything at all. My mother's hand tightened on my shoulder.

I was looking for Dog to say goodbye. He must have been scared of the loud angry voices and run off to hide. I wanted so badly to see him that I kept on searching, trying not to stumble as my mother pushed me out through the scuffed green door and into Fletcher Road.

We opened the gate and walked fast. My mother's sharp steps cracked down on the pavement. She was gripping my hand very tightly to pull me along in a cutting cold wind that made the little string bag of clothes fly right out alongside us. We passed the cobbler's shop and kept striding down the long straight road towards St Peter Ad Vincula: the Church of St Peter In Chains. I almost had to run to keep up and I was very out of breath. I tried to pull my mother's arm to ask her to stop, but when she looked down at me, she seemed to be so angry that I started to cry.

"*Shut. Up*," she said to me, in a very soft voice.

I felt much more afraid when she spoke to me that way than I had when she'd been shouting at Gran.

"*Just. Shut. Up.*"

For the first time, I looked into her face. For just a few seconds, we stared at each other. I swallowed my crying right down.

I'd never been inside Stoke station before. This was a far smarter part of town, just over the road from a very grand hotel. The grey shape of Josiah Wedgwood, founder of the potteries, loomed on his plinth. I thought all the columns and arches made the station look like a palace. My mother already had tickets in her hand. She pulled me up the steps very fast to find the train, and all the climbing made my legs hurt. When we reached the narrow bridge right up in the roof, a train went by underneath our feet with a huge whooshing roar and hiss. I jumped. Steam streamed up all around me. The big, moving world made me feel very small and I started to cry again. I knew by now that my mother would be angry, but it hurt in my throat when I tried to hold back my tears.

Then – when my mother looked down at me – silence.

"I thought I told you," she said, "to s*hut up*."

As the train moved off, I thought of my Dolly. I'd been holding her tight in the back room at home. After that, I wasn't so sure. Did I have her as we walked down the road? By the church? By the statue? Where was she? Dolly wasn't stuffed in my pocket, or in the string bag, or in my mother's hand. She wouldn't fit into that black shiny bag. I tried not to fidget but inside I was frantic, looking all around the carriage, turning my head back and forth and catching my breath.

Dolly had been left behind in Stoke. My eyes filled up with tears. Now she'd be all alone and frightened.

My mother didn't say a word. She gave me one single look and I knew that I couldn't cry for Dolly.

***

It was night-time when we arrived in London. After the long ride on the train, we caught an underground train, and after that we walked up a wide straight hill. Not all the houses had gates, not even the big ones. There were spaces in front between their high white gateposts, and I knew that was from where they'd taken the metal in the war to make guns for the fighting.

We passed a big dark church with brick turrets rising like spears and a pointy, narrow tower. Then there were more long streets filled with pale square buildings. The walk seemed unending, then we turned into one last road and arrived at a big white house with a gateway and pillars. There were six tiled black and white steps up to a front door with columns either side. My mother took out a heavy black key from her black shiny bag.

She opened the door and we stepped into a dim and silent hall. A lamp stood on a table, its yellow light gleaming down on dark shiny wood. I could see the door of a very big cupboard.

A man came towards us down the stairs. He must have heard the rattle of the key. He was small, tidy and clean-looking, dressed in dark trousers and a very smart waistcoat. He didn't say anything to me, just murmured to my mother. Then he pointed down the passageway that ran towards the back of the house. I walked down the passage and he followed me. It was totally silent in the house, with no footfall sounds on the thick blue carpet. I'd never been anywhere I couldn't hear footsteps approaching.

Down some steps at the end of the passageway was a room with a small single bed. I'd never slept in a single bed, or had any bed to myself. The clean little man showed me in. I thought he might follow. Instead, he just closed the door behind me.

I was too tired and scared to do anything, so I waited. I started to follow the swirls of the carpet around with my eyes and then with the toe of my shoe. The pattern helped me drift into a dream. It looked like long blue grass, so deep you could lie right down on it and rest. But then I thought the quiet man might be angry with me.

A few minutes later he came back, but still he didn't say a word. He was carrying a cloth which he wrapped around his hand, and then he stretched up his arm. The ceiling was low and in one sharp movement, he twisted the bulb from inside the light shade on the ceiling.

Now the room was dark, apart from the thin line of light round the edge of the door. I heard a rasp as he turned the big doorknob to leave, then there was a heavy click as the door swung closed. They'd left me there on my own. Nothing else happened in the darkness for a very long time.

I stood there feeling terribly confused and afraid. Far away outside, I heard cars. My stomach felt twisted in a hard, tight knot. I was thirsty, but I didn't know where to get a drink or who I should ask if I could have one. I was so tired by now that I thought I might fall over. My eyes and the back of my throat and my chest ached hard from not crying for Gran and for Dog and for Dolly.

I climbed up on the bed and fell asleep with my coat on.

***

I am six years old. I'm standing in a big, bright room in a smart London house. My mother is angry with me because I pulled out the ribbons in my hair when they were tight, and now both my bunches are coming undone. She punches me hard around the ears. I see the sharp white bones in her hands through the skin, then her knuckles turn red.

Her punches are big dull bangs in my head. It grows foggy. My ears ring. My mother slaps my face. I lose my balance and fall. I hit my head on the edge of the table. I'm dizzy and everything feels far away.

She grabs my hair in a big tight grip with her fingers twisted through. She lifts me right up off the ground. The clean, small man I know now is her husband is watching us from his chair. He doesn't say anything. I'm kicking, but she carries me all through the house and opens the door of the cupboard in the hall with her other hand. Her breath comes in puffs as she drops me inside. She ties my wrist to the heater. It's not turned on. She slams the cupboard door and it's dark.

Inside the cupboard I curl in a ball on the floor with one arm up over the heater. Above me are coats on hooks. I close my eyes tight. I miss Dog so much. I miss Dolly too. I know I mustn't cry, or make any sound. I stay on the floor of the cupboard and keep quiet as a mouse.

***

I learned about my new life in London as the weeks went by, although no one told me why I had come here. My mother was rich now. She lived here in this big white house with her husband Lionel. Her name was Mrs Mirvis.

She was a singer, and sometimes her singing flowed down the stairs and echoed all around. Her voice was as beautiful as Uncle Vernon told me, and she practised her music, just like he did in my grandmother's room back in Stoke.

My mother didn't work as my grandmother had to do. Here a housekeeper, Mrs Anand, came to do the daily work of washing and cleaning, and a dressmaker made all our clothes. Every day I had to look very smart, wearing clean socks and those tight, tight hair ribbons. I kept on trying to pull them loose.

I lived all by myself in the basement downstairs. Mrs Anand gave me meals in the kitchen. She didn't really speak to me, or mind what I did, so I ate on the floor between the legs of the chairs. Sometimes I closed my eyes very tightly and pretended that Dog was sitting there with me.

My mother had four other children, my three younger sisters and my little brother Peter who was born after I came to visit the house, and once I heard her asking her husband if I could be called the same name as theirs. "Please," she said to him, "because she is my daughter too." But Lionel Mirvis was angry. That was the only time I ever heard him raising his voice, with my mother or with anybody else.

"That little bastard in the basement is a visitor in this house! She's not one of our proper children. No – she can't have the same name."

My mother hurt me and I didn't know why – but she loved me too, and she wanted me. Here was the proof. It must have been her who had decided to bring me to London, because I was her daughter and a part of her family. This is what love must be like, I thought, so painful and confusing. Even though she beat me, she still came all the way to Stoke to fetch me. She argued with my grandfather, and with her husband – all because of me. Nobody else ever wanted me like that. No one else ever seemed to care much where I was or what I did. I didn't understand how my mother behaved – but I could feel that she cared very much in every blow that she gave me. And so I began to love her too.

***

"This is your cane."

I am seven years old. My cane is long and yellowish-brown. My mother holds it out to me, turning it over in her hands.

"This is only for you. All children have one. If you do things that are wrong, I will fetch your cane and I will punish you."

When I've done something wrong and she's angry, she hits me with the cane. It hisses in the air but makes no sound as it touches my skin. The pain of each blow is so big and I feel so small. I wait for its whisper – the next stroke, then the next. I don't know how to make the pain stop. I can't make a sound. I'm frightened I might die of the pain. Panic spreads like beating wings, all through my body, like the flapping of an injured bird that's struggling to be free.

When she's finished the beating, she pushes me down onto the floor. She crouches over me, her face close to mine. Her mouth's dragged out of shape just as if she was screaming, though she's talking in a very low voice.

"Shut. Up. If you cry when I hurt you, then I will hurt you more."

The panic wings beat wildly inside me, but by now I've learned always to keep very still.

***

Sometimes I saw my little sisters in the hallway, or heard their footsteps upstairs in the house. I was terribly afraid that my mother would lock them in the cupboard, or beat them like she used to beat me, but there was never any sign of this at all. Later, when Peter was born, I would sometimes see them playing outside in the big back garden.

In London, I had to go to school. It was bigger than Boothen Juniors in Stoke, and it was a long walk to get there on my own. At first I was frightened when I set out on the noisy wide pavements. Then I learned the way and I liked my morning walk. I saw streets full of cars and sometimes the wide bomb-spaces and rubble from the war still piled around.

Sometimes at school, when my mother had been hitting and punching my head, I would mix up the ringing in my ears with the lesson bell and the other children laughed at me. I felt happier when I made a friend – a girl called Winifred. One day, my mother made me go to school in wellington boots as a punishment for pulling my hair ribbons. I was worried the other children would tease me for wearing wellingtons in school, but Winifred lent me her plimsolls. I put them on, then we hid my wellingtons outside in the hedge. We did it several days in a row, until my mother let me wear my shoes again.

***

It was nearly the long summer holidays. Then, even though she'd told me I was never going home to Stoke-on-Trent, my mother sent me back there on the train. She came with me to the big station and put me in the guard's van by myself with a label on my coat. On the label, she wrote our address in Fletcher Road. When I got to Stoke, I saw my gran waiting there to meet me.

Dog was so happy when I came back home. He jumped up and wagged his tail and licked my face all over. I sat with my arms round him under the table. That was the place I liked the best. Then I took him out for a walk and we climbed up the slag heaps together.

***

My world was split into two, London and Stoke and then back again. Nobody explained when I would next go to London, or when I would come home. When I was with Dog, I never wanted to leave, so I tried not to think about going away, just in case thinking bad thoughts made the bad things happen.

I would stay in the big white house on my visits for many, many weeks at a time. Sometimes it seemed to be so long that I thought I would never leave again. I missed Dog very much every day. I tried not to think about him, or Stoke, or my gran. The happiest days were the days when I walked in through the back door at home, and Dog would lick my face and jump up at me and lash his stubby tail.

***

I'm eight years old and we're walking with Dog on a Stoke summer's day, Uncle Vernon and I. He's dressed in his shirtsleeves. Of everyone I know, I am still the most afraid of him.

My grandfather makes a big noise when he's angry, but each time he stands me in front of the fire, before he touches me he'll pause and glance over his shoulder. He's listening for footsteps. I know he's afraid that someone will catch him. Soon he stops and furtively does up his buttons. Then he gives me a sixpence so I won't tell my gran.

Uncle Vernon is different. His eyes don't slide to the side to keep watch, or glitter like grandfather's. There's no light in them at all. When he comes home on army leave, he takes me out of the house on walks, then when we're far away from Fletcher Road, he does the same things to me my grandfather does by the fire. But no matter what happens, his cold eyes never change. Sometimes I think that Uncle Vernon must be mad.

I dread it whenever he comes home. I hate going walking with him. I hear his big boots in the backyard ("here I am, Ma!") and then I know that soon he will want to take me down to the river. We walk Dog right along the path, where nobody comes. There are bushes very close to the water. Uncle Vernon takes me into the undergrowth with him. He tells me to touch him, then he touches me. Each time he does this, he says he will kill me if I tell. When I look into his face, I know without question that he would.

Dog runs to and fro, sniffing and wagging his tail. This time Uncle Vernon tells me to do the thing which always makes me sick. When it's finished and I'm retching, he looks angry. He turns away and does up his buttons.

My cheeks are hurting. I spit out the mess in my mouth and wipe my chin with my dress. But his slimy stuff goes all over the place: now it's on my hand and I bend down and rub my palm on the leaves. But everything's still sticky, and horrible all over me, on my face and my hand and my clothes. I crouch there, looking for more leaves to wipe myself clean. I can't find any. I feel so dirty that I start to cry.

Dog wriggles up to me. There's no wagging tail now, but he licks the tears from my cheek. He stares at Uncle Vernon, and then he growls at him.

Uncle Vernon's eyes go dull. He's a few steps away and he strides and grabs Dog by the string round his neck. He twists his hands round and round. The string pulls tight and lifts Dog up. He's a little dog, but he whines and tries to bite and he kicks out with his legs. His back leg claw scrapes a long red gash on the inside of Uncle Vernon's arm.

Uncle Vernon curses, then swings round. He's carrying Dog with his string pinched tight. He disappears through the bushes. I hear splashing.

I run out onto the path. I see Vernon nine or ten feet away, up to his knees in the river. He's holding Dog underwater. Dog is frantically clawing and scrabbling with all four legs. I can't see his head – it's below the surface. I cry out in panic.

I'm much too scared of Uncle Vernon to run into the river to try to save Dog. I stand on the bank screaming as loud as I can with my hands by my sides. Screaming and screaming: "No! Stop! No!."

It's only a minute until Dog goes still, but Uncle Vernon holds him under for a very long time. When he straightens up, Dog's body slides down beneath the surface and disappears. There are red lines across Vernon's hands where the twisted string collar dug into his fingers. The long clawed groove on his right arm has started to bleed.

I can't stop screaming. I fall to my knees because my legs won't hold me up. No. No.

Dog. He killed my Dog.

No, no, no.

Uncle Vernon walks out of the river. He grabs me by the shoulders and lifts me right off the ground. His fingers grind me to the bone. He shakes me so hard that my head bounces backwards and forwards.

"Fucking shut up! Fucking shut your mouth or I'll drown you as well!"

His eyes are staring.

"Not a word! Not a fucking word at home or I'll bring you back here and I'll drown you! Quiet now!"

The horror inside me hasn't come out with my screams. When I stop, I can feel it still swelling. Its ripples billow and burst in my chest. I don't make a sound. Dog. I love you so much. Dog.

Vernon grabs me by the hand. He's cold and wet from the river. Dog, Dog, Dog. We stumble along the path towards Fletcher Road without him.

My gran asks us where Dog is.

"Bloody thing killed the chickens, didn't he? Had to drown the bugger."

I miss Dog so much. I crawl beneath the table and curl up tightly all alone.

***

Sometimes, when I was in London, I was taken to a different house. Mrs Anand came with me. The first time she took me there, she didn't tell me where we were going or what was going to happen. She never spoke to me once, all the way there and all the way back again.

The house was next door to the fire station, big and tall and made from red brick, with "London County Council" on the front. It had great high archways for the engines to come and go, and sometimes I could hear the engine bells ringing. A smart, quiet man in a crisp white shirt and shiny shoes always opened the front door.

"Come in," he said to me, the first time we knocked, but I noticed how he didn't smile at all as he said it. "Would you like a drink of orange juice?"

The orange juice smelled strange. It always made my throat and eyes sting, and afterwards the world would go dreamy and I didn't know why. I drank the juice because I was thirsty from the walk, and soon I got used to the taste. Sometimes in hot weather, the man would bring a second glass and I would drink that too. He left me to wait in the hall on a high wooden chair.

***

The very first time, I sit there and listen for voices and footsteps. Later on, I'll learn how to tell who's coming from their tread. The men in the house are very strict about keeping things tidy; they tell me to take off my shoes and leave them neatly by the wall. In winter, I hang up my coat on a peg. There's a very strong smell of tobacco.

The first time, I sit there and wait, and I don't know what's going to happen. But I know that it's better not to think too far ahead, in case there's a bad thing coming. Minutes go by in the high silent hall, and I start to feel terribly uneasy.

The hall has thick brown wallpaper, almost like velvet. Its creamy, chocolatey swirls make it look as though the walls are melting. I run my fingers over them, tracing the coils round and round like the grooves on a seashell for minute after minute so the minutes don't move forward. These big slow loops stop time. I don't want the man in the crisp white shirt to come back. And he won't, not while I'm lost in the pattern in the wallpaper, just seeing circles of toffee, sand and butterscotch, constantly changing direction. I sink into a dream amongst the rich brown spirals, until the door opens and makes me jump.

I learn there are five men in the house, or maybe there are six. They all dress alike in smart dark clothes – businessmen, I think, with shiny leather shoes just like the ones that Lionel Mirvis wears. I've heard people say that your shoes always show if you're rich. So these men must have a lot of money. They aren't the same men every time and it takes me many months to know all of them by sight.

But quite quickly, I'll start to know them by their smell. I know what they've been eating, and I catch the scented cream reeking from their slicked-back hair. They sweat on warm days, and stain the underarms of those crisp pale shirts with the burnt tang of laundry.

On another of my visits, months later, I peep round the living room door and see that they are having a tea-party. There's a big china tea pot on a table, with crumbs left on plates and squashed raisins by a platter of fruit cake. There's my jug of orange juice too, and next to it a dark green bottle with a square white label and black writing.

The first time I go to the house, once I've drunk the sour-tasting juice that makes the world go dreamy, the quiet man comes back into the hallway in his crisp white shirt, dark trousers and shiny, glossy shoes. He walks towards me with a strange little smile. I know that his smile isn't real and I don't smile back. Then he reaches out and grips me by the wrist.

"Come upstairs with me now."

We walk up through the house. It seems very high. I try to count the steps but every minute that passes I'm more anxious and confused. On and on we go, up and up in the stillness. On the very top landing, there's a room. We go inside. Heavy red curtains are closed in the middle of the day. I see a big wooden bed. Then the man shuts the door behind us with a crunch.

My fluttery, wild-bird panic stirs – the beating wings. I look into his face and I see his eyes are cold, just like Uncle Vernon's.

I stop all my thoughts. The only things around me that are real are the things I can see. There are bluish water stains up high on the ceiling. Dust specks mottle the air. Streaks of gold lie on the floor as daylight shines in round the curtains. There's the bloodlight glow of the sun behind. The house is quite still. The man hurts me very very much. But whatever he does, I know that I mustn't make any sound at all.

When Mrs Anand comes to fetch me, I'm already sitting waiting in the hall, ready to put my coat and shoes on. In silence, we walk back home.

***

Whenever I was taken to the house, Mrs Anand would leave me once the front door was open. I don't know if she knew what was going on inside. She made no sign of knowing. There was just one time that was different.

That was the day when a stray dog in the street ran towards me as we got to the big front step, snapping and snarling. Then it bit my leg. Mrs Anand stayed to help clean the wound. I was pleased I'd been bitten by the dog because just for a few minutes, it meant I didn't have to go inside.

***

The morning after my first visit to the house, I walked to school just like always.

All night I'd had very bad pains in my tummy. The pains travelled all down my legs. A shivery, splintered feeling came and went away, and then came back again. I felt very far away from everything, as though I was watching things around me through a thick pane of glass. Mostly in my lessons I kept still, except once or twice when I fluttered with panic and my teeth began to chatter. Whenever I looked up, I was sure I was going to see the man in the crisp white shirt standing watching me.

Just before lunch, we all went outdoors to play rounders. But as soon as I started to run, I grew hot and wet between my legs. A thin line of blood crept down the inside of my thigh. It stopped before it reached my sock. Then a second one appeared, which didn't get as far. I went over to Miss Thompson, my teacher. I pulled at her arm and pointed because I was far too frightened to say a single word. My teacher took one look at the blood on my legs, then she led me inside.

***

Miss Thompson, my PE teacher, is very kind. She talks to me calmly and quietly and holds my hand until I stop shaking. She tells me that I'm not going to die because there's blood between my legs. I must have had an accident this morning, she says, or yesterday. When she asks me three times about my accident, I say yes, yes I did. She nods and gives a quick little smile. She sends me home from school early with a note for my mother, but I hide it and don't give it to her. I know she will be dreadfully angry if anyone at school finds out what has happened.

So when the doorbell rings that evening and Miss Thompson is standing on the black and white tiled steps, I'm so astonished that I don't know what to do.

My mother is friendly and invites her inside. Miss Thompson looks flustered and embarrassed, while my mother is smiling and calm. They quietly talk in the hall. My mother calls my name and I stand alongside her, so close that I can hear her quick breathing. She tells Miss Thompson that I hurt myself yesterday afternoon, playing on my bike in the garden.

I don't have a bike. I've never been in the garden.

"Her foot slipped off the pedals, I think, and she sat down rather hard. I must say I didn't realise it was serious and she didn't tell me it hurt — funny the things that children won't say! You poor dear — we must go to the doctor's and check there's no lasting damage been done."

Miss Thompson smiles a careful smile.

"I don't think it's too serious," she says. "I think this is an – an unfortunate thing – perhaps a little sooner than is usu – but perhaps it won't have done her lasting harm."

"But we must make sure," says my mother, determinedly. "Perhaps a hot water bottle, darling, if you have a sore – tummy, and you must rest tonight."

"Yes," says Miss Thompson. "It's certainly important to make sure."

She glances down at me.

"Sometimes," she continues, "I've noticed that your daughter has bruises. Nasty bruises. I've been feeling quite worried about her."

"Oh dear," my mother says lightly.

Miss Thompson is a very kind teacher. But the only thing I want is for her to stop talking to my mother and leave.

"She really is so clumsy – aren't you, darling? She's always dropping things. Dropping things and falling over. We're at our wits' end with her, my husband and I."

"It's certainly very difficult," says Miss Thompson, "to have a child who is always hurting herself. Thank you so much, Mrs Mirvis, for understanding my concerns."

"Of course – but of course. It's – unfortunate and embarrassing, but no harm done, I think. Thank you so much for taking the trouble to find out she's alright. Say thank you, darling."

I say thank you to Miss Thompson, then I stand with my mother and watch from the drawing room window as she walks down the black and white steps. She vanishes into the dusk. I'm very, very frightened of what is going to happen next. I know that my mother will punish me.

When the garden gate shuts with a click, she pulls the curtains closed across the big front window before she speaks a word. Her lips are white and pressed close together.

Then she says in a very quiet voice. "You – bitch. How dare you? You. Little. Bitch."

She drags me up the stairs to the bathroom. She takes off my clothes, lifts me in the bath and pours jugs of water down my legs where the thin brown blood lines are still faint traces. There are brown flecks and specks on my skin. The *salty blood smell rises when the warm water touches them. The water runs down and makes a brownish puddle at my feet.*

She picks up the scrubbing brush and scours me. The harder she scrubs, the higher and louder her voice becomes. She's nearly screaming through white lips that scarcely move: "Bitch! Fucking horrible little bitch!"

She scrubs me a very long time, until my skin is red and sore. Now you can't see where the blood marks were before. The water that flows down the plughole runs clear and clean.

***

When Lionel Mirvis's father died, the family went on a visit. I went too. It was the only time I ever remember that all we four children – me and my three sisters, for Peter wasn't born yet, with me on the end as the eldest and tallest – stood together in a row. We went to Finchley, to another big house, and all filed solemnly upstairs.

The man who had died was laid out in a bedroom. There were candles all around and people sat quietly on chairs, watching him. His dead face was yellowish and pointy and I could see pale ridges of bones through his skin. I didn't feel afraid of him because he was dead. I realised that no matter what happened in the room, he wouldn't hear and he wouldn't see. He wouldn't feel it if you touched him. But everyone still tiptoed and whispered, even the children. Everywhere around him lay the deep, deep peace and stillness of death.

As I stood and watched him, I understood that I would die too. On that day, there would be no more hearing and no seeing and no feeling – just nothing at all. When I looked at the quiet and the candles all around where the dead man was lying, it didn't seem to me as if the ending of my life was really anything to be afraid of.

***

When the time of my two divided worlds came to an end, it seemed like a dream, just the same as it had seemed in the beginning. It happened in bright flashes, like photographs being taken, but the minutes and hours in between them have all disappeared from my memory.

Flash! It started when I couldn't jump a rope in PE. I try, but when I land on my left foot, I fall to the ground.

Miss Thompson is taking the lesson. She stops and crouches down beside me.

Flash! She rolls my sock down my leg to the ankle. She doesn't go further: my foot is so swollen that my plimsoll won't fasten. There are long red-brown marks on the front and the side of my leg, purple-brown patches and raw, broken skin. She looks straight up into my face. I think that she must be angry with me.

"What happened to your leg?"

I can't answer.

Miss Thompson pulls down my other sock. That leg looks the same.

"My love, I'm not cross with you. I just need to know what happened. Can you tell me how you got these marks?"

This morning my mother was angry and she beat me with a broom. She hit me on my legs and my feet, and bashed the broom down hard on the side of my left foot. It hurt a lot then, and it wouldn't take my weight. When she saw this, though I didn't make a sound, it made my mother stop. I waited until the pain went further down inside me. Then, when I could walk on my foot, I made my way slowly to school. The pain stayed deep down all morning – but then I tried to jump and suddenly my leg wouldn't hold me any longer.

Miss Thompson touches my foot and the pain comes right up in a rush.

"All right. All right. I think we should get you an ambulance. You've hurt your foot and we need to take you to a hospital."

Flash! The worried face of the school caretaker, helping lift me up. He and Miss Thompson support me indoors. I hop along between them with an arm round the shoulder of each. I can't touch my foot to the ground.

Flash! I'm in the ambulance. Men in black uniforms with bright silver buttons. They make me lie down on a stretcher.

Flash! There are nurses in white aprons in the hospital. My foot is broken. Now it's in plaster. The nurses keep on looking at the marks on my legs. They're asking me questions but I don't know how to answer them.

Two days later, two policemen climbed the black and white tiled steps, and knocked on my mother's front door.

Soon after that, almost ten years after my world was split in two, I took my last train ride home to Stoke.

***

The police had so many questions: asking my mother and her husband, asking me. I had no idea at all what to tell them, or what it all meant. All I could think of was that I mustn't get anyone I knew into trouble, or make anybody angry. But that didn't help me answer all the questions. I stammered and stuttered and kept on saying that I didn't remember.

They asked me where I wanted to live, and I told them that my home was in Stoke with my grandparents, and no one in Stoke had ever hurt me. Then they said that I was going home.

Grandfather Edwin was older now, less and less the man of the house who rode on his bicycle and brought home the big sacks of coal. He didn't pound his fists on the kitchen table. Instead he sat all day by the hearth, listening to the radio and swearing at it. I didn't know where my mother was now, or where Lionel Mirvis was. No one even mentioned their names. No one said a word about anything that happened in London. No one talked at all in Fletcher Road, not about my leaving, and now not about my return.

As time went by, the past and the years I'd spent visiting London faded away. Dog was the only memory I had that seemed real. I didn't feel like a real person either.

Now that I was almost fifteen, I didn't go to school any more. Instead I found a very good job, down at the Spode works in the middle of town. My job was painting china, and out of all the boys and girls I used to know from Boothen Juniors, all of us heading for a life in the factories now, I was the one who would earn the most money. I walked through the town each morning, down to the factory gate. End of day on Fridays, I proudly gave my wages to my grandmother.

The factory rooms at Spode were very long and low and their floors were thickly carpeted with dust. Long trestle tables were laden with crockery and workers wearing overalls with nets on our hair, sat in rows before the plates we had to paint. One by one, they were spun on a drum while we added streaks of gold to their patterning.

I loved all the patterns of Spode: leaves and branches and roses with delicate tendrils. I could have gazed at them for hours, and before the pattern finished, I could see where it should go and exactly what the colours should be. I saw exquisite green birds with tails that fanned right out behind them. There were Chinese ladies with coiled black hair and clothes that spiralled to the ground. There was beautiful tobacco leaf – blue, gold and orange, and a ship setting sail for a distant shore. I was very, very good at painting china: everybody told me that my work was exceptional. For the first time in my life, I was proud.

But I was very clumsy in the tight, narrow space, and disaster often struck. As each plate was finished, its paint still wet and glistening, it had to be balanced in a stack. Three blocks of cork stopped it touching the others whilst it dried. The other painters finished each piece, then tossed the new plate lightly in an effortless arc, and it landed on the corks. The stack rose up to twelve plates high before it was lifted and hefted from the room on a plank to be fired. But my plates often tumbled to the ground, ending up smashed or smudged and useless. I lost the job at Spode.

There was silence at home in Fletcher Road. It seemed that the house had grown much bigger. No one else slept in the upstairs bedroom now. I lay alone at night beneath the rough brown blankets. These days we even had a television, but it didn't get clear pictures – its thick little screen was filled mostly with buzzing grey grit. Then we found the answer – if someone sat outside on the high backyard wall and held up the aerial, figures would emerge from the blur. Sometimes you could even make out what the foggy little people were saying.

I sat out on the wall with the aerial up above my head.

"Gran! My arm hurts, Gran!"

"Just another minute, duck!"

"Graaa – an!"

***

Now I am 15 years old. I have never in my life felt so alone as I do now.

The beatings and blows that my mother used to give me were the only way she knew how to love me. Now her love is gone. No one ever mentions her name. No one tells me where she is, and I'm far too scared to ask. What happened to her after the police had asked her all those questions? Violence once held me to the world, and now that violence has ended, I feel that I barely exist. Without my mother to pay me attention, it's as though I have become invisible – even to me. I drift through endless days as though I'm floating in space.

Next I find a job at the Mich, making inner tubes for tyres. At least they don't shatter when I drop them on the ground. I don't know what to say to the other girls on breaks when we eat from our snap tins. They are making plans to visit the pictures at the weekend. I have no idea why they laugh as they do. Perhaps they are laughing at me. I don't understand why I don't fit in with them, or why it's so hard for me to work out what the right thing is to say.

Gran arranges for a boy to collect me and walk out with me by the lake in Trentham Park. He gets there on time but I won't go with him. Gran tells him that she's sorry; the boy shrugs and leaves. Gran says I'm strange.

At home I still sit beneath the table, and I eat down there too, in my secret place where I used to hide with Dog. That's the only place where I really feel safe. Sometimes I think about him still, and I still miss him very, very much. But it's hard to be so sad, so I try to block it out just like I block out the rest of the past and so many of the things that have happened.

I miss my mother too, but no one ever tells me where she is, or if I'll ever see her again.

There's so much empty time all around me. This silence seems somehow worse than anything – much worse than any kind of pain. This is the loneliest time of my life.

I spend my days of nothing time just dreaming. I dream about patterns on wallpaper, patterns on china, slivers of light on the floor and the glow of the sun. Circles and spirals go round and around till they curl into emptiness and air.

***

I saw an army poster and decided that I wanted to sign up. Everyone around me was talking about the Cuban missile crisis. The world seemed a terribly dangerous place, filled with threats of war. Surely a soldier would be strong in such perilous times. To help keep people safe seemed a good and worthwhile thing to do.

After I applied, the army sent a khaki green canvas case with a thick black handle. With it came a big pile of forms and a list of all the things that I had to take with me. I saw that I needed my birth certificate.

That certificate was part of our family story. I knew that it was with me in the box when I was left as a baby by Stoke football ground, just around the corner. I'd never once seen it. Even to this day, my gran still wouldn't show me, although that might be because I'd never asked.

"Gran – I need it. I have to prove that I'm British, that I was born in Britain."

"Of course you was born in Britain. Listen to you talk."

41

"But this is for a form. This is official. It's the army! They have to see the paperwork."

"It should be obvious that you can join the army, duck."

"Uncle Vernon did the forms for the navy, didn't he? And Granddad did. Gran, you know I have to have it. The day I report to the barracks to sign up, I have to show them my proper papers. They won't let me join unless I do."

I was very determined. And I didn't want it only for the army: I wanted to find out about me. My mother, when I knew her, never told me how she came to leave her baby labelled in a box by Stoke City football ground long ago. Now she had vanished again, and I felt like the child from nowhere. But tomorrow I was leaving. I must take my birth certificate with me.

"Gran. I need it, Gran. *Graaaaan.*"

"You know it isn't right, what it says," Gran muttered. "I don't know where it came from. I don't think it's official. I don't know if the date on it is right."

"They won't know that. It says I was born in England, doesn't it? It says I'm British."

"It says you was born in Surrey. I don't think Syl went all the way to Surrey then came all the way back with a baby. I think it's a funny certificate that somebody made for her here when you was born, a friend of hers maybe. I don't know what she did to get it but what if it's —"

"Give her the certificate, Sarah," said grandfather Edwin suddenly from his chair.

Gran went upstairs and fetched it.

My mother's name I knew, though she wasn't Mrs Mirvis back when I was born. I came in 1945, before she was married and rich and had beautiful new clothes. What I wanted to see was the other name written on the form – the name of my father.

But then when I saw it, I thought there must have been a mistake. I read the name. Then I read it again.

"Gran? Gran? I don't understand."

The name on the form was Edwin. The year of his birth was 1890. That was just the same as my grandfather. I tried to speak again.

"Gran – it says – gran –"

Through big, clumsy lips I tried to ask the question. The words wouldn't come.

"Gran – is he – is he –?"

Then my gran wept and I knew.

I was Edwin's daughter as well as his granddaughter. My grandfather Edwin made my mother have a baby. Having his baby was the reason she must have run away.

I remembered my grandfather in his chair by the fire and the things that he did to me there. I felt his rough hands touching me, caught the stink of his breath and saw the glitter of his eyes. My stomach turned over. But it turned over twice now I knew that I wasn't the first little girl he had forced to do all this. My mother Sylvia had stood there before me.

I remembered how she scoured my skin in the bath long ago. How the brownish blood water ran down, and the way she kept on scrubbing, as though she could never get me clean. I remembered Auntie Opal, and how she would cut herself in the kitchen. I could see where the dark brown stain of her blood still marked the floor. I thought of Uncle Vernon down by the river, and the dull empty look in his eyes. I understood now what the secret of our family really was, and why no one here would ever speak. I felt as if the shame of knowing all of this would burn me up completely.

Upstairs, I finished packing my khaki canvas case with the things I would need for the army. Half-ready beforehand, I'd done in ten minutes. I'd nothing left to say to my gran or to Edwin my father.

It was spring 1963, and I was seventeen. I left the house by the green front door as Auntie Frieda once did, and slammed it behind me in the way that she had done. I walked down Fletcher Road towards the station alone.

Chapter Three

I joined the army to see the world and got as far as Bicester

Qui-ick… march! Eyes right, eyes left, on the spot, in unison. March and salute. Eyes left! Eyes right! About turn! Halt!

I don't know which way I'm going. On the parade ground, I just can't seem to follow orders. The others can, faster and more smartly every time. But I spin around too soon and crash straight into Paddy who's behind me. The girl behind bumps into her. The collision runs right down the line like dominoes toppling.

We have to start the drill from the beginning. The other girls hiss at me to get a grip on myself and just listen to orders, can't you, else we'll be here all day. But I'm listening hard already. It doesn't make my body join in.

"Count your steps, you idiot!" Sergeant Kathy barks. "Count them! You can count, can't you!?"

She never hits anyone, though. I'd expected beatings in the army. The sergeant's so fierce that the others sometimes cry when they get the drills wrong, or fail kit inspection, or turn out late on parade. But I don't cry once. And however much she shouts, when I realise that she's never going to hit me, I smile. I can't think of anything better than knowing that I'm safe.

"And wipe that bloody grin off your face!"

***

The train pulled into the station in the late afternoon. I was tired from my long journey south, and thirsty, though I didn't feel hungry. I never really seemed to feel hungry, as though a hard tight knot in my stomach that never went away could take the place of food.

My khaki case banged against my legs as I walked, containing all the things on the long list they'd sent me: a brush and a comb, new socks, toothpaste, soap, hairpins. All the clothes I owned. At the bottom of the case was my birth certificate, tucked where I didn't have to look.

When they asked us to present our papers, the certificate was ready in my hand. As I passed it over, I stood holding my breath, certain that the office would know the truth about me the moment she saw it. She glanced, but made no reaction – instead she just ticked off my name on a list and handed the certificate back. What did I think she would say? Of course she wouldn't show the disgust that I knew she must feel for somebody like me.

This was Surrey, the place where the certificate said that I'd been born. Women's Royal Army Corps recruits reported to Lingfield for training. The green army lorry that met us outside the station was full to bursting with dozens of girls, all of us with suitcases like mine. On the journey to the camp, the others were giggly and nervous with excitement, glancing at each other then down at the floor. We were closely crushed together as the lorry took the bends on the narrow road.

We arrived at camp at dusk and saw neat rows of huts in a field inside a high encircling fence. The rooms where we would live were very plain, with grey metal beds and square white lockers. There were eight girls to a building, four beds each side and a bathroom at the end for all of us to share. There were nine altogether with Joy, our platoon lieutenant, who had her own private room.

We went to pick up kit from an office at the end of the field, called to a counter four at a time to be issued with our garments. Our uniforms were scratchy and rough, just like the big army coat

I'd slept beneath in Fletcher Road: a jacket, white shirt and tie – always to be fastened with a Windsor knot – then khaki trousers, spats, boots and beret.

As soon as I put my uniform on, I felt bigger and stronger and more real than I ever had before. I was a soldier now. I was recruit number W416068.

At first, nothing fitted. We scratched at the sides of our necks where our stiff new collars chafed and scraped: for days the skin was red raw. Alterations could be done by a seamstress: where it needed taking up or taking in, she made chalk marks to follow with her needle. I was small and slight and my uniform hung in great folds. The seamstress drew white lines down my sides where she needed to gather it in. Although I was a soldier now, I flinched when she pressed her stick of chalk to my hip.

On our very first night, Sergeant Kathy gave a talk. She was stocky and dark, with tight muscles and thick black eyebrows. She stood there, solid and confident. Welcome, she said. She told us that this was a proud and special place, which made us special too: we were a part of the British army. We stood for its values and lived by its standards.

And if we broke the rules, we'd be punished. This mostly meant docked pay, but she told us that far worse was possible. Harshest of all was dishonourable discharge – to be sent away from the army in disgrace. The shame would last your whole life. Everyone would know that you'd betrayed your country, betrayed your army comrades, let down your family and let down yourself.

I didn't understand all she said, but I did like listening. I wanted to help save the world – from Fidel Castro, the atom bomb, the crisis with the missiles in Cuba and the threat of nuclear war... all those awful things that could happen to innocents. I wanted to make the world safe from disaster and fear.

Still, on our very first night in Lingfield, some of the girls were unhappy. Quiet tears fell once the lights were turned out. But no one was homesick for long – we were all too busy. It was only in the evening that sadness could sometimes peep in through the small square windows of our hut.

I didn't cry for home. There was nothing there for me, and I knew it. I couldn't look back. This was my new world and I would have to learn to live in it.

***

But trouble came right from the start.

On the very first morning came the new routine: maintenance of barracks, kit inspection, drill and basic training. Inspection was hard, with everything just so or else – uniform folded on each girl's bed with the beret placed neatly on top and the bedsheet and blanket in a pile. We never quite seemed ready when the inspection alarm was raised: "They're coming! They're coming!" I was the last every time, and always the one who would get into trouble.

We did physical training with press-ups and star jumps and bunny hops, and long runs all round the perimeter of camp in all weathers. We travelled by lorry into nearby towns where we'd use the empty buildings, some of them still with real wartime damage, to practise what the army called 'rescue': saving people from explosions, accidents and fires. Some of us played victims, lying on the ground or covered up in chunks of rubble, waiting to be found and then carried outside. I quickly found out that I'd rather be rescuer than find myself thrown over someone's shoulder or dragged inexpertly down a flight of stairs.

On our very first night, we filed across the compound to the cookhouse. It was steamy-hot and crowded, with pink, shiny faces all in dark green clothes, like a room full of plants. Everybody chattered and laughed. The big crowded cookhouse made me feel very anxious. I'd never seen a meal served like this, or any place at all like this before.

We picked up our mess trays then went past a counter, holding out the tray. The cooks served everyone a big scoop of everything. I wasn't hungry – I never seemed to be hungry – and didn't know what all the food was. I'd never paid attention to it before, or liked to eat much, just gulped down quickly whatever I was given so that I could get away and hide. No one ever asked me what I liked, or taught me how to cook, and I'd never minded. I didn't want to pay attention to my body in any way at all.

The mess tray was heavy. I was scared of dropping it, so that everyone would turn around and stare at me. I wobbled along, eyes fixed on my tray, hoping a seat would appear somewhere close. My heart beat fast and hard. At last – an empty chair, but now I couldn't eat. I pulled the piece of bread I'd been given to bits and sprinkled the crumbs on the tray. Now it looked as though I might have been eating.

After that, when meal times came along, I'd grab my slice of bread from the square brown basket by the soup. Then I took it back to the hut and ate it on my own. I tried not to drop any crumbs so that no one would know. That was all I ate.

I noticed how my body would skip past all the things that the others found important – endless small needs, so that life in the barracks was filled with their clamour. "I'm starving!" they'd say, and "it's freezing in here!" or "it's stuffy!." They were constantly opening and closing the windows. I had no idea why they took such notice of the way they were feeling. I felt numb all the time, so whether it was hot or cold scarcely seemed to matter at all.

I watched them as they formed their friendships, joking and laughing, saving places in line and heading to the cookhouse in groups. I couldn't understand how they knew how to do it.

***

I grew more and more afraid of lying in my bed. Whichever way I faced, there was somebody behind me. I thought of asking the girl in the bed at the end to swap so that I could lie with my back to the wall. But she had sharp black eyes and nudged the others and made jokes that I couldn't quite hear. Then I heard them giggling and saw them look towards me. I didn't want to ask her after that.

I hated the way the springs on the bed gave a creak when I sat on it, no matter how slowly and carefully I bent my knees. I hated the firmness of the mattress, pushing back at me with tight little springs. It felt just like the big bed in the house by the fire station. If I closed my eyes even for a moment, I caught the smell of bed rising up – the hot stink of blood.

The biggest fear of all was falling asleep. When I shut my eyes, I had started to see pictures. I saw the hall of a quiet house in London, as clearly as if I was sitting there on my chair, sipping my orange juice and waiting. There was thick brown wallpaper, almost like velvet, patterned in creamy, chocolatey swirls. In a moment, I knew someone would come for me. Then I gasped and forced my eyes wide open to melt all this away and bring back the barracks and the smooth shapes of seven quiet sleepers there. The fear grew worse every night until I only had to see the bed to feel a lurch of dread in my belly.

I lay as still as I could, always watching, my head propped up high on a pillow folded double. I could hear the others' deep slow breaths. From time to time, someone muttered in her dreams. Then each morning, at last, the pale window squares grew bright, the bell rang and everybody woke.

I knew that if I slept, a man in a crisp pale shirt and smart shiny shoes would come in my dreams. He'd tell me to follow him, up and up the house on those zigzag flights where I always lost count of the stairs, to the room with dark red curtains kept closed even in the afternoons. Where was that man now? What if he was here? My heart beat so fast that I thought my ribs might splinter and break.

I started to tremble as lights-out approached, so hard I could barely keep the others from noticing. I felt the sweat running down my sides. What if the quiet man was outside the barracks, pressed against the window, watching me? What if he got inside? I dug my fingers hard into my palms. I mustn't make a sound. The weight of him was crushing me. Panic wings beat and thrashed in my bed.

"SHHHHH will you!? Shhhh! Why are making all that noise?" came a voice from close alongside.

"Huh? Uh?"

"Just keep still! Some of us are trying to sleep! And stop squealing!"

"Sounded to me like she had company!" another voice said, followed by a burst of laughter.

***

I wait a bit longer until everyone's asleep, then carefully climb out and pull my sheet and blanket right off. The pillow comes too, and I push the whole bundle underneath the bed then roll myself up in it.

Down on the floor I am safe. Now there are watchtowers: four bed legs, one at each corner like guard posts all around. I curl up in a ball with my arm around Dog, who will stay with me through the night and always.

If the man in the pale shirt approaches, I know that Dog will growl. He will never let anyone hurt me. He will bite the man and chase him away.

***

Next morning I was woken by a bare foot prodding me in the ribs.

"What are you doing under there?"

Blurry and sleepy, I couldn't think how to reply.

"She slept under the bed, look!"

"Did you fall out?"

"Yes."

"You fell out of bed with all of your bedclothes and pillow as well?"

"Uhh… I must have done."

"You're not right in the head, you."

"What do you think you're doing down there? Hahahaha!"

I became a space in the room. Army life was all about learning to fit in. The others could make friends. I didn't know how. I didn't understand how they could know this, or where they had learned. What was it that they talked and joked about so easily? They weren't unpleasant, they just left me alone – until I began to get them into trouble.

There were big problems out on the parade ground. I couldn't get the drills right although I tried and tried: I turned left when the others turned right, saluted with the wrong hand, lost track of my steps and stopped when I shouldn't, walked into somebody's heels when I'd not been counting right. Out there for hours in all weathers, up and down and up and down while the sergeant yelled louder and louder, the rest of the squad got angry. Then the sarge found breadcrumbs on the barracks hut floor and the whole room was punished with a long extra run on a freezing cold morning. They all knew it must have been me.

No one invited me over to the NAAFI in the evenings. The NAAFI was the camp's social place, with a shop and a bar and a launderette. I noticed how people did chores over there with their friends. Everyone drank at the bar until last orders at 10pm, laughing and joking, getting friendly with the men. I sat in the hut alone and smoked. When I entered, a hush would fall, which meant they'd been talking about me. Then I'd hear them giggling, or see them roll their eyes.

Weekends meant home leave; the camp was almost empty. Two of us always remained, me and dreamy, quiet Paddy with her southern Irish accent I could scarcely understand. I think that we were friends, though I wasn't sure that I deserved a friend. We never told each other why neither of us had anywhere to go, but I liked her, and found that her company was peaceful.

Sometimes she wrote letters, sitting on her bed and turned to face the wall with her head bent low. She wrote for a very long time, pushing her hair off her face and sighing. She couldn't be writing happy words, with her high hunched shoulders, pressing down so hard with her pen. But at least she had something to say to somebody else in the world.

***

Some of the girls made special friends. I knew that these friendships must be secret. To me it made more sense that you'd want to be friends with a girl – much more than you would with a man. Men in their uniforms scared me, especially the thud of their feet. It sounded to me like Uncle Vernon's boots in the yard in Fletcher Road.

The girls who were special friends with girls were the ones I liked best. They dressed the smartest, marched the sharpest and wise-cracked the fastest. They seemed not to need the men at all: instead of flipping out their hair and looking up sideways and smiling and not saying much, they laughed and joked with each other. They looked very strong. But I knew they would never talk to me. If they did, I'd no idea at all what I would say.

One afternoon I was smoking alone, and two girls ran in through the door. Neither of them was from our barracks, and I wondered what they were doing there. Down at the end of the room, I was sitting on the floor with my back to the wall.

They jumped in the bed near the door. Both of them were giggling. Then their laughter changed into sighs and moans. It sounded as though one of them was hurting the other. The thought of that kind of hurting made shivery dread run right through me.

I knew they'd be angry if they found I was there. I lay down on the floor with my fingers in my ears, waiting for the noises to stop.

When I tried to join in conversations, I found my throat grew dry and my lips became stiff. I worried I would say something strange because I couldn't talk and laugh the way the other girls did. The longer I went without speaking, the stranger my voice sounded if I tried. I felt my strangeness growing and growing inside me. I didn't know how to make it stop.

***

I didn't pay attention to my wages. I knew that I had an account and that money was paid to me, then after that, the costs of my barracks and my meals were taken out. The NAAFI shop sold everything we needed: toothpaste, soap and washcloths when an old one was worn right through. The shop opened late, because we were so busy all day. I walked there one warm spring evening, then back through the compound in the dusk. Nobody else was around.

Close to the ground by our hut glared a red fiery eye. Somebody was sitting there smoking on the grass, her back leant up against the wall.

"Want a ciggie, Private?"

Sergeant Kathy's voice. I knew from the slur of her words that she'd been drinking. I wondered why she'd come back so early from the NAAFI.

I didn't want a ciggie. "Yes, alright."

"Siddown over here next to me."

I didn't want to sit with her. "Okay."

I crouched on the ground and took a cigarette. The match flared and lit up her face. She smiled.

I inhaled. "Thanks."

"You don' like going to the NAAFI with the others, then? Not made many friends here, have you?"

"No."

"Iss' because you're too tense. You need to relax more, Private. Relax an' join in, you know what I'm sayin'?"

I smoked more quickly, so that I could get away from her.

"You don' drink, do you?"

I didn't drink at all. I didn't like the noise in the NAAFI. I hated the beer smell, like something that was starting to rot. I was frightened of the men and the way they would grab you when they'd had a few pints. Sometimes they'd grab with their hands, but always with their eyes. The other girls just giggled and slapped the hands away.

"I don't like the taste."

"You'd get to like it, you would, if you joined in."

A last quick pull on my cigarette. I tried to stand up.

"Well, I –"

Kathy leaned nearer and pressed her hand down on my knee.

"Sorry, Private. Sorry sorry sorry. 'S none of my business if you don' wan' to get friendly while you're here."

She was very close now.

"But – don' you wan' to be – you know?"

She meant did I want to be her special friend. I didn't. I wanted her to leave me alone.

"It'd make things nicer for you here, Private, wouldn' it, eh? If we were… you know…"

I needed to tell her that I couldn't be her friend. I was frightened. I didn't know how. But then she didn't wait for me to answer. Instead her hand snaked up my leg. Her fingers gripped hard.

Panic.

Everything slid sideways, as though I'd been thrown from my body. There was no space to breathe – just Kathy's face pressed up to mine. Her smoky mouth was big and wet and wide. In a dazzle like a flashbulb going off, I saw the close-up pores of her skin and the fine downy hairs on her cheeks. Her raw pink tongue came flicking and licking at my lips.

I sprang back in horror, lost my balance and went sprawling on the grass. Spiky blades bristled at the back of my neck. I was terrified that Kathy would jump on me and try to pin me down. The thought of the pressure of her long, heavy body filled me with fear. My arms and legs flailed.

Kathy started laughing.

"Wha's the matter, Private?"

"No!" I said, but the word was a gasp on an indrawn breath. I didn't think she'd heard.

"Tha's not very nice now, is it?"

"*No!*" Surely she could see the violent tremors running through me. I leapt up from the ground with all my might.

I feel as though I'm spinning away from my body and from Kathy and the huts and the compound. My arms and legs move although I'm not telling them what to do. I plunge forwards as fast as I can, tilting so far over that I stagger. I've no idea at all where I'm going.

Footsteps shake the ground, or perhaps it's the pounding of my heart. Someone's coming after me. Running, I see splashes of silver and black – the night sky above and the lights of the huts. Kathy's footfall crashes at my heels. My eyes must be staring. The sound of my voice is too high for anyone to hear: an endless scream made out of silence.

Now there's a man shouting too, and other more distant voices. Nothing seems real. I lash out at anything that gets in my way. I run and I run.

***

"Step inside, Private!"

I walked in through Captain Nicholson's office door and saluted, though I probably used the wrong hand. She was seated behind her big desk with piles of paper on top of it, and grey ring-bound files full of army business. There was one open file on the top, with typed sheets of paper inside.

Three words on the very top sheet were in dark, bolder type: clear enough to read them upside-down. The first two words were my name and the third was "absconded." I wasn't sure what this word meant.

Alongside me was another sergeant, whose name I didn't know. In all the confusion since they brought me back to camp, nobody had said. Everyone I saw was very angry. No one really spoke to me at all.

The sergeant and I both stood to attention. Captain Nicholson put us at ease.

She had streaky grey hair in a regulation bun and her lips pressed together in one straight line. She was going to say something, then she frowned. She looked hard at the densely typed text on the top sheet of paper.

"I think it's fair to say that army life hasn't worked out well for you so far, Private."

"No, ma'am."

"Why do you think that might be?"

I didn't know why army life hadn't worked out for me. I wished very much that it had.

"I don't know why, ma'am."

She tilted her head to one side.

"Other people have told me why they think it is, Private, but now I'd like to hear it from you. You might have a different explanation."

In the silence, I heard the sergeant next to me let out a tight little sigh.

"I don't know, ma'am."

"Alright then. So can you tell me where you went on Tuesday night when you left camp without permission? And before you tell me where you went, can you tell me why?"

I knew that I could never tell her why. As for where, I was not at all sure.

"I can't remember, ma'am."

She frowned.

"You can't remember why you left, or you can't remember where you went?"

"I can't remember much about it, ma'am."

"Private, I want you to understand that I am trying to help you. It's clear to me, from what your commanding officer has said, that you are a hard-working member of your unit. You have some difficulties with the basic skills the army requires, but what I'm hearing is that you have been trying hard to acquire them."

I didn't think that she would be so nice. I thought she was going to be angry.

"We're not just here to punish you. When someone has tried hard, and things have not gone right, the army can give a second chance."

She paused.

"But to do that, I need to overlook a serious offence. You have absconded from camp." She saw that I didn't understand. "Absconding means leaving camp without permission. You were absent without leave overnight. And of course, there was an – incident, when you left on Tuesday evening. Quite a serious incident. I have statements from those who saw you leaving – and in two cases tried to stop you – and I'm worried by what they've said. They describe your behaviour as out of control – shouting and screaming, pushing other people around. But they don't say that you seemed angry, Private. They say that you seemed terrified. Are you able to tell me why?"

Nothing that had happened two nights ago – or three nights ago, or maybe only one, I really wasn't sure – seemed real any longer. Remembering was like thinking of a long time ago, when you've lost all the details. You're left with just a series of bright little blinks, and nothing to string them together.

***

I'm on a train, but I don't know how it happened; then in a big, bustling station with lights all around. London Victoria, I read. I feel as though I'm here but I'm not here at all. It's like looking at a picture on a screen.

Time keeps jumping forward, like fragments of film snipped from a reel. Sounds are faint but then boom really loud. Everything I see curves like a fishbowl. The edges seem very far away but anything in front looms right up in my face and startles me.

I still have my wallet in my pocket. Somehow I've managed not to lose it, even though I know I was running on a long narrow road in the dark for a very long time. I remember falling over; there's mud on my trousers and the palms of both my hands.

Faces come up to me; people are talking and laughing. Somebody pokes me in the ribs; I shrink away from this and there's even more laughter. I realise I must look very strange, because I'm gathering a crowd in the middle of the station. Everyone is staring. My panic begins to bubble up. If they don't stop pressing in around me, I will scream and run away.

Then I see a woman with a very kind face and lots of blonde hair that looks stiff, like a fluffy helmet. She pushes her way through the crowd and asks me if I'd like a cup of tea. I must say yes because next there's a jump and now we're sitting in a cafe. I'm burning my fingers on a blue china teacup. I have to put it down very quickly; my tea slops into the saucer and drips on the tabletop too.

The blonde woman takes out a handkerchief and dabs at my face which is streaky with dirt. I can see brown stains on the cloth. I try to say thank you and she smiles at me again. This time she rubs my cheek gently with the backs of her fingers. She seems very kind.

Another blurry jump to a big black cab. I see the city and the glitter of its brilliant shop windows. The London lights make streamers in my vision if I turn my head too quickly. I squeeze my eyes tight shut. When I peep, there are theatres going by, with chains across their wide front doors because by now it's late at night. There are beautiful photographs of actors and actresses on billboards.

Shaftesbury Avenue. Old Compton Street. Dean Street. Then a tiny little door without a sign. A flight of steps leading to a basement. It's very warm down here. There's music playing loudly and people are dancing.

The blonde lady sits with me at a table and talks. I can't follow most of what she says. I'm dizzy and the lights all have halos hanging round them. I rest here and float while the music comes and goes. In a little while, the lady stops talking. She smiles and strokes my hair, and then she lets me be.

I stare blurrily out across the room. Something here is strange but for a moment, I don't know what it is. Then I notice that the people who are dancing are all men; there are no women on the floor at all. The men dance in pairs, very slowly, with their arms around each other. Whilst I'm still understanding this, the two nearest to me start to kiss.

And then I can't stop watching. These kisses are like nothing I have ever seen or dreamed.

These men don't look guilty or ashamed. They don't grab their kisses, like the boys and girls who stepped out in Trentham Park or went snogging round the back of the Spode works when I worked there painting china long ago. They turn their heads sideways, break off, then kiss again, as if they're being careful to plant each one in just the right place. They move gently, lost in a slow, deep embrace. I'd never seen such tenderness, or even imagined it. I'd no idea that any man was capable of this. When I see it, the sadness and emptiness inside me seem to rise and fill me up.

I sit there and watch them for a very long time. Colours swim and merge and run as if it was raining indoors. Or perhaps that's the tears without end that come streaming down my cheeks and drip onto my grubby army shirt.

***

"Private? Pay attention, please. Answer my question. Can you tell me why?"

"Why what, ma'am?"

'Why you absconded, Private."

"I don't know why I left camp, ma'am. I – went to London."

"You handed yourself in to Charing Cross police station at five o'clock the following morning. The officers describe you as 'confused'.

Do you have any idea where you had been?"

"No, ma'am."

"Do you have friends in London?"

"No, ma'am."

There was more silence.

"They tell me you never go home at weekends. Is there not somewhere you could go?"

"No, ma'am."

"You don't have relatives? In your file, it mentions your next of kin as your grandparents. Do you never visit them? Do you not get on?"

For a moment, I saw my grandfather's face. I smelled his breath and felt his rough hands. *You are not a proper child. You're dirty. If you were a proper child, I wouldn't have to do it.* I closed my eyes tight, and turned my head to push the image of him as far away from me as I could.

"No, ma'am. There's no one I can visit."

"This may be a strange question, Private, but do you have nightmares?"

"I don't know, ma'am."

"Other members of your barracks say that sometimes at night you seem anxious. They say you don't sleep very well."

I didn't know the others had been watching me underneath my bed. How did they know I was awake? Even when I'd been the most scared that the smart, quiet man would come down the stairs to fetch me, I'd tried to hold tightly on to Dog and to never make a sound.

"Can you tell me about your family, at all? Or – perhaps it's too hard for you to talk about the past?"

Ma'am, I could never ever tell you. No one knows the truth about me or the truth about my family. No one will ever know about where I came from. Nothing that happened in our house in Fletcher Road can ever be spoken of.

The words were so clear and so sharp in my head that it seemed as if I'd said them aloud.

Captain Nicholson placed her hands flat on her desk.

"Alright, Private. I think that sometimes we all need a fresh start in life. And it can help us to put the past behind us if we change some of the things that remind us of it. I can think of something which might help. To make a fresh start, have you ever thought of changing your name?"

Her words made no sense. My name was my name. Of course I couldn't change it, just as nothing else about me could ever be changed.

"Perhaps you don't know this is possible. But it is – it's something you can legally do. I knew someone else, a junior cadet, who did the same thing – quite a long time ago. She had had – a difficult time. I think she gained some peace of mind. You have to pay a lawyer. But you've hardly spent your army pay at all – it's building up and now I believe you have almost enough. If you would like to find out more, I will ask someone to give you the information about what you should do."

"I can change my name, ma'am?"

"Yes, Private. Didn't you know?"

For a moment I couldn't speak at all.

"Do you think you would like to do that?"

In a burst of hope and excitement, all my words came out in a rush. "You mean – I'd get a different birth certificate? If it had a different name on it would it be a different one? A new one? Ma'am, I mean. Sorry, ma'am."

The captain gave a very small smile.

"I believe that you would get entirely new documentation to record your change of name, Private, yes."

"Would I have to show anyone my birth certificate then, ma'am?"

"The new document would be more important. You could show people that instead and explain that it replaces your birth certificate."

I could scarcely believe what I was hearing. I'd believed I would carry my grandfather's name like a scar. I thought he would always be with me.

"I suggest we make a plan to help you, Private. I'll order the papers to be sent to you and you can take a look at what you have to do."

"Thank you, ma'am!"

"But I need something from you in return."

"Yes, ma'am."

"A fresh start means just that. You must start behaving differently here. I know you find it hard, but one thing that helps above all is to have comrades. It's important for anyone who serves in the British army."

"Yes, ma'am."

"You can't find comrades sitting alone. You need to join in with the others. You must try to get to know them. It would help if you went over to the NAAFI and spent some of your leisure time there."

Noise and jostling as everyone crowded in together. The dank smell of drink. I didn't want to go to the bar in the NAAFI. But the captain would help me to get a new name. For that, I was ready to do as she said.

"Yes, ma'am."

"You agree that you'll do as I've suggested? That you'll make a real effort to start afresh?"

"Yes, ma'am."

"You did the right thing to come back to the army, Private. To hand yourself in to the police as you did was brave. It's right for us to face up to the consequences of our actions. Sometimes when we do that, we find our problems aren't as serious as we thought."

"Yes, ma'am.".

"Very well, Private. Dismissed."

***

"Well now, look who's here!"

"Hey! It's —"

"– Nicky now, remember!" someone else butted in.

"Oh yes – how could we forget? It's Private *Nicky Nicholls*, isn't it? Hello Private Nicky!"

I liked it because it sounded butch and tough. My old name was soft, a real girl's name, and my new one was a chance for me to become a new person who was strong and who couldn't be hurt any more. But it still seemed very odd to be called something else.

The Deed of Change of Name, when it finally arrived through the post, was covered in curly black script with a big red seal in the bottom right hand. It seemed so much more solid than my yellowed, scrawled, shameful old birth certificate. I stared and stared at it. Someone with her name on a document like this could surely be proper at last. With my brand new name, a brand new life was possible, everything different and better for new proper me.

I cleared my throat. "That's right – I'm Nicky Nicholls." I thought of the captain's words. *You can't find comrades sitting alone.* That's why I was here, standing stiffly alongside the other girls, wondering what on earth I should order at the bar.

"Well done, anyway," said Paddy. "I think it's a nice name. It suits you."

Now they were all smiling. Someone must have told them to be friendly to me, and how I was having a fresh start. But even when they were all nice, there was thinking and talking to be done, and working out how to fit in. I wasn't sure what I should do next.

"We should have a toast! To your new name! Let's do that. What are you drinking?"

I didn't want to drink and get noisy and shouty and out of control. I didn't want men to be near me and not be on my guard.

"Um…"

"C'mon now! What you having?"

"She'll have a Coca-Cola, please," said Paddy.

"Faaah! She can't have that! She needs a proper drink!"

"If that's what she likes then she can have it, can't she?"

Paddy was a quiet one, but still no one giggled or laughed behind her back. She never seemed to care what anyone said. There wasn't much fun in winding her up.

"Cola for Nicky, then."

The curvy glass bottle was placed in my hand.

"Cheers, Nicholls!"

I muttered "cheers" and drank from the bottle.

"Gee and tee for me!" said Joy. When her drink was passed across the bar it was short and clear, like a little glass of water. Gee and tee looked nicer than the pints of brown, soapy-looking liquid most people seemed to drink, that smelled of wet floors and old vegetables.

Joy saw me looking.

"Want to try it, do you? Go on then — have a sip."

I didn't really want to, but now she thought I did. I wasn't fitting in if I told her that I didn't. I needed to fit in.

"What is it?"

She laughed. "It's gin and tonic," she said.

I lifted the glass.

***

That smell. I recognise that smell. Gee and tee is the smell of my strange orange juice, long ago in the big London house by the fire station. When it catches in my nose, I cry out. I lose my hold on the drink. It tumbles onto the bar and tips over. The liquid shoots up like clear shiny fingers, splattering the sleeve of my shirt.

One time I peeped round the living room door in the house and saw that they were having a tea-party. There was a big china tea pot next to crumbs on plates and some left-over fruit cake. There was a big jug of orange juice too, which must have been mine; right next to that was a dark green glass bottle with a square white label and black writing. I realise now that this was a bottle of gin. I can see the same green bottle, right there behind the bar, and read its black writing.

Gin in the orange juice, sending me drifting in a haze. Gin so that nothing seemed quite real. Gin on the breath of the men in their crisp white shirts and dark shiny shoes. I can see the stairs that lead me up and up through the house. I can hear their footsteps coming. Gin. They gave me gin. Gin to make me dreamy and confused, so that they could –

The stink of gin makes me want to throw up. My shirtsleeve is soaked. The smell of it is everywhere, half bitter, half sweet. I gag and retch and clap both my hands to my mouth.

"What do you think you're doing?"

"Oh for chrissake!"

"Why didn't you say you don't like it?"

"I told you she's nuts!"

"Oh my God! What's the matter with her?!"

***

I thought my army uniform would change me like clothes that you put on inside as well as out. But I'm still me. I'm strange and I'm bad. I am not a proper child. I am not a proper soldier, however hard I try. I'm not like any of these other people here. I can't be one of them.

No matter what I do, the walls of my strangeness rise higher each day, closing me off and leaving me alone.

***

"Your beret's too big – haven't you noticed?" said Paddy.

I'd heard the other girls complaining how droopy theirs were. I didn't think it mattered.

"Did you know you can shrink them to fit?"

"No."

"They look better when they properly fit your head, don't you think?"

I hadn't thought about it, but it was nice of Paddy to explain.

"Well, yes."

"So we should do yours, this weekend when there's no one else around."

"What do you mean – do mine?"

"Shrink it. Boil it. Only for a minute, though. You put it in boiling water then it goes straight into cold water, then you shape it to your head. When you dry it, it fits you!"

"Is that what they've done?"

"Yes – most people have. The sarge gets cross but she can't say much if you're still wearing it and it's clean, can she?"

"Okay."

"Not if you don't want to. But – it would look nicer."

"I don't mi – yes, okay, I'd like to. Thanks."

I felt a bit strange and very shy, but still, it was nice to have a friend. I went to the kitchens with Paddy on Saturday afternoon. She fetched a big metal pan and filled it with water, then lit the gas and put it on to boil. We stood side by side and watched the little bubbles form in silence.

"It takes a long time," I said to her.

"That's because a watched hat never boils!"

We both thought that was funny. She smiled at me and I smiled back.

"Where are you going to go, then, Nicky, at the end of training? Only two weeks left now. You applied for anything?"

"I've tried a few."

"What did you try?"

"I wanted to join the army band, but I can't read music. Or I wanted to be a vet, but you have to be qualified for that."

"Why did you want to be a vet?"

"To look after the horses," I said. That had sounded wonderful. I'd hoped I could train for it. But they only wanted people who'd passed their School Certificate.

"So what will you do?"

"Ordnance," I told her. "That means supplies – it's looking after everything the army might need, all the guns and equipment and things. They might need things urgently, sometimes."

"Sounds exciting!"

"So I'm going to Bicester, to be trained for the Royal Army Ordnance Corps," I explained to her, stumbling a bit with the words.

"Well, good luck to you,"said Paddy, and she gave me a proper little grin. "It's been very nice to meet you and wherever you go, you're going to have a well-fitting beret!"

She was right: when we were done, my beret shrank just like she said. I had to squeeze my fingers inside it to tuck in the stray bits of my hair. But I still didn't try to hang around with Paddy or talk to her, even though I thought she was nice. I felt too awkward to talk to a friend. And anyway, what would I say?

***

Bicester Garrison was different from Lingfield, much bigger and noisier, with trucks and jeeps coming and going on the roads that criss-crossed the camp. A group of us travelled there by lorry. As we came to the perimeter fence, I saw long blocks of red-brick buildings, modern and clean with white metal windows. The camp lay in a gently sloping valley with a big square parade ground at the bottom, and halfway up the slope was a larger building, two floors high with a wide glass frontage.

My new job here was to organise the transport. I was based in the radio hut which was right at the top of the slope, very close to the perimeter fence. Our orders would come through on a big black telephone, or sometimes on piles of official slips of paper, densely typed then threaded together with a spike. Through the hut's window, I would watch the lorries heading up and down the long road that ran to the garrison gate.

I didn't like the job because I found it hard to concentrate. I was easily distracted, with long chains of worries going round in my head, jumping when the phone rang and forgetting things I'd only just been told. I was supposed to record the details of the bookings in a log: who was going where and taking what, and how many vehicles they needed. Sometimes I had to make changes to the schedule but it was hard to think clearly and I often got it wrong. They saw I was confused, and told me to ring the garrison sergeant major's office if I didn't know what I ought to do. The GSM would come up to the hut, or on busy days he'd send someone else, to make the extra phone calls and changes and do the crossings-out. But then I was worried that everyone was angry. I knew I was making extra work.

Some days the schedule was busy, with new orders every few minutes. On others, the big black telephone stayed quiet. That was the only time I really felt safe. I sat there in a dream with my chin on my hand, and was startled when the radio crackled into life.

***

The NAAFI bar at Bicester was right next to the cookhouse on the first floor of the building with big windows. Halfway up the slope, it looked out over the parade ground. Beyond that, a line of trees circled the low, wide valley.

The people in my barracks here were welcoming and friendly. They asked me to come along drinking in the NAAFI. I knew I had to try to join in.

"What are you having, Nicky?"

"Um – um – what are you having?"

"A pint."

"Um – well –"

"Here –" said someone "– have one of these!"

The glass was short. The liquid was deep golden-brown.

"That doesn't taste like gin, does it? I definitely don't want –"

"It's nothing like gin, okay! I promise! It's whisky. Relax and drink up!"

The scent from the glass came scratching at the inside of my nose.

"Get it down you!"

I tried to take a sip but the stinging taste of whisky made me splutter.

"It's strong!"

"Yeah, it's strong! But it'll make you sooo happy – you'll forget all your worries!"

"Drink up!"

I didn't like the crowd in the NAAFI. I felt trembly and shaky, jostled in the back as a big group pushed towards to the bar. The only way to speak was to lean in very close to another person's ear. But no one else seemed to be frightened. They were all laughing. Suddenly I wanted – really wanted – to forget all my worries just like they said. I wanted to forget me altogether. I grabbed the glass of whisky and drained it in one go. It blazed down my throat, between my ribs, all the way to my stomach. I gasped. A burning wave rose through my body.

"That's the way!"

"Get her another in, quick!"

A second shot of whisky. This time I gulped at the warm yellow glass.

A slow strange ripple took hold of me. Instead of being crushed by the crowd, I seemed to be floating. I was bumping and bobbing, rubbing elbows and shoulders with them all, but even when they touched me, I still felt relaxed. I stumbled into someone close beside me, but now it just seemed funny. She gave a great big laugh as well.

"Well – it didn't take you long to get legless!"

Everybody grinned, and now I was grinning too. It was easy to be here if you only drank whisky. I didn't know why nobody had told me this before. It was easier to talk, although afterwards I couldn't remember how the conversations went. The tightly clenched knot in my stomach seemed to loosen.

I went to the NAAFI bar each night, and thought about whisky all day as I sat in the radio hut. I was still very scared when the phone rang and the transport schedule had to be changed. But when I had a drink in the evening, the world slipped sideways. Nothing much mattered any more.

Best of all, my whisky nights would always end the same – in quick black sleep, the minute I closed my eyes. By the time we left the NAAFI I'd be spinning, sometimes walking into doors or falling on the ground, and they'd laugh at me and pull me to my feet. Nothing really hurt me in the warm whisky bubble. When I lay in bed for just a few seconds, unconsciousness rushed in and there was nothing but silence until morning.

The smart man in a crisp white shirt and dark shiny shoes, waiting there to grab me if I closed my eyes, was gone. There were no endless stairs up through the house, no blood red room, no army boots banging in the yard, no grandfather's hands. Dog was gone too, and I missed him, but the big golden blank was worth his loss. The day's first glass of whisky stopped the world.

In the mornings, my mouth felt rough and dry and I was thirsty, but that passed soon enough. Time split apart, into hours before I drank and the hours that came after. I spent each day just waiting for my first taste of whisky.

***

"Um – you're drinking quite a bit, Nicky."

Ann and I were giving our boots a regulation spit-and-polish. Ann slept two beds away. She was smart and organised and got along with everyone. Some evenings she came with the group to the NAAFI; other times she didn't.

"No, I'm not."

I didn't care anyway.

"Look – I know it's none of my business," said Ann. She started scrubbing hard at her boots. "But I think – look, I think that you – well – I'm not trying to interfere. It's just that you've changed a lot."

I scratched at the toe of my boot with a stiff little brush. I wished that Ann would just shut up.

"Anyway, I've said it now. I'm trying to be – just – please just be careful."

"Alright."

I knew that she was right. But I didn't want to think about that. I drank until I didn't even remember that she'd said it.

***

Each time I drink, the shutters fall faster and faster. Whisky wipes me out. It's a walk into a wall, a great big bang in the face and then beyond it… fade. When I lived in focus, I winced at the colours of the bright, real world. They jabbed at me – they hurt my eyes. Now I can smooth the pain away. And I need to do that more than someone like Ann will ever know. I can't stop. I won't stop. No one is ever going to take this away from me.

***

One night there was a band playing live at the NAAFI. The tables were pulled back to the edges of the room, and everyone was leaning up against them, talking and drinking. More and more of them had started to jive.

The jive looked fast and crazy. You threw yourself about with one arm up in the air and your whole body jerking side to side. There was only your dancing partner's hand to keep you from flying over backwards.

"Can you jive?"

"Can I wha'?"

"Can you jive?"

"Wha's that, then?"

"It's dancing! Like those over there, look!"

"No way… can't do that!"

The room was hot and crowded. Someone had opened the doors that led out onto the balcony. The dancing spilled towards the top of the steps.

I was drinking fast. I drank beer now too, when the weather was warm and my throat was very dry. I didn't like the taste much but that didn't matter. What mattered was a drink. Then my arm was grabbed. A tall blond man with a pink sweaty face tried to pull me towards him. I pulled back.

"She's going to dance with me!" he yelled. He even had sweat on his palms. His hands felt slippery. I didn't like the way he was pulling at my arm.

"I'm Roy!" he shouted. I didn't care.

Someone else gave me a push in the back.

"Let's see you two dance!"

"Oh go on – be a sport!" said Roy. "Dance with me!"

I took a long drink of my beer.

"A'right!"

As I followed him across the room, I walked hard into the corner of a table. It jabbed right in the middle of my kneecap. My right leg half gave way. I stumbled. Roy hauled me to my feet, then he squeezed my waist and laughed. I felt I had to laugh although I didn't like the squeeze. My knee was hurting quite a lot.

I could see the bar's lights all reflected in the big glass windows, mixed in with the last streaks of sunset outside. The headlights of a lorry were still moving on the road. Everything around me seemed to shimmer. I was dizzy. I screwed up my eyes. There were couples jiving fast all around. The band played louder.

"C'mon then!"

Roy pulled me towards him and we started to dance. The jive seemed pretty easy – jump in the air then hold on tight to his sleeve and spring backwards. He tried to spin me round with his arms above my head. But as soon as I spun, the floor seemed to tilt. I weaved off into someone else's dance. Roy came after me and kept me on my feet.

"Sorry, mate – she's had a few!"

He grabbed me by the shoulders, steering me back to the middle of the floor.

"Watch where you're going!" He was yelling in my face. "Stay here with me and don't bump into people!"

I didn't like the way he was shouting.

"I wanna drink!" I said. His grip on me was very tight.

"Let's dance first!"

"Drink first!"

"We can't get back to the bar now!"

He grabbed both my hands and we started to jive. I jumped backwards and forwards with my foot stuck out in front, and swung my knees first one way then the other. It was very hard to balance when my right knee still felt weak. The pain was getting worse. I was wobbly all down my right side. I lost hold of Roy and I staggered. I smacked my hands hard against the big glass window.

Roy came diving after me.

"What do you think you're doing? Hold on to me properly this time!"

He came up very close and grabbed my wrist. Then he whipped my arm right up above my head with a twist that sent me spinning like a top. I couldn't keep hold of his slippery fingers. As I reeled away from him, my right knee gave way.

Then there was a wild blur of white and a terrible crash. I felt something smash into my back. Everything went dark as I fell sprawling through the window, shattering the big sheet of glass. As I tumbled in a shower of ice, I heard screams.

When I hit the ground below, it knocked me out.

***

"Nicky Nicholls, you are hereby dishonourably discharged from the Royal Ordnance Corps."

My new life had ended before it had really begun.

No more second chances. They held a brief hearing, but I was very drunk. They read me the charge sheet and asked if I had anything to say. I didn't. They were absolutely right, after all.

Under the influence of alcohol, they said, I'd behaved in a riotous manner. I'd disgraced myself and everybody else. I'd let my comrades down. I'd let the army down, and the country and the Queen. I'd damaged army property by falling through a window, seriously injuring myself both from the fall and from glass lacerations. My left foot was cut to the bone. Over all the stitches, they had to graft skin from the inside of my arm.

Ann came to see me in Halton military hospital. She looked scared, and told me that I could have been killed when I crashed through a first-floor window. I tried to feel frightened when I thought about that. Roy came to see me as well, and brought me a bottle of vodka. He looked so guilty that I asked him to bring me another.

Ann wanted to know where I would go. She'd noticed that I didn't take leave at weekends like the others, and wondered if I had a family.

"Do you have anyone, Nick?"

I was lying in bed with my foot up in traction. I'd drunk half of Roy's vodka before Ann arrived. I didn't reply.

"Nicky, this is serious. You've been living here in Bicester for months. Where else can you go? Can you go home?"

Home? No, I certainly couldn't go home. But I was sorry for Ann, who looked so worried and sad.

"It's okay," I told her, trying to sound as though everything was under control.

"Nicky – have you been drinking?"

"No, 'course not."

"Oh my God, you have! Nicky – I'm not sure, really. I think you need help. I think maybe we should talk to someone about this."

"Look – they're discharging me dishono – dish – dishon – discharging me," I told her roughly. "It's not your fault an' you're trying to be nice but there's no one I can talk to here. They're done with me – all done. They gave me a second chance already, didn't they? An' I – anyway – too late for that. Now they jus' want me to get out."

Ann twisted her hands in her lap.

"I seriously think you need help, Nicky."

"They did help me. They did. Captain Nicholson –"

I didn't want to talk any more. I wanted her to leave so that I could have a drink.

"OK, but you'll still need somewhere to go. A place where you can stay while you try to get a job, earn some money so you can –"

But everything Ann tried to say to help just made the world outside come closer. Soon there would be so many problems that I had no way to solve. Problems I couldn't even bear to think about. I had to have a drink. A drink a drink a drink.

"Ann..."

"Yes?"

"Ann... I can't... I don't know..." Inside I did want her to help me, but I couldn't find any words to ask.

She looked at me so sadly, wanting to make things better. She was ever so kind.

***

I didn't save the world from Fidel Castro or the atom bomb. Nothing I did helped at all. I tried to be a soldier, but I'm still just me. I'll always be the same, no matter what my name is, no matter where I go or what I do or what uniform I wear.

I'm not a proper person at all. The dirtiness inside me goes with me and makes everything go wrong. It's like constantly falling down a deep dark hole, yet somehow never vanishing.

Whisky takes this feeling away. Whisky and vodka and beer. My world is split in two all over again: the one side where there's drink and the other where there's not. I can't even think about not drinking. If I can't have a drink, the badness and filth that's inside me will take over and I won't exist at all.

***

The last thing I received from the army was a train ticket. They asked me where I was going, and I said Darlington. Ann's parents had agreed that I could spend some time in their house. I was amazed that two strangers had offered to help me, but Ann said her parents did a lot of work with their church. Sometimes they had visitors who stayed while they were having problems. She was sure that her parents would be able to help me too. It was only for a while, she said – just until I sorted myself out.

I didn't know what everybody meant by "sorted myself out" though they all kept saying it. But they all seemed to know, and they seemed to think that I should know too. I didn't even know where Darlington was. Ann explained how I should get there.

."... and Nicky – don't start drinking when you're on the train. It's quite a long way. If you drink you'll be confused and you might get lost."

Okay.

"And please don't drink in my parents' house. They really wouldn't like that. I've told them that – you've had a bad time. I'm sure they'll be able to give you some ideas, you know, about looking for work. They'd be happy to do that. They want to help you sort yourself out."

Okay.

"They're nice, my parents. They help people a lot, through the church and everything, like I said. My mum's in the Mothers' Union."

I didn't know what that was either.

The journey to Darlington was long. It was late autumn now, and very cold, and the days grew darker early on. I almost got lost changing trains at Birmingham station. I had a bottle of vodka in my suitcase, but I was sure that if the railway staff saw it, they'd take it off me. So I waited, and didn't start drinking until the train was moving.

We travelled to the far north of England. Darlington was almost in Scotland, Ann had said. Her father met me at the station, holding up a sheet of paper with my name on. Ann's mother smiled when she greeted me at the house, and showed me up to the spare room, telling me to make myself at home while she cooked us all some tea. The room had a pretty patterned bedspread and flowery paper on the walls. I still couldn't sleep in the bed, but the sheets and blankets kept me warm when I piled them in a heap underneath it on the floor. Ann came from such a nice, safe home and I knew I was lucky to stay there and have help from such generous people. I wanted to show them I was grateful.

But the kinder they were, the bigger the sadness and guilt grew inside me, weighing heavier and heavier until it was hard for me to breathe. I wondered if Ann's parents would still help me if they knew about my past – the real, shameful truth about me. I was sure that the answer must be no.

Next morning, and more mornings after that, I tried to have breakfast at the table by the window looking out onto the frosty winter garden. Ann's mother always cooked such lovely food and I felt ashamed because I couldn't eat. Each day her father kissed her mother goodbye with a quick little peck on the cheek. Then he left for work with his briefcase. I went back up to the spare room and my bottle of vodka. After that – the void.

Dark blanks opened in my days, different from the stuttering jumps I'd sometimes known before. These were much more scary. Hours had started to go missing. I'd curl up in the armchair in the corner, and then there would be nothing. Hours later, the weak wintry sun had moved right round.

Sometimes I went to the shops for Ann's mother, who gave me some money and a list. But the darkness could still creep over me while I was away from the house. Instead of buying the things on the list, I bought more vodka with the money, and drank it in the park near the children's playground. Then there'd be another jump in time – and now I was back in the kitchen with Ann's mother, who was talking and talking. She had an angry face, though she said she was only disappointed. Everyone was always disappointed in me. She went on and on. I couldn't really hear what she was saying.

I knew that the black gaps came because I was drinking. I started to dread coming round, not knowing what might have happened, but the thought of never drinking was much more scary than the gaps. Ann's parents were saying that I needed to sort myself out, but they didn't explain how to start. I didn't know what time it was, and started missing breakfast. In the hard wintry darkness of the north, it never really felt like morning.

One day, they both came knocking on the spare room door. I was in the armchair and didn't say come in, but they came in anyway. I tried to hide the vodka bottle standing on the floor but I just knocked it over instead. In any case, the bottle was empty.

They had such serious faces. They sat on the edge of the bed side by side and told me that of course they weren't angry, just that they were sad. This couldn't go on. I was welcome to remain in their home, they said, but only on condition that I sorted myself out.

I heard a high-pitched noise, like somebody screaming, though I didn't think I'd made any sound.

I have no idea at all what you mean! No idea! Why do you keep saying this?

It doesn't make sense! I can't do what you want unless you tell me what it is!

They both jumped up from the bed. I realised that the screeching noise was coming out of me. They waved their arms and seemed to be terribly upset. Ann's mother started to cry. Her father passed his wife a handkerchief.

I was all alone in a stranger's house being shouted at by strangers. I began to cry too. I'd run out of vodka. Everything was loud and sharp without it, like being stuck with pins. The more and more I cried, the more frightened I became.

I slid onto the floor and curled up in a ball. Ann's mother said that she was phoning for an ambulance.

Chapter Four

Two great escapes

I'm feeling very sick. My legs are wobbling. I shake uncontrollably. Someone has got me by the arm. There are two of them, nurses. I can hear the jangling of keys.

We're walking down a very long corridor. One nurse unlocks a huge green door. I don't want to go inside. I'm scared. I struggle. The nurses hold me tighter then pull me forwards. The green door closes. There's a crunch as the key turns behind me. I'm told to sit down on a hard wooden chair.

The room stinks of urine and carbolic soap, just like the soap my grandmother used. Outside the door, I hear running footsteps, then wailing and desperate crying. Where am I?

I'm given a small plastic cup full of syrupy liquid. "Swallow this down" – but my hands are shaking too much for me to hold it. The nurse pours the stuff into my mouth. It's pungent and vile, but after a minute a heavy warmth moves through my body. I fall asleep sitting there.

When I wake up, a different nurse tells me that it's bedtime. The word "bed" throws me into panic. I stand up and scream. I hear an alarm go off. Three of them come at me and hold my arms tightly. I'm terrified.

This is my new world of liquid largactil and straitjackets.

***

When the ambulance arrived, the two attendants talked to Ann's parents outside on the landing. I couldn't hear what they were saying. Then one of them sat down beside me on the floor. He tried to touch my shoulder. I told him to leave me alone but the words came out as a moan.

As the ambulance man got to his feet, he kicked the empty bottle of vodka. It rolled across the floor and chinked against the others tucked underneath the bed.

They lifted me up by my arms and led me out of the bedroom and down the stairs. The ambulance was waiting in the rain, its back doors standing wide open. We all climbed in. Before the doors closed, I saw Ann's mother standing crying on the pavement with her wet hair sticking to her head. Ann's father was watching the ambulance, distractedly patting her arm.

***

Where am I? How long have I been here?

The women here are frightening: at first I don't know what's wrong with them. I've never seen anyone behaving like this: howling and rocking, taking off their clothes, crying in the night and crouching down in corners with their arms across their faces. A young girl is given a Mars bar: she throws the chocolate on the floor and shoves the crumpled black wrapper straight into her mouth. The woman in the bed next to me strips naked and bounces: she has big floppy breasts and as they fly up and down she keep shouting out how much she loves Jesus.

There's a terrible smell. It's shit, sweat, old food and drains. There's something else too, but I'm not sure what. Maybe all the breaths that carry all that terrible wailing have made the air turn sour. I want a drink very, very much. It's difficult to think about anything else. A drink a drink a drink.

"Where am I?" I say to the nurse.

"You're on a mental ward," she tells me, kindly enough, but I don't understand what that means. If I'm on a ward then I'm in hospital. Why would I be here when I'm not sick?

They bring trays of food, and the woman in the next bed along just eats it with her hands, shoving it up towards her mouth and smearing mess all across her cheeks. I gag and refuse to eat anything at all. One morning, the others start walking in a circle in the dayroom, so I join in. It doesn't make sense but perhaps it's what the people here expect me to do. We wander round and round for a while. Then our straggly roundabout collapses and I drift away.

I won't sleep in my bed. That's because the white-shirted man with shiny shoes and a strange little smile comes walking down towards me a hundred times each night. I hide my face and tell myself again and again that he isn't really there. But more and more my eyes go on seeing him, in nightmares that don't belong to sleep.

I'm too afraid to lie there and wait for him to come for me and lead me away. I hide under the bed until the nurses drag me out by my ankles. The next night I do the same thing, then the next and then the next and the next one after that.

Whisky would shut it all out. But all the doors are locked and we're not allowed to go to the shops. We can't ever leave the ward at all, unless the nurses take us on a special trip for people who are starting to get well. They don't take me.

I long and long to have a drink, but there's nothing here but water or the thick sticky juice in plastic beakers that they bring round on a tray. If a woman makes a noise or seems to be upset, she gets extra juice and then she's quiet. When I drink it, the ward goes far away, like looking down a tunnel. The juice makes me fall asleep by daylight, curled up in a chair.

***

Dr Simpson asked to see me in the dayroom. She had thick golden hair that was parted at the side and held back with a slide. She brought along a clipboard with lots of sheets of paper and made notes at the side as she asked me all her questions. I couldn't read her upside-down writing. A nurse sat right alongside me. When the nurse saw I was trying to read the notes, she tapped me on the arm and made me pull my chair further away.

I wasn't sure how many days had passed since I was brought here from Ann's parents' house. When were they going to let me out? But Dr Simpson wouldn't tell me anything like that.

She asked me what had happened in the army, how long I'd been in Bicester and in Lingfield, the reasons why I'd left. I thought she might be angry and tell me that I'd let my country down, but she seemed to be more interested than cross. She asked about parades and the problems I'd had marching and with kit inspection and drill. I said that I was clumsy and did everything wrong, and I'd tried to be a soldier but it didn't work out because I couldn't count my steps or keep my kit tidy. Then they put me in the transport hut at Bicester and I didn't understand what to do. And then – I didn't want to tell her why they dishonourably discharged me.

"I see. And you had to leave the army because you got drunk in the camp and had an accident?"

Ann's parents must have told her about that.

"Yes."

"You had a very nasty accident, didn't you?"

I showed her the scar on my arm where they'd taken the skin graft for my ankle.

"You were lucky. You could have been more seriously hurt."

"Yes."

"So then you came to Darlington, to stay with friends?"

"To stay with Ann's parents, yes."

She turned through her pages of notes.

"Were you sorry to leave?"

"You mean was I sorry to leave the army?"

Oh yes. Yes, I was sorry about that. I was so very sad and sorry that I couldn't change the world. I was sorry that the new me had turned out as big a disappointment as the old me ever was.

"Yes."

"I want to go back before that, Nicky – before you were a soldier.

Let's go back to when you were a very little girl."

I didn't want to talk to her much about anything, but certainly not about that.

"Where am I?" I blurted out. "I don't know the name of where I am."

"I'm so sorry that no one has told you. You're in Spring Bank hospital."

"Where's that?"

"You know where you are, surely? You're in Durham – a beautiful part of the world."

"Why am I in hospital?"

"This is a mental hospital. I think you understand that you're not very well. You have had a breakdown, but already we can see that you are doing much better –"

"What's a breakdown?"

."..so it won't be too long before you can leave here, and go back to living a normal life. You need to be patient for a while, and co-operate with your treatment."

"What treatment?"

"What we're doing now is your treatment."

I stared. I couldn't work out how she was treating me for anything.

"So as part of your recovery, I think it would be helpful for us to talk about things that happened when you were a small child."

I didn't know why she thought that.

"I think that you've been drinking too much because it helps blot out things that make you frightened and sad. Things that you remember. If you can tell me about them, it might help you feel better."

"Does everyone in here have – treatment?"

"Some people have different – well, yes. We don't go down the same route with everyone, of course. But yes."

So the women in the ward, the women who wailed and cried

and howled and sat there naked and ate chocolate wrappers instead of the chocolate inside, women who could only be still and stop rocking to and fro when they were filled up every day with sticky drugged hospital syrup – they were being treated for their bad memories too.

This is what will happen if I open the door and let the past get out.

I didn't want treatment. I sat on my chair in the dayroom and looked at Dr Simpson and I didn't say anything else.

***

Deep down inside me is a scream. If I ever set it free, my scream will fill the world. It will bend trees before it and break apart buildings. It will send storm waves a hundred feet high through the streets, unleash roaring volcanoes and rain burning ash on the heads of anyone caught in its path. My scream will obliterate everything. Beyond all shadow of doubt, it will obliterate me.

Sticky largactil syrup will muffle it a while. Whisky blocks its big black mouth. At least I understand what I must do to keep the scream locked inside.

***

I grew used to Spring Bank and became less afraid. Women would attack one another sometimes and the nurses had to drag them apart, but the fights were very clumsy – lots of shouts and screeching, but slow. No one here could move very quickly. Besides, there were warnings if you knew how to read them. Alice on the far side of the room, always rocking, would sway forward and backwards to comfort herself: that showed that she was feeling sad. If she tilted side-to-side, that was danger. That meant that you should stay away.

Our beds were made of iron, the bars of metal all painted white, and we each had a narrow grey locker alongside and a chair we could sit on in the daytime. I barely slept at night so I often sat half-dozing in the chair. When I'd had no sleep at all for lots of nights, the nurses explained that they wanted to give me something called temazepam. "It's extra strong," they said, "but it will help you. We're worried you'll be ill if you don't go to sleep."

But I was scared to take temazepam, in case it made me sleep and then trapped me in my dreams. What if I was dreaming that the white-shirted man came to take me away, and then I found I couldn't wake up? I longed and longed for whisky-sleep: the certain, sudden darkness with no moving pictures from my memory at all.

They made us take baths in four deep tubs in a big shared room. The first time they took me there, I wouldn't get undressed, but the nurses stripped my clothes off and dunked me in the water anyway. Other people didn't like the baths either: one girl, Virginia, really fought them and they dropped her as she struggled. She hit her head hard on the edge of the tub. The streaks of her blood trickled down until they mixed with the water on the floor and spread out in a pale brown puddle.

But most of the nurses weren't unkind: they spoke gently and told us their names. My favourite nurse, Joan, brought me scones when I told her I liked them. She seemed to be so worried because I wouldn't eat. She told me more about Spring Bank hospital: because I was young, she said, under twenty-one, the doctors had the right to make me stay on the ward. But that was so that they could look after me. Somebody like me must be protected so I wouldn't hurt myself, or get hurt by anybody else.

But I remembered how the nurses had dragged me that first day, how frightened I had been when the big green door slammed shut and the sound as the lock was turned behind me.

"Hmm," said Joan. "Yes, well." She frowned and looked quite bothered about it. "Well, it shouldn't be done like that. Not when you don't understand what's going on. They should try to help you calm down first."

She sat alongside me while I nibbled on a scone, and when I said thank you, she gave me a wide, warm smile.

"Is it just scones that you like, then, Nicky?"

"Yes."

"Not any other sort of cake? I could bring you some in if you tell me your favourite."

"What could you bring?"

"Fruitcake, maybe, or biscuits. How about Victoria sponge? Or a jam tart?"

"I like scones better."

"Okay, then – scones. Or what about a doughnut?"

"What's a doughnut?"

"You know! They're round and they have sugar on the outside and jam in a hole in the middle."

"There's a hole in the middle?"

"Yes, but it's meant to be there. Doughnuts are made like that."

"I feel like the hole in the doughnut," I told her. She looked very interested in what I'd just said.

"Why, Nicky?"

"A doughnut's made with part of it missing."

"And that's how you feel about yourself?"

"I am that way," I said. "There's part of me missing."

"Maybe we can help you find the part that isn't there?" She smiled at me hopefully.

She wanted to use doughnuts to get me to talk about the past. But there weren't enough doughnuts in the whole of the world to make me do that. I knew she couldn't help me at all, but at least it was kind of her to try.

***

The nurses brought newspapers with them when they came in for their shifts. Copies of the Northern Echo were dotted all around the ward. I found a pen in the nurses' station and doodled on them.

At first I thought they'd stop me, or even that they'd hit me, but no one seemed to mind me making pictures. Soon I was drawing every day, cartoons and little figures, all along the edges of the papers, and sometimes in the big grey spaces in photographs, where there was a big plain object like a wall or a wide expanse of sky.

I loved to draw. Hours slipped by in the details of the little biro-ed figures, the shapes of their bodies in outline and the movements of their arms. Even when the ink from the newspaper made long dark streaks up the side of my hand, I carried on drawing.

Joan brought me in a big pad of paper and a set of coloured pens.

"There you are," she said. "You keep on with that – I can see how much you like it."

"Thank you."

"Better than getting your hands all grubby on those Echoes, eh?"

***

"Nicky!"

"Yes, Dr Simpson."

"I've been having a look at your pictures ."

I didn't say anything. I thought she was going to make me stop.

"Don't look so worried – they're great!"

"Oh."

"This is something you really like to do, isn't it?"

I wasn't sure at all what she wanted.

"It's OK, Nicky, I'm not going to take them away. I think you should do more drawing. Our talking therapy is – it's – well, we need to try to move things along, don't we? I think drawing would be helpful to you."

"Oh."

"You draw really well. Has anybody ever told you that?"

"No."

"We have an art class here – wouldn't you like to join it?"

No. No art class. It was mixed, with men and women together, and I found that frightening. How could I think about colours and shapes and shading and shadows when I didn't know who might be watching me?

There was a very long silence. I kept on looking down at the floor.

"Okay, then – let's not worry too much about joining the class. Let's do what we can as we are. I'd like to get you more materials. Or maybe even get you some paint. I think you'd enjoy using it. We'd all like to see what you can do!"

I didn't believe she meant it, but it turned out that she did. Two days later, she came to the ward on her rounds and handed me a brown paper parcel. Inside was a square lidded box with sixteen different paints in bright little rings. There were two small brushes. I was so pleased and happy that I smiled straightaway when I opened the tin.

"Ooooh!"

Dr Simpson smiled back.

"I thought that you might like them. Happy painting!"

***

I am eight years old and I'm drawing. I don't often sit at the table in the big bright kitchen in London. But today when I came home from school there was a visitor in the house — a friend of my mother's — and I was brought into the kitchen and given a glass of squash. When outsiders are here, I'm treated like the others. The friend talked to me for a while but I didn't reply so she smiled at me and gave me some paper and a pencil from inside her handbag, to keep me busy whilst she chatted to my mother.

It's soft, thick paper and the pencil's soft too, with a grey-black lead that's extra-good for drawings although it wears down quickly. You can smudge it for shadows in corners and clouds. I draw a secret garden like the one in a story we were listening to at school. The garden has a high wall and a gate that's all overgrown, with ivy hanging down. I draw all the leaves up close. I can see how they rustle and move and make shadows on the ground. I blur and smudge the shadows at the bottom. It makes my hands dirty but I don't mind that because the smudges and shadows look just the way I want them to.

My mother's friend gets up to go but I hardly notice: the rustling leaves have all my attention. The grown-ups leave the room and I sit there and keep working on my own.

All of a sudden my mother's behind me. I see her for a second from the corner of my eye. Something heavy strikes the back of my head. My face hits the table top hard. There's a very loud crack and a really sharp pain in my nose. I cry out, which I don't usually. I wasn't expecting a blow.

My mother's face is white with fury.

"Get out! Just get off that chair and get out!"

She slaps me again, hard on the side of my face.

"What do you think you're doing, you little bitch? You're not allowed to do that!"

I make myself quiet by biting my lip very hard. I can taste blood in the back of my throat. My top lip is warm and wet as well: when I bring up my hand to touch it, there's red all over my fingers. I realise how much my nose is bleeding. I try to stand up but I can't see because the pain in my nose makes my eyes stream with tears. Everywhere's water and the saltiness of blood. The blood from my nose is on my drawing too. There's blood on the leaves and the smudgy pencil shadows. It's scarlet and charcoal and black.

My mother grabs my drawing and rips it into pieces. She crumples the thick soft paper in her clenched white hands and stuffs it into the rubbish bin.

***

I used my new hospital paints with a set of three brushes, all in different sizes, sitting at the table in the dayroom. Sometimes the other girls came and looked over my shoulder.

At first being watched made me feel very anxious. I kept hearing footsteps behind me, and ducking my head down in case there was a blow. But no one here seemed angry or upset. Once or twice someone even sat down to watch me working for a while.

A few days later, Dr Simpson came and sat down too.

"Who's that in the painting?" she asked me. "Is it Joan?"

"Yes."

Dr Simpson put her head on one side and looked closely.

"That's very good, Nicky. I can really see her there."

"Thanks."

"And the colours – the feeling of life. Just as if those figures are moving."

Now I didn't trust her: this was too much praise. There was a pause.

"Anyway, I have a suggestion for you."

"What's that?"

"I'm sure someone must have told you about the death of Mr Churchill."

Winston Churchill was the British Prime Minister, back in the war, when the bombs were falling. I'd learned all about him at school.

I said, "Joan told me."

"A sad day for the nation, to lose our greatest wartime leader," said Dr Simpson seriously.

"Yes."

"Would you like to paint Mr Churchill?"

"Paint his portrait, you mean?"

"Yes – exactly."

"Um…"

"Marvellous! There are lots of pictures of him in the papers. Maybe you could choose one and use it as your base for the portrait."

"Okay."

"Are you sure about doing this? I thought you'd be more pleased. We'd really like it if you could do a painting to hang on the wall. A tribute to our greatest Prime Minister."

"Er…"

"Well of course, you don't have to if you don't want to. But – we've talked about it, and we think there's a lot to be gained from you doing your art and your painting. And Spring Bank would love to have a proper memorial to Mr Churchill!"

"Yes, I'll do it. I'd like to."

They gave me a big sheet of paper and a new box of paints. There was a little plastic palette for mixing up the colours. Joan brought in pictures of Mr Churchill that she'd cut out from the newspapers, along with some coloured ones she'd found in magazines. I chose one to copy.

Before I started painting, I stared at the pictures Joan had brought me for a very long time.

"Is something wrong, Nicky?"

The more carefully I looked, the more I could see that skin isn't just one single colour. Neither is hair. People were all different colours, many shades that change when the shadows and light move around. To paint a person right, you had to watch them very closely and take in all of this, then turn what you'd seen into paint.

Mr Churchill's skin took ages. It kept coming out looking wrong, though I wasn't sure why. I'd mix paint and mix a little more, covering the palette with little yellow splodges that weren't the same colour as he was at all. But then I saw the problem – Mr Churchill was purple. I wasn't sure at first how to mix it – too much red, then too much blue – and then at last just right. Now Mr Churchill was exactly the colour he should be.

***

Virginia had long black hair and a very white face. She wasn't much older than me, but even thinner, with great big hands and feet like a doll. Her fringe was cut all crooked. She had huge dark eyes. She was the one who hated bath-time, and always made a fuss when the nurses tried to put her in the deep tubs filled with steaming hot water. When she was undressed, her ribs stuck out like railings.

After the day she hit her head, I saw that they were being more careful, talking to her gently and telling her to keep herself clean so they didn't have to force her to wash. Virginia still smelled, though; you noticed when you walked past her bed. The gash on her forehead needed stitches: now you could see the jagged red scar across her brow.

She seemed to like watching me painting. I got used to her there, though I still didn't like the way she smelled. She didn't say much and when she talked, she left spaces so she didn't quite make sense. She told me one day that she enjoyed how I'd painted Mr Churchill.

"Thank you," I said.

"My house was bombed in the war," she told me, "and my family had to move out somewhere else."

"Did they rebuild your house?"

"Yes. I wasn't born, though. Everything was burnt up by the bombs and the fire. All burnt. My mother used to cry about that. I remember her crying all the time."

I thought about how people in Stoke used to talk about the war; how some of them would still get upset when they remembered.

"It must have been awful."

"Then my mother killed herself."

"I – I – I'm sorry."

"It was when I was small. I don't really know much about it. I only remember her crying and talking about the night the house was bombed. They were down in the shelter and they heard it really loud, and when the all-clear came and they came outside to look – just ruins and fire. That's what she used to keep saying – it's all in ruins! It's on fire! Ruins!"

Virginia wrapped her skinny arms tightly round her chest and rocked.

"Perhaps she just couldn't stop thinking about it," I said. I knew what it was like to have terrible pictures on your eyes.

"She was very sad. I know how she killed herself – my mother."

"How?"

"She did it with alcohol and tablets."

Virginia made this sound very easy. Could it really be a simple thing to do, to decide you'd had enough and to make your pain stop?

"What kind of tablets?"

"After she died, no one ever said her name again."

"How many tablets did she take?"

"My granny said it was a sin that she committed. She told me that my mother went to hell."

"To hell?"

"That's why they didn't like talking about her. My brother was a baby."

She still hadn't told me how exactly her mother had died. I wanted to know.

"How many tablets did she take?"

"When I was a child, whenever I remembered my mother, I knew she was burning in hell like they said."

Virginia rocked so far back that I thought she might tip her chair over.

"I wonder if Mr Churchill went to hell too," she said.

"Mr Churchill!" I felt quite shocked. "But he was a great war leader!"

"We never know who's going to hell," said Virginia solemnly. "The angels are sent to fetch you when you die, and they take you up to heaven or they send you down to hell. Nobody knows until they tell you where you're going. So maybe if he –"

I cleared my throat and she broke off talking. I was sure that we shouldn't be discussing Mr Churchill like this. It seemed rather lacking in respect.

Then Virginia burst out laughing out of nowhere.

"Wouldn't it be funny if Mr Churchill ended up in hell when

he wasn't expecting it? If the angels said — not that way! This way! And carted him down there when he thought he was going to heaven!"

"Look – you know you said that thing about your mother, a minute ago?"

"What thing?"

"She killed herself, you said."

"Yes."

"How many tablets did she take? Do you know? What were they?"

"Oh – just normal stuff!" said Virginia lightly. She didn't seem to care very much about it now. "Just tablets that she bought at the chemist."

"Like aspirin?"

"Yes, she used aspirin. It was ever so easy. If you mix up aspirin and alcohol you'll die. I think about doing it too."

Aspirin and alcohol mixed up together. I didn't think that sounded very hard.

"Do you think about killing yourself?" I asked Virginia.

"Oh yes, I do sometimes. Maybe I shall. I'd like to see old Simpson's face if I did! Wouldn't you?"

***

I finished my portrait of Mr Churchill.

It was going to be unveiled in the entrance to the ward. Everyone filed along the corridor, patients and staff, and stood there in a wonky half-circle. When an important-looking man in a smart striped suit arrived and stood up at the front, everybody lowered their voices. Our whispers rushed around the ceiling.

I could see the outline of my portrait, bang in the centre of the big front wall. The picture had been framed, and covered in a sheet with a cord rigged up so that somebody could pull the sheet off, when the most important man in the suit had made his most important speech.

My stomach turned over and my heart started beating in a way that I could feel. My hands began to tremble. I wanted a drink very badly. If I could just have whisky, the shaking that was spreading through my body might stop.

"The nation gives thanks... Spring Bank is proud... at this sad time... our finest hour... fight them on the landing grounds... a man of destiny... this remarkable portrait by one of our patients, Nicky Nicholls!"

My mother grabs my head from behind and slams it hard onto a table. I've been working on a beautiful drawing – now my face smashes right into it. There's a terrible pain in my nose.

"What do you think you're doing, you little bitch? You're not allowed to do that!"

My heart raced so fast that I thought I might faint. The man pulled on the cord and the sheet from the painting fell onto the carpet. Everyone clapped and the sound was like a roar.

My mother's face is white with fury. She rips my drawing into pieces. She crumples the paper in her clenched white hands and pushes them into the rubbish bin.

"You're not allowed to do that!"

Panic wings were beating back and forth inside me. I felt a scream rising and forced it right down deep inside.

"YOU'RE NOT ALLOWED TO DO THAT!"

As dusk falls each night, the man in a crisp white shirt and dark shoes comes quietly walking through the shadows of the ward. He's coming to lead me away. Even with temazepam, I can't go to sleep in case he reaches out his arm and seizes mine.

Ruins. It's all fire and ruins, like Virginia's mother said. Everything around me is burning and I'll never find a way to put it out.

***

Nurse Rhoda was angry with me.

"You spoiled the unveiling ceremony, you silly girl, making a fuss like that!"

I didn't know what I'd done. I couldn't remember.

"You don't know what happened, do you?"

Now I just felt weak. My body ached as though I'd run a very long way.

"You started acting silly and crying and we had to bring you back up here instead of staying there with the others for the celebration. There was nothing to get so worked up about."

I remembered the noise of people clapping, then my mother grabbing hold of my head. The crash onto the table and the awful pain. I reached up my hand to touch my face, to find out if my nose was still bleeding.

Rhoda was standing by my chair looking down with her arms tightly folded. I wished she wasn't there.

I'd started to know the nurses' shift patterns: three of them a day, the morning, the afternoon and night. Right now, Rhoda was working afternoons. I didn't like having her near me.

She had big brown eyes and her hair was dark and short, with little curls that wriggled round the edges of her starchy nurse's cap. When Alice started rocking back and forwards, Rhoda would laugh, and sometimes she mimicked her, whether or not Alice could see. Some of the other nurses laughed when she did this, but some looked unhappy. I noticed that Joan would always frown and walk away; the two of them didn't like each other. When they had to sit together at the nurses' station, both of them looked angry and tense.

Rhoda had a special friend called Pauline. She was smaller and thinner and I didn't like her either. When Rhoda mimicked Alice, Rhoda's friend Pauline would always be the very first to smile.

"Anyway," said Rhoda, "it's just you and me here now and it's no fun at all, instead of being downstairs having cake."

"I'm – I'm sorry, I –"

"What was the matter with you, anyway?"

I couldn't think of anything to say.

Rhoda gave a big, deep sigh.

"So... I think you owe me for this."

I didn't understand what she meant, but I didn't at all like the way she said it.

"You made us both miss out on a party, didn't you?"

"I'm sorry," I said again. "I didn't mean to."

She smiled a little smile which I didn't like either.

"You'll have to make it up to me, Nicky."

"What do you mean, make it up?"

"We could have a little party of our own."

Something in her voice made my body grow tense.

"What – kind – of – party?"

Rhoda gave a little light laugh.

"Oh, I think you know just what I mean. I spotted you the day they brought you in. You've got the look, you do."

She smoothed her apron down and patted my arm.

"So don't you be playing the innocent! We'll have a little party just for us. Something tells me you'd enjoy it. We'll have to find a way to do it soon."

***

Rhoda was on nights now, with Pauline. It was late. The ward's only light shone out from the nurses' station.

I watched her leave the desk and walk towards me. I was curled up in my chair, wide awake and staring. They mostly left me sitting there now, and didn't try to make me go to bed.

"So – would you like a drink, then, Nicky?" she whispered.

"A *drink*?"

"Shhh now!." Rhoda put her finger to her lips then gave a very wide smile.

"Have you got some?"

"Oh yes. Just you look at this…" She had one arm held behind her back. She slowly pulled it round across the front of her apron. A bottle of clear liquid gleamed in her hand.

Vodka. When I saw it, I wanted it so much. I wanted it more than anything else. A drink a drink a drink.

"Please!"

"Only if you come along with me and Pauline."

"Why?"

"Oh – don't you want a drink?"

"Can't I have some here?"

"If you want a drink, you'll need to come with us and do what we tell you."

Vodka. I wanted the vodka.

"We'll have a nice time, and you can have a drink. You want to have a drink, now, don't you?"

I didn't want to do what she told me. But she half turned away with the bottle and I gasped and reached out my hand. Rhoda smiled.

"You can have as much vodka as you want if you come along with us. Pauline and me don't think they should stop you from having a drink. You're a big girl now, aren't you?"

"Okay, I'm coming."

I got slowly to my feet and walked down the silent ward. Alice was sitting up in bed, rocking back and forth with her eyelids squeezed together. As I passed, her eyes flickered open and she looked straight at me without seeing. The nurses' station light gleamed briefly in her flat blank stare, as if she was a cat.

Rhoda went on past the desk, right down the corridor and

turned a corner at the end. I'd never been to this part of the ward. She unlocked a door.

"So this is where Pauline and me sometimes have a little party with our very best girls."

"Can I have a drink now?"

Rhoda switched the light on and glanced at her watch.

"I promise you can have a drink in a minute."

Inside there was a chair and a narrow single bed. In the corner was a pile of old boxes and a couple more folded-up chairs.

A low sound of tapping at the door, and Pauline came inside. She closed it behind her. She looked up at Rhoda and I saw Rhoda wink.

I wanted them to give me a drink.

Rhoda sat down on the edge of the bed. She leaned right back on her arms and tilted her head to one side. Then she lifted the edge of her nurse's dress right up. I could see the tops of her stockings. Behind me, Pauline gave a giggle.

"Would you like a drink now, Nicky?"

"Yes."

"You'll have to say it a little bit louder!"

"Yes," I said. Pauline's hot breath was on my neck. I was sweating and frightened.

"Come here and do as you're told, and you can have some vodka."

I didn't want to go towards Rhoda.

"There's going to be no vodka if you don't!"

Then Pauline whispered in my ear. I didn't know that women could behave like my grandfather. I didn't know they used the same words that he did, or gave the same orders. I wanted a drink. I knew that if I had one, everything would stop being real. But I was still too afraid to do what she said.

"I can't."

Pauline slapped me hard across the back of my head.

After that, I did what they told me. Then they gave me the bottle of vodka.

***

"Nicky! Nicky!"

I can hear Joan saying my name.

"Nicky, wake up now."

I can't lift my head. I can't move my arms or my legs. I feel completely floppy like a puppet.

"Nicky, you need to get up and lie down in your bed. I know you don't like it but you can't stay down there on the floor."

I can't speak. My lips and tongue won't work. My face feels swollen and bulging. My stomach clenches tightly and I vomit.

I hear Joan calling for help from the others. Arms lift me up and I'm laid on a bed. They turn my head sideways and I feel the cold edge of a bowl placed underneath my chin. I throw up again and again, as though I'm turning inside out. I'm hollow and trembling.

Joan sits beside me, and gently strokes my forehead with her hand. I don't have muscles or bones any more, just liquid for a body. I can't move at all.

"You had a drink, Nicky, didn't you?"

She doesn't sound angry.

"You had quite a lot." She pushes my hair gently back from my temple.

"It makes some people ill if they drink while they're taking medicine. You've had a nasty reaction."

I can't be sick any more, but my stomach keeps trying. It makes my whole body scrunch up.

"Don't worry — you'll feel better very soon. Then we can find out exactly what happened."

***

Dr Simpson asked me where the vodka came from. Joan asked.

The sister in the ward asked me too. I didn't say anything. Rhoda and Pauline stayed away from me.

For days I felt too weak to sit up at the table in the dayroom and paint. All I could think of now was vodka. Weeks and weeks had passed since I'd left Ann's parents' spare room with the empties piled underneath the bed. The thick sticky syrup kept me numb all this time, but underneath – a drink a drink a drink. The longing had never gone away.

***

"I think I know who gave you the alcohol, Nicky," said Joan. "Alice told me."

"Alice!"

I didn't think Alice noticed anything.

"But she can't… I didn't think Alice could talk."

"Well, she can. She talks to me sometimes, and tells me how she feels. She can't talk to very many people. But Alice sees lots of things that happen in here. Can you tell me a bit about what happened when you had the vodka?"

I didn't want to think about the hot little room. I turned my head to push the images away.

"I –" The words dried up.

Joan touched my forearm with the tips of her fingers. I flinched.

"Nicky, no one is angry with you, please remember that. Alice has told me what she saw. I believe that this has happened here before. I don't think things like this should go on in a hospital, where patients are supposed to be looked after, do you?"

She was right. But I knew I couldn't help her. Instead I closed my eyes.

"Okay, Nicky. I'm not going to keep on worrying you. But if you want to talk about what happened, you can. Remember that I'm always here, every day."

I couldn't even nod.

"I'd like to do something about it. I really hope you'll help me."

I heard Joan's apron rustle as she got to her feet, then the tiny little shrieks of her shoes as she walked away. I squeezed my hands tightly into fists. I wanted more vodka.

***

I knew straightaway that Pauline was angry. When she brought my evening medicine, she pushed the cup of syrup so hard into my hand that it gave a heavy slop in the beaker. A slow, thick gob of it oozed down and landed on my knee. The outside of the cup was all sticky.

"*What did you say to her?*" she hissed.

"Say to who?"

"To Joan, of course."

"Nothing. I didn't say anything."

"Good! And you're not going to!"

I tried to hold the cup in my other hand. Now all my fingers were covered in mess.

"What if Dr Simpson found out?" I asked her.

"*You what?*"

She was frightened. The fear in her face spread instantly to me.

"*What did you say?*"

I tried to take a sip from the little sticky beaker. My fingers had started to tremble.

"*Don't you be having ideas about getting me and Rhoda into trouble! If you try that, you'll be sorry!*"

I thought she might hit me again, like she had in the room along the corridor.

"No telling tales to Simpson, you understand!"

'I won't tell Dr Simpson."

"Well, my girl, you'd better not!"

When Rhoda came to see me later on, she sounded quite

different from Pauline. She sat down on my bed, leaned forward and laid her fingers all in a line along my arm. Her big brown eyes looked straight into mine. It was hard to imagine how she'd lifted up her skirt and giggled in the room at the end of the passage.

"Nicky, I don't want you to be scared, but I need to tell you something that's important."

"What?"

"Look, please don't worry – the hospital will always keep you safe. But some of the other girls here – they would like to kill you."

"Why?"

"What do you mean, why?"

"Why do they want to do that?"

"You don't seem very worried about it."

That was because it didn't sound true.

"How do you know?"

"I overheard them talking in the dayroom. It's because of your portrait."

"Because I painted Mr Churchill?"

"Yes!"

She glanced down the ward, as though someone might be creeping towards us with an axe.

"I'm not sure when they're planning to do it!"

"So how are they planning to kill me, then?"

For a second, Rhoda looked annoyed.

"You need to take this seriously. It really is true. Of course, we'll protect you if we can."

"You just said that the hospital would always keep me safe."

"I said we'll try."

"No, you didn't."

"Yes I did, Nicky. We'll try very hard, of course we will, but none of us can be here every minute."

"But there's always someone here."

I could tell that something wasn't right. She was working out what to say next. There wasn't any tremble in her fingers on my arm. She was lying. When she saw me looking at her hands, she pulled them away.

"They want to drown you in the bath!" she hissed.

"Drown me in the bath?"

But how on earth would they do that? None of them could organise it. No one could move fast enough. There were always nurses when we had to have a bath.

"They're very, very jealous, because you were chosen to do the painting of Mr Churchill!"

But Mr Churchill and the painting were long ago. Weeks had gone by, though I didn't have any way to count them. I didn't think that anyone could even remember the painting.

"If – you – stay – here," said Rhoda emphatically, "something very bad will happen to you. I'll try not to let it, but I might not be able to help."

I knew that the things she was saying weren't true. But still, it was hard to keep my thoughts clear in my head.

"I think you should leave Spring Bank tonight – for your own protection!"

Rhoda looks frightened. She thinks that if I stay here, I'll tell Joan what she did in the room at the end of the corridor.

She didn't seem to know that I was never, ever going to tell anyone. I would never be able to repeat what Pauline whispered in my ear. But explaining all this was much too hard. I couldn't make my brain turn corners like hers did.

"Get dressed and I'll let you outside!"

She said this in a very fierce voice, like an order.

"Won't they want to know where I've gone?"

"Leave that old army bag of yours in here. Then they'll just think you saw a door left open and you legged it."

All the nurses knew I was scared and upset about the night I was given all the vodka. They knew I kept worrying that I was going to get into trouble. Joan would know different. She'd guess what must have really happened. But who was going to listen to Joan? I realised that Rhoda was right.

I put on my clothes and walked to the nurses' station. If Alice saw me leaving, she didn't give a sign.

Rhoda led me down to the ward's back door and unlocked it, just as it was starting to grow light. The sky was full of purple-black clouds. I heard the wind moving in the branches of the trees. I'd not been out of doors since –

I suddenly realise that I have no time. In the hospital, no one's even told me the days of the week. I am outside time. I've fallen right through it.

The sky was growing lighter every minute. Low mist lay across the ground. I walked down a wide straight path through a garden. White flowers glistened on the banks beside the path.

Snowdrops. Outside the ward, it must be spring.

***

Now I start walking. On and on I go. I can't work out directions. Anyway, I've nowhere in particular to find. I keep on going. I walk further, out onto roads that have more traffic, where the road signs are bigger and much higher. I don't read what they say.

In Spring Bank now, it's time for my morning medicine.

Hours go by and my feet start to hurt. I grow colder and colder in the loud hard wind that blows along the big wide roads.

It's time now for my lunchtime medicine.

It's springtime but the days are still short; light begins to fade from the sky up ahead. Behind me there's a sinking pastel sun, throwing my shadow on the tarmac at my feet. As I watch, the shadow girl dissolves right away. Dusk drops down. The car headlights wake.

It's time now for my evening medicine.

I've spent the whole day in a daze. I've no idea at all how far I've come, or even why I chose to start walking the way that I did. The thick sticky syrup always made me so confused. Now, at last, my thoughts begin to clear. With the deeper cold of night comes a wave of horror.

I am homeless. When I left the army camp at Bicester, I had a place to go – somewhere out there, somebody expected me. There would be a roof and a bed when I arrived. Now there is nowhere where I can go indoors. As my thinking grows sharper, I understand that I might die tonight.

I'm so tired that I climb a garden wall and flop down on the grass. As soon as I'm down, it seems as though I'll never get up on my heavy, twitching legs. If they threw me in deep water, these deadweights would drag me to the bottom. Then I see the shed with its door half standing open. It's ten feet away in the corner of the garden. I crawl across the grass and through the shed door. Immediately I clang my head against a enormous brown metal drum. I stare at it in shock. It's the front end of a lawnmower.

There are sacks in a pile on the floor. The shed feels a little bit warmer than the night air outside. I lie down with my head on the sacks. The beams of the cars passing by on the road weave and cross above me like searchlights. But I'll never be found, and in any case, no one's out looking. I'm falling into nothing from a high cliff edge and no one even saw me let go. As I drop through empty space, nobody has noticed.

Here, where there's no medicine and no whisky and no vodka, I remember Dog. He's close alongside me, smelly and rough, and I wrap my arms around him. He licks my face. I feel the little bump of his stubby tail wagging.

I dream that I fly far away with Dog and the angels. We go into a storybook from long, long ago, where turtles with their pebbly flippers sail like great ships along the eye-popping reds and jewelled blues and metallic hot yellows of the reefs down deep beneath the sea.

They are bluer and kinder and wiser than anything. I hope that the beautiful turtles will sail me to heaven.

***

I wake up in the pitch black shed. Suddenly I know quite clearly that I can't take any more. What shall I do?

"My mother killed herself with alcohol and tablets." I remember how

Virginia said these words in the day room at Spring Bank, staring straight at me with her big, dark, faraway eyes.

"What kind of tablets?" I ask urgently. "I need you to tell me. How many tablets did she take? How many tablets, Virginia?"

"When I was a child, whenever I remembered my mother, I knew she was burning in hell."

And I am in hell here too.

"How many tablets, Virginia? Do you know? What were they?"

"Oh – just normal stuff!" says Virginia lightly. "Just stuff that she bought at the chemist."

"Like aspirin?"

"Yes, she used aspirin. It was ever so easy. If you mix up aspirin with alcohol, you'll die."

I can buy alcohol and aspirin, and then mix them up. It's going to be easy. I still have money in my wallet. All I've left behind at Spring Bank in my khaki army case is the Deed Poll – the piece of heavy parchment with its big red seal that promised me a brand new name and a whole new life to match. It promised that I'd be a proper person. But it turned out not to be true.

In the morning light, I see there's a gate in the garden wall. I don't need to climb back over. I walk down the road and I keep on walking. Seagulls start to circle and scream overhead. The air is speckled with rain. I walk for a very long time. The morning traffic starts, fills up the roads and then thins out. I see a school bus with children in their uniforms climbing on board. Then there's a sign saying "Welcome to Redcar". Beyond it, I see a row of shops. I buy myself a bottle of Guinness and a green and white packet of aspirin.

It seems as though I've travelled as far as I need to, so then I just walk across the road and sit down on someone's garden wall. I don't feel anything at all about what I'm going to do. I made my decision to die on the floor of the shed. It's simple. When you can't bear something anymore, you make it stop.

I swallow every tablet in the packet of aspirin. I gulp down the Guinness, though I still don't like the taste.

***

The curtains in the house behind me kept on twitching.

I had no idea how long I'd been sitting on the wall. There was very little light now. The night wind was rising. This would be the second time the sun went down and I had nowhere to go. When I swallowed all the tablets and drank down the Guinness, I thought that I would die at any moment. I wondered if I'd fall off the wall.

The curtains in the house behind me moved again. I'd wanted to die before anybody noticed I was there. I'd started to feel dizzy. My mouth grew very dry. It had to mean there wasn't much longer left to wait. Seagulls were wheeling up above, their wings like spinning lights in the cocoa-coloured sky. I stared into the brown and grey and whiteness full of churning, circling birds.

At the side of my vision was a thin strip of grass along the edge of the pavement, broken up with pram wheels and feet. Every single blade was a different shade of green. Its bright slash of colour made me blink. I seemed to have blinked myself back into my body. I began to feel less dizzy. How long had I been here?

The curtain flicked right over to the side and a face peered out from the window, a worried pale oval surrounded by silvery hair. It was hard to be sure if the watcher was a man or a woman.

The seagulls screamed suddenly much louder. Their cries became a giant blare of sound. The air flashed electric blue. A ambulance drew up by the pavement, and then a little blue and white car.

Lights. Sirens. Police.

There were uniformed men, talking in loud official voices. One of them crouched down in front of me. They lifted me up by my arms and hoisted me into the ambulance.

It was meant to be easy to die, but it turned out that it wasn't. I realised Virginia had lied.

***

This time I know straightaway where I am. I recognise the stink of a mental hospital. I read the sign above the door when they lead me inside: St Mark's.

St Mark's is modern and shiny and made out of glass. There are long clear corridors with walls like windows. The rooms are all sunshine-y bright. Everyone can see into everything.

I feel as though the light is going to blind me. I curl up on the floor with my arms around my head. When they try to make me stand, I fight them, lashing out and kicking them as hard as I can. There's a sound like an animal screaming. I think the sound is coming out of me.

Now I'm down on the ground in a room which has walls made out of eiderdowns. I can see the stitches in the lumpy grey padding. The room is very small. There's a gutter on one side and a trickle of open water flowing. The place reeks of piss.

I don't know how I got here. It's difficult to breathe because my arms are tightly folded round my chest. I can't unfold them. They're tied. What feels like a canvas sheet is wrapped around my body and knotted at the back. The little bumps of knots are digging in. I slump to the side and without my arms to help me, I can't sit up again.

***

I'm lying on a trolley being wheeled along a corridor. I can hear the whirr of its wheels. Striplights on the ceiling streak by. My arms have been freed now but my cold stiff fingers still won't work. I wiggle them. They hurt. My shoulders are knotted and cramped.

I see a row of curtains, then one of the curtains swishes back. Behind it in a cubicle, a woman is lying on her back. There are two people standing there: a doctor in his shirtsleeves and a nurse in a uniform dress. On her head, the woman's wearing what looks like a diver's helmet with electric wires coming out of it. She's jerking and mumbling, and trying to lift herself up. I'm absolutely terrified.

The curtain's pulled back quickly into place and the trolley moves a little further on. Then they push my trolley inside another cubicle that looks just the same. They put a diver's helmet on me. I want to scream and shout, but my jaw locks shut. I'm mumbling and moaning with fear.

They tie me down tightly with big buckled straps and light me up.

***

"Hello, my name's Maureen."

A young woman in a white overall was standing by my bed. She was smiling and holding a cup and saucer.

"Would you like a cup of tea?"

I didn't want to lie down in bed. I instantly felt frightened and tried to sit up, but my arms and legs were much too heavy to move.

"Don't try to get out of bed now," said Maureen. "You need to rest after your treatment."

"What… treatment?" My lips are clumsy and stiff. It's as though I've not spoken for so long that I scarcely know how. I fumble to find the words I need.

"You're allowed to eat and drink. If you don't want tea, I can bring you something else."

I didn't want anything.

"What's your name?" asked Maureen.

My name. I reach around inside my brain to find it. How could I forget my name?

"Er… Nicky."

"They gave you ECT – can you remember that? It was three days ago."

I'm searching in my mind, but there's nothing behind me but blank.

"Don't worry if you can't remember, that's normal. When you come back from the treatment, you never remember what happened. Then later on you do, or some people do. Not everyone."

"What's – what's EC – what is that?"

"They put electricity into your brain, to help shake you out of your depression."

Maureen put the tea on the table alongside me.

"Let me help you sit up and drink it. It'll do you good."

I tried to sip the tea. My lips wouldn't close around the edges of the cup. I tipped a lot of liquid down my front.

"It's going to be okay, Nicky. You're going to be fine. When the ECT starts to work, you'll feel better. Next week will be your second treatment."

"They're doing it again?"

"I know it's not nice, but the first time is the worst, with not knowing what to expect. When the funny feeling afterwards wears off, you'll be a lot happier."

"How many treatments will I have?"

"Of ECT? Honestly, I don't know. I'm not one of the proper nurses. I'm the orderly." She smiled at me again. "But please don't be scared. Finish off your tea and try to have a rest."

***

Any minute they could take me away. They could tie me to a bed and put wires on me.

I had to get out.

Early next morning there was wailing and screaming, just like there'd been at Spring Bank. Then the medicine tray went round and the ward grew quiet. This time, they didn't give me the sticky syrup – I was having a different sort of treatment.

There weren't so many kind nurses here. Instead there was swearing and slapping when the women wouldn't do as they were told. A lady with no legs in a wheelchair wet herself. One of the nurses hit her. I raised my arm to hit the nurse back. She caught my wrist and twisted it and yanked me away.

"We'll have you if you start any trouble!"

If you made a fuss or a fight got out of hand, they rang the alarm and then everyone piled in. They stripped off people's clothes and tied them up in jackets with those long tapes attached, so you couldn't move your arms.

I know that I have to get out.

In the next bed to mine was Dorothy. She wore an olive green coat the whole time, and clutched an enormous leather bag. She smoked a lot and hardly said a word.

But she seemed to mean well, smiling at me sometimes, and offering me her cigarettes. Did I have any money? she asked me. I told her I still did, in my wallet.

"Keep it," she said to me. "Useful."

"Be careful of Dorothy," Maureen told me.

"Why?"

"She's a paranoid schizo. She's dangerous."

I didn't know what Maureen meant by that.

"I'm leaving," Dorothy told me.

"What do you mean, you're leaving?"

"Getting out. Do you want to come?"

"Er… yes. Yes I do. But how?"

Dorothy opened her big leather bag. It seemed to be full of crumpled paper. But then she held it out so I could see right down inside, and when she did that I saw a gleam of shiny silver metal.

"What's that?" I asked her.

"That's… my… knife… see?" said Dorothy very slowly and softly, drawing out the words. I remembered how Maureen had warned me that Dorothy was dangerous.

"I'm going to break out of here," she whispered.

"When?"

"You coming?"

"Yes."

"Bring your wallet. Your money."

"Okay."

"I'll tell you when."

Two days later, she came tiptoeing over to my chair. It was dusk. "We're getting out tonight. Meet me in the dining room!"

"When?"

"Five minutes." Then in a low urgent hiss: "*bring your money.*"

I made sure my wallet was safely in my pocket. Outside the dining room window was a big black nothing. Rain tapped the windows. Car headlights glimmered far away.

"I'm here."

"Keep watch!"

She crouched by the door and twisted the blade of her knife in the lock. It wasn't very strong; in just a few seconds, I heard a sharp crack. She pushed the door open and we stepped outside.

I realised that St Mark's was almost in the country. Around us lay pale moonlit fields. Very far away there was the muttering of traffic. The rain was falling faster. This wild, wet night seemed unreal when just a moment ago had been the locked-up ward with its lights always shining.

As we climbed a wooden fence, I caught my sleeve on a nail with a long grating tear. The ripped sleeve flapped as we went running through the grass. The ground was uneven and we kept on tripping and stumbling. I was getting out of breath and very scared, and I realised that I'd no idea at all which way we were going.

"Stop!"

Dorothy turned back to face me, her bushy hair all flattened down with water.

"Not this way. This isn't right. Let's go into town," I panted. "Over there, towards the lights!"

"Where?"

"We need to find a bus stop."

"Where?"

"Where?"

"*Where?*" Now she sounded angry.

"I'm telling you! Towards the lights."

"Where?"

"Don't you have a plan which way to go?"

"What plan?"

"Somewhere we can go."

"Where?"

It was getting very hard to think clearly at all.

"We – ahhh – look, we need to get a bus, to get away from here."

"There isn't a bus."

"In the town, there will be!"

"Where?"

Dorothy reached into her bag. Then her knife glinted in her hand. What if she tried to attack me, in the middle of this big dark field? I was starting to panic.

"It's okay, it's okay! We just need a bus."

"Where?"

"Let's – um – let's get to the road. If we follow the road, we can probably find a bus stop."

Dorothy twisted the knife in her fingers. She stared at me so wildly that I thought it might be safer to run back to the ward.

But then they will strap me to the bed and put on the helmet of wires.

We followed the road until we came to houses. Then Dorothy couldn't walk any more. She sat down puffing on the verge by the roadside. I left her there. I thought that if I could find a bus stop and a timetable, surely I could plan where we should go. Perhaps I could buy us some tickets. My legs grew heavier. The damp of the grass had soaked through my shoes.

Now I saw the glow of the Fly and Firkin pub up ahead. It was late but the door was standing open. At last, I was going to have a drink.

***

Whisky is a wipe-out for me. Each time I drink it, the shutters fall faster.

Whisky is a walk into a wall.

When the pub closed, I found my way back to the place where I'd left Dorothy sitting on the ground. There were no more cars on the road, just silence and the raindrops' patter on the leaves.

But as I came around the last long corner, I saw that the air was filled with blue shimmering light.

The flash of a police car, shining through the rain. I watched as two policemen hoisted Dorothy up off the ground. She'd been waiting by the roadside for me to fetch bus tickets. I pressed myself down into the soaking verge and buried my face in the grass. The police car doors slammed shut. The blue blur of light moved away. They were taking her back to St Mark's.

Slowly I got to my feet. The water on the ground had soaked my clothes. I stumbled down the road through the night.

***

Now I was travelling by bus. A day had gone by since I'd left St Mark's, lost in a big drinking blank so I didn't really know how far I'd travelled. I knew I had nowhere in the whole world to go, and when my fear rose in peaks, I drank some more whisky from the flat little bottle in my pocket. That pushed the fear down, although I couldn't make it go right away.

We came to the edge of a city. The rain was still falling and I had no idea at all where I was. Getting off the bus, I saw a petrol station, closed-up and dark. There was no one around. I needed a cigarette very badly.

The tear in my shirt had run right up to my shoulder. I wrapped the loose cloth around my hand and punched out a pane of glass in the door. Inside I found the cigarettes and I took one. Then I heard the sound of an engine. A police car drew up on the forecourt.

***

I didn't mind a night in the cells – it was indoors and dry. I gave a false name and next morning, the police let me go. After all, I was only a nuisance who'd stolen just one cigarette and broken a pane of glass in a door.

Now I was right in the centre of a city, surrounded by tall buildings with high arched windows. Some of them even had statues at the front. My clothes were drier now, but my socks were still so cold and wet that I threw them away.

I bought a bottle of whisky with the last of my money. The customers were staring because I was so dirty and my shirt had one sleeve. My ankles were bare and my shoes were squelching when I walked. I hurried round the corner, sat down in a doorway and drank. The morning sky was pale hazy grey and became more hazy the longer I kept drinking.

The next thing I knew it was starting to grow dark. The streetlamps came on. The wind swept around the tall buildings, so I took a wide road that led away from the middle of the town. The rain began again, then grew much harder. I drank more whisky as I walked, stopping under a streetlight and staring upwards through the shining torrent of water.

Around the next corner, I saw a little glow. There were lights in a building set back slightly from the road. The Lucky Star cafe, I read. Its windows were cloudy and I couldn't see inside. I pushed the door open, blinking in the glare. Immediately a woman's voice cried, "Coom in, loov, you're soakin'! Coom inside and 'ave a sit down!"

Chapter Five

Nicky No Socks

The woman's voice was warm and kind. As I pushed the cafe door open, everyone turned round. Rain streamed off me. I blinked in the glare.

The Lucky Star cafe was small and very full. The customers were all Asian men with brown skin and beards, wearing tunics in pale brown and white. Some of them had sweaters and waistcoats on top of these as well. Over in the corner was a big blue jar with a thick pipe coiled around it on the floor. It was making a low bubbling sound, filling the air with sweet-smelling smoke.

The woman who had spoken looked English, with brown hair tied back off her face. She put down two plates of food on the edge of a table and hurried towards me.

***

"Where am I?"

"Bradford, my loov! You're in Bradford!"

Fazil and Rita ran the Lucky Star cafe. They were married, though he had come to England from Pakistan and she was born two streets away. I didn't know that was allowed.

Rita hurried off to fetch me a towel. Somebody else offered me a cigarette. They gave me a plate of chicken curry but I didn't want food. They all fussed around. Someone else put a chapati in front of me. I didn't know what it was. I realised they were trying to be kind, but the cafe was small and full of men. Their closeness frightened me. It was difficult to speak but I managed to stammer out a thank you.

Rita patted my hand.

"Ee, loov, but you've nowt on your feet!"

"I lost my socks," I told her, in a daze.

Fazil shook his head at me, and smiled.

"What's your name?"

"Nicky," I said.

"Nicky No Socks, you!"

"She's proper gone, Faz," said Rita quietly. "We'd best 'ave her tek a lie down."

She led me upstairs. The back bedroom door opened slightly as we reached the narrow landing. I heard giggles and whispers from inside. Little girls' faces peeped out.

"Our lasses," said Rita with a nod. "Off to sleep now!"

She gave me clean dry clothes. Then they let me sleep on the sofa.

***

The house behind the Lucky Star cafe was crowded. Rita and Fazil's eight daughters all shared a bedroom.

Fazil needed help in the cafe, he told me. He cooked the food and Rita cleaned, but most of her time was spent looking after the girls. Sometimes in the daytime he would stop his work to pray. He told me I could stay with them and sleep in the little back cupboard if I wanted a job. "You work to pay your rent!" he said to me. I didn't want a bed, but Rita found a crochet blanket and a cushion, and put them on a bucket in the cupboard to make me a seat.

Late in the evening, long after Fazil had locked up the cafe's front door, a different group of customers knocked and were shown upstairs. They went into a tiny back room – the shebeen, Rita called it. The men would stay there drinking until the small hours of next morning. This was Fazil's secret: the Lucky Star cafe had no licence for selling alcohol.

He was an elder in Bradford's Pakistani community, respected by his friends, and by younger men too. He was gentle and kind. He noticed I was frightened when I helped to pour drinks in the tiny shebeen, and told me there was no need to worry.

"They are my friends. Only here for a drink," he said. "You pour – they are happy. Then there is no trouble for no one!"

Fazil was wrong about that. One of the men tried to touch me. I flinched. The man wouldn't stop and I panicked. I swung out my fist and I punched him. Fazil took charge. "Anyone touch Nicky," he told them, "you will puckin' die." He wouldn't ever swear. A puck was the furthest he would go. I hated those words and liked Fazil because he wouldn't use them.

He didn't think that women ought to drink. It just wasn't right, he said – but he made an exception for me. He was happy so long as I could keep on pouring, taking the trays of glasses down to the kitchen for washing and bringing the clean ones back up. Then I could have all the whisky I wanted. And so long as I made sure I stayed drunk, I didn't feel afraid of the men and their rumbling voices in a language I didn't understand.

Now I no longer needed money. The days grew warmer and the door of the cafe stood open. In the corner, the radio played: we listened to the Kinks, Elvis Presley, Cliff Richard. I drank through the day and slept when I had nothing to do. Nobody sighed or looked impatient or got angry, or told me to sort myself out. Sometimes I slipped into a blank and a long stretch of hours would go missing. But Fazil didn't mind, just so long as my work got done in the end.

***

One of Fazil's customers gave me a sword.

His name was Rafiq. I was amazed at the gift, long, curved and gleaming in a dark red sheath. He said that it came from Pakistan. When armies fought on horseback, a curved slashing blade allowed the rider to kill without jamming the sword in the enemy's body and getting it stuck. When I ran my finger along it, I shivered.

One late spring day with a high, hot sun, a woman came into the cafe. Her cheek was bruised brown and her lower lip was cut. She'd only been there for a moment when a man came in after her. He didn't say a word. He reached out and gripped her wrist hard. Then he pulled her out of the door.

Time took a big jump forward. Now I was outside in the road and striding after them. Somehow in my hand was a long swerve of metal. I heard a screech of car brakes, and then cries.

"Christ!" "What the bleedin' 'ell is that?!" "Get that bluddy thing off 'er!" "Mind out!"

I didn't know how, but I was holding Rafiq's sword. It flashed in the sun. I swung it to and fro. The man and the woman heard the shouting and turned back.

"*Get away!*" I screamed at him. Already he'd dropped the woman's arm. She covered her face with her hands. I still slashed and swung. "Get away from her! *Get away!*"

"Alright, loov, tek it easy!" A older woman came towards me, holding out her hands with the palms facing up. "'E's let her go now, my loov, so jus' you relax!"

I stood there with the sword held high. It was heavy. It made my wrist ache. I felt as though I was holding fire. Everyone was shrinking away.

Then Fazil came out of the Lucky Star's door.

"Alright, Nicky No Socks," he said to me gently. "You put it down now."

He ordered that no one should call the police. "We don't have that here!' he said. "We don't want it!" I still thought they'd come, and waited until nightfall for a car to pull up outside the cafe. But nobody came.

***

Weeks are passing by. Everything's a blur – I have no idea how long. I drink. Every day seems the same but none of them seem real. I wonder if the Lucky Star cafe can perhaps become my home.

When I think about the past, back to the times when the terrible words and the pictures and the nightmares filled my head and I couldn't sleep at all, I know that I would rather live like this. I like the way drinking makes this long, quiet nothing.

***

I'm high up in the air. Even with my eyes shut, I can feel there's a big space around me. Below, I can hear people shouting.

"Drop the clock! Drop the clock!"

None of this makes sense to me at all.

There's a sharp pain along my left arm. I realise it's holding all my weight. My muscles are protesting.

I can't understand where I am. I open my eyes just a chink. It's night. I see a line of street lamps a long way below. Across the dark valley all around, the tiny lights of houses are sprinkled. Right down past my feet, which are swinging in the air, a bright little circle is bobbing, moving quickly. It's somebody running with a torch.

Somehow, I'm halfway up a wall. I'm standing on nothing. My left arm's wrapped tightly round a drainpipe.

More shouts drift up from below.

"Drop the clock, will you! Just DROP THE CLOCK!"

However I got up here, I can't work out how to get down. Perhaps if my arm becomes too painful, or just can't support me anymore, I'll let go and fall into space.

I'm holding a cuckoo clock tightly in the crook of my right arm. The cuckoo's wooden beak pokes my throat. As I wriggle, searching for a place to rest my feet and take the weight off my arm, the bird bounces backwards and forwards and pecks me on the windpipe.

Down below I see blue lights flashing. I'm going to be meeting the police.

***

They hoisted me up to the roof and arrested me. The building was a Bradford cotton mill. They told me I'd been trying to break in, then the owner arrived in a car. When I heard the engine, I'd tried to climb down the drainpipe. Except that I got stuck halfway. Where the cuckoo clock had come from, nobody knew.

I didn't remember a single thing about it.

I gave the address of the Lucky Star as mine. Surely, when they'd done with their questions, the police would send me home. Instead, they remanded me in custody. All I could think of now was a drink. They put me in handcuffs and pushed me in the back of a police car. We drove across the moors.

I was desperate for whisky to stop my hands from shaking. The cuffs were very big and my wrists were so thin that my hands could slip free. When the officer next to me saw this, she offered me a Woodbine. We sat there and smoked. Then I saw a high fence topped with wire. I thought that perhaps this was a mental hospital. Except that this time, I'd never get out.

A drink a drink a drink.

I was taken to a room filled with cages. The cages were low and made from wire, like chicken coops. They put me inside. There was no room to move. I couldn't change position, stretch my arms or stand. There was nothing to drink or to smoke.

I have to have a drink soon. A drink a drink a drink. The next room held a bath tub and stank of carbolic. They made me have a bath, just like they had at Spring Bank, then put on an orange prison dress. They told me that now I'd see the doctor and be checked. In the next room was a black and metal chair facing stirrups that were hanging from the ceiling.

Horror.

I wouldn't put my feet in the stirrups. They started to force me: I screamed and lashed out. When they tried to push me down, I bit and kicked and spat. They couldn't make me sit in the chair.

"I think she's had enough," said the doctor.

After that, they didn't try any more. It was autumn 1965. I was ready for admission to Risley Remand Centre.

***

I'd been inside for quite a few weeks before they took me back to court. I was fined five pounds for trying to break into the cotton mill. I knew there was no way I could pay. But I told them that I would, so then they let me go. I walked all the way to the Lucky Star cafe. I wasn't sure that Fazil would let me come back, but he told me Nicky No Socks was welcome. He didn't even ask me where I'd been.

At the cafe, I could drink whenever I wanted. But when I remembered how I'd found myself halfway up a wall, clinging to a rickety old pipe, I started to panic. The scary drinking blanks meant trouble, and now I could see it. It was dangerous to go around doing things like this – stealing cuckoo clocks, climbing down drainpipes – with no idea at all what I had done. What if I had some terrible accident? What if the worst that could happen to me hadn't happened yet?

Nothing made sense when I was lost in that big black space. I must drink to keep my nightmares at bay, but not tumble down into oblivion. If I could manage this, perhaps I could still keep whisky as my friend.

***

The Lucky Star's customers were mixed. Builders and workmen in overalls stopped by for a full English breakfast with their vans parked outside. Retired people came wanting just a mug of tea. There were street girls, the imam from the mosque and conductors who worked on the buses.

The clippies always seemed to have fun, very smart in their ties and peaked caps for the women as well as for the men. I thought I'd like to stand at the back of the bus and ring the bell, then walk up and down between the seats and sell tickets to passengers.

And I was more and more frightened about how much I drank. Spending every day in the Lucky Star cafe made the whisky just too easy. A job as a clippie would surely be a help, and I liked the idea of wearing a uniform again. I filled in the forms and applied. They sent me a letter inviting me for interview.

On interview day, a Lucky Star customer told me to suck lots of mints to hide the booze on my breath. It worked – and I was going to be trained as a clippie. My training day was down at the depot the following week. But as the day went on, I grew more and more worried and unhappy.

There was quite a lot more than I'd thought to working as a clippie. There was handling the money: the float at the start of each shift must be counted out and signed for. You put all the cash in a big leather pouch which you wore on a strap across your chest. At the end of your shift, the whole lot would be counted again. Then the float was taken out and the balance was compared with the print-out of the tickets you had sold.

There were lots of different tickets which you printed by turning a handle on the silver machine around your neck. You had to make certain you were printing the right one. You must also make sure that everyone pays – so watch carefully as passengers climb on board the bus. You don't approach the same ones twice, but keep an eye to make sure no newcomer gets missed. Then there were the fare dodgers: up to you to stop them if they try to get away without paying.

No one must be hurt on the bus, so check that everyone's safe and sitting down before it moves. You had to keep in touch with the driver in his cab, watch for the traffic outside and be sure that everything was ready before the bell was rung. But you couldn't take too long or the bus would be late.

Working as a clippie had turned into a big scary problem.

I numbed out my worries with whisky through the night before my first shift. As the sun came up, I drank a load more. Then I grabbed my booze-busting breath mints, put on my uniform and headed for the depot.

At the depot's main office, I signed in for my shift. I was far too drunk to count my float, so when they handed me the money, I tipped it on the table and jangled the coins in the palm of my hand. I'd no idea at all how much there was. After I'd pretended to count, I dropped all the coins in my pouch and strapped it on right across my chest. It was hard to make the pouch's flap stay down. My first bus departed from the stop around the corner in five minutes' time.

The blue double-decker pulled up and I hauled myself aboard. My stomach lurched queasily as soon as the bus started moving. We drove round the corner to the very first stop, and several passengers got on. I swayed along the gangway selling tickets. I wasn't sure at all how much they cost, or whether I was selling the right ones. If I tried to count the change, I couldn't keep my balance, so I dropped the coins they gave me straight in the pouch without checking. So far, no one seemed to mind. The flap on the pouch kept popping open. I had to push it down to stop it slapping passengers right in the face.

Seven twenty nine. Time to go. The driver glanced over his shoulder. He must be waiting for the bell. I pulled on the cord.

Ding ding! The bus moved off. I clung to the conductor's pole. The road went spinning past. It made me feel giddy.

At the second stop, the bus filled up. It was hard to tell who'd been on board before. I headed to the upper deck to sell more tickets. The bus swayed and swung from side to side. Coming down, I missed a step and slithered all the way to the bottom. The coins in my pouch gave a great big clatter. The passengers nearest to me stared.

The bus stopped again and even more people crowded on. I'd no idea now who'd bought a ticket and who hadn't. The passengers were shuffling along to find a seat. I couldn't see over their heads to the driver. But if I waited, I'd make the bus late.

Ding ding! Forward we went. Except that this time, I didn't. Instead, I felt myself toppling. I grabbed at the conductor's pole but missed. My feet left the floor and I crashed off the bus, landing flat on my back in the road.

The flap on my pouch flew open. Coins sprayed all around. One second later, the ticket machine around my neck landed too, thumping me hard in the chest. A couple of lads ran forward, laughing and scooping up the money from the ground. Somebody yelled that the money wasn't theirs and they legged it up the road, still cramming coins in their pockets. The bus was disappearing out of sight.

I'd been a clippie for twenty-eight minutes. I lay there and looked at the sky.

***

Back at the depot, I was fired. Everyone was angry. They were angry that the float had flown out of the pouch ("It should have been secured!") and even more angry that I hadn't stopped the lads from grabbing all the money. They were angry that the bus had gone roaming off through Bradford with no conductor aboard and the passengers all banging and shouting for the driver to stop.

All I could think of was a drink.

Then someone noticed I was drunk. They were even more angry

and I told them I would bring back my uniform next day. Then I had to leave. Slowly I walked back to the Lucky Star cafe. Fazil was sitting at the door in the sun.

When I told him the story, he laughed.

"I puckin' love you! You are crazy woman!"

When Fazil laughed, I tried to laugh too. Then I found the whisky and took it to my seat in the cupboard. I opened the bottle and made everything go black.

Next morning, Fazil gave me a waistcoat. From my country, he told me – from home in Pakistan. The waistcoat was black with red and white brocade around the edges, then patterned all over with birds and leaves and flowers in vivid greens and oranges and white. I stared and stared at its colours, shining like jewels in the plain little caff.

"You wear this, you will feel happy! Nicky No Socks is a friend here! We are always happy when you work here for us!"

My eyes were tired and sore, but Fazil was so kind and I could see that the waistcoat was beautiful.

***

Two young women sat down in the Lucky Star cafe. Both of them had pale round faces and long untidy hair. One had a pregnant belly. They were hungry, and Rita made sure they were served a big meal. She asked them lots of questions, and wanted to know when the baby was due.

Very soon, they said. They'd travelled here from Liverpool. The girl who was going to have a baby was looking for her boyfriend. He was the father. She was hoping that he would give them money and somewhere in Bradford to live. I could see straightaway that Rita didn't think that the boyfriend in Bradford was going to do anything like that.

Rita loved Fazil, but I don't think she really liked men. She thought that they were trouble – that the way they treated women wasn't right. She'd listen to them talking sometimes, and then you'd see her give a little shake of her head. She never asked questions about my life before I came to the Lucky Star cafe, but she did tell me once that I should put the past behind me and try to find a good man one day.

"It 'asn't been easy for you, my loov, 'as it?" she said, and I wondered how she knew.

The girl who was having the baby was called June. Her friend's name was Alice. Alice looked lost and scared and unhappy. I'd sat here in the cafe just like her, with nowhere to go, and people had been kind. That memory made me want to help them.

They left. They had June's boyfriend's address and they said that it wasn't far away. Rita watched them from the Lucky Star's window as they walked up the road. When they were gone, she gave a little sigh and shook her head.

Then a week or so later, Alice came back. She was pushing a pram. For a minute or so I was confused; she hadn't been the one who was having a baby, had she?

"Where's June?" I asked her.

"The ozzie!"

"Where?"

"'Ospital! Gav 'ad to tek her back! She's 'ad the baby and she brought it 'ome, but she didn't stop bleedun after that!"

"Is she okay?"

"They 'aven't phoned."

"Where's Gav?"

"Dunno." She looked at the ground. "'E's a proper dead beat, Gav."

Both of us peered into the pram. A dark little head, with tightly closed eyes.

"I dunno know wha' tuh do!" whispered Alice. "Ju's been gone fer hours, an' wha' about whun it wakes up?"

I didn't know what to do with the baby either.

"It's asleep now."

"'It'll wake up when it's starvun'!"

Rita had been kind to them last week; Alice had remembered her and hoped that she might know what to do. But Rita was busy with her daughters. I thought that we should take the baby back to Gavin's house and wait. Surely he'd turn up, and then he'd have to help. And when June came out of the hospital, that's where she would go. That's where she'd expect her baby to be.

Alice just seemed muddled and helpless. I explained my idea.

"Only if yous come too!"

I stashed some whisky in my pocket and we set off back to Gavin's. When we got there, his house was a horrible place, dirty and crumbling, with great big gashes in the lino and a jagged crack right across the glass in the door. There were men in the kitchen who Alice didn't know. To get away from them, we took the baby upstairs. But the bedroom was horrible too − piles of sheets with stains in a heap on the floor and unwashed plates and dishes all around. The baby was still sleeping.

"It's cold in 'ere," said Alice anxiously, "fer the baby."

"Where shall we put it?"

"Put it whur it's warm."

We put the baby down in the big bottom drawer of the chest, and padded all round it with the sheets from the pile in the corner. We both noticed that the baby was beginning to smell.

"It stinks!"

"Can't you take it home − take it back to Liverpool?"

"June's dad's dead angry wi' er. Fer gettin' the baby. Her mam would 'elp, but not if 'er dad really does one."

"Do they know where you are?"

"Nah. We ran away."

"What about your family?"

Alice rubbed her eyes with the back of her hand.

"I dunno... I got five brothers. Me mam's dead skint the 'ole time. Me dad..." Her voice trailed away.

The baby started wriggling. We looked at each other.

"It's 'ungry now," said Alice.

"Can it have some curry?"

She stared at me.

"No! Course not!"

"Well, what then?"

We heard its first lurching little cry.

"It needs to 'ave milk."

"Is there any milk?"

"We'll 'ave ter buy some."

Alice sent me down to the shop on the corner, to try to get milk. I drank some of my whisky on the way. I didn't know what sort of milk the baby wanted. When I got back with a bottle of Sterimilk, Alice was pacing the hall, with both her hands pressed against her head. From upstairs I could hear the thin scary wailing of the baby.

"We'll 'ave to ring June's mam!"

"Yes! That's a really good idea."

"There's a phone box down the street."

She didn't seem able to do anything without me to help. She gave me a scrap of grubby paper with a phone number on it and asked me if I'd call. When June's mam answered the phone, I could hear straightaway that she was very upset.

"Our June 'ad the baby?"

"Yes."

"Wha' is it?"

"It's a baby."

"Is it a boy or a girl?"

"Um..." I didn't know. I didn't think that Alice knew either.

June's mam said, "Oh my God." She told me to give her the

address and to wait until she got there. She said that it would take a few hours and that while she was coming, we needed to try to give the baby some milk.

As we were waiting, Gavin turned up. He had a closed, tight expression on his face and didn't seem to care about the baby at all. He didn't seem to want to help June either. When Alice said that June's mam was coming very soon, he left the house.

When June's mam arrived in her car, she had a big bag of things for the baby. She said that she was going to the hospital, to find June and take her back home. She seemed very angry with Alice, and left her just standing in the hall. She picked up the baby and took everything away.

***

The men who drank in the Lucky Star shebeen were unhappy. I couldn't understand what they were saying, but Rita said they talked about their problems. At school, their children were called names. Their wives were insulted in the street. It was difficult for them to get jobs. Sometimes people threatened to beat them up and even to set fire to their houses. I heard Fazil being called a Paki – Paki bastard! Fucking Paki! Sometimes I saw the word sprayed up on walls around Bradford: Pakis go home!

"It's easy for uz, dook," said Rita. "If ah'm not wi' 'im, no one bothers uz. Same wi' you too. But 'im, he gets no rest wi' it – them lot allus call 'im names."

It was strange to think that all the time I trusted Fazil, he felt he was lonely and in danger. I understood how that must make him feel. Nowhere in the world was truly safe, not for him and not for me.

***

Another of the Lucky Star's customers made an advance. It happened very late, in the shebeen. This time, Fazil wasn't there. I hit the man as hard as I could to make him stop. But he didn't seem hurt – he just carried on laughing.

"You come home with me!" he shouted. "Then we have babies!"

I thought about the stink of June's baby. I remembered the pinched, empty look Gavin gave it, even though he knew that it was his. I was very, very sure that I never wanted anything like that.

"No!"

He laughed even more. He came up close behind me and tried to wrap his arms around my chest. He rubbed himself up against my back.

His arms circling round me made me panic. I tried to fight him off. A few seconds later, he was lying on the floor. The man started shouting. Somebody ran out of the shebeen and called the police from the phone in the cafe. When he rushed back up the stairs and said that the police were on their way, everybody else ran down and straight out of the Lucky Star's door.

By the time the police arrived, the customer I'd punched had got up off the floor. He was holding his nose and starting to complain. The police asked lots of questions: the man called me names. I argued. They told me I was under arrest for being drunk and disorderly.

I was terrified they'd take me off to Risley on remand. I screamed and fought the policemen. Then they changed their minds about arresting me, and called for an ambulance instead. I went on screaming in the ambulance, until they gave me medicine which made me go to sleep. Next day, I managed to stay calm because I thought that if I didn't, they might send me to a mental hospital. I told them I was sorry that I'd had too much drink. They cautioned me and let me go home.

But when I got back, I found that Fazil was angry. The police had been called to the Lucky Star cafe.

"We don't want no puckin' policemen in here! I say this to you! Why you involve the police?"

I wanted to tell him that I hadn't. But it was hard to think clearly and explain. I'd not seen Fazil's lips buttoned up like this before. He'd never once shouted at me. When anyone was angry, it made me very frightened. I went out looking for signs in shop windows for jobs, and spotted that a petrol garage in Manningham, just up the road, was wanting a manager.

I still had a sheet of paper saying all the things about myself that I'd made up to get my job as a clippie. The garage didn't check if they were true: they just gave me the job. Now I could work at the counter in the day-time selling petrol and sleep in the back room at night. I didn't tell the man who ran the garage what I was planning to do. That was how I left the Lucky Star. I never said goodbye to Fazil and Rita, which made me sad, but it seemed to me that everything was ruined now that Fazil had been angry.

Every day at the garage, so long as I opened on time, helped all the people buying petrol, and kept on sucking mints, I could carry on drinking. I bought myself whisky and vodka with the takings.

I met Mr Brant, who was the area manager for Bradford. He came to the garage each week to collect all the money from the safe. Sometimes he couldn't make the totals add up right and then I had to blag about what had happened to the money. I started to dread seeing Mr Brant's big car drawing up on the forecourt. I kept on expecting him to tell me I was fired when the cash was all wrong. If that happened, there would be nowhere indoors for me to sleep.

***

"Alice!"

When she came into the garage, it was difficult for me to recognise her. She was dirty and dishevelled. Her hair was very tangled and her round face had grown much thinner.

"Alice, what's the matter?"

"I been lookin' everywhur fer yous! At the caff, they diddun know whur yous went!"

Ever since June's mam took her home with the baby, it turned out that Alice had been trying to find somewhere safe to live in Bradford. She said that Gavin's friends were making trouble. They were telling him that she'd put June up to making out he was the father of her baby, just so they'd have somewhere to stay when they ran away from Liverpool.

"But I never!" said Alice. "I never dun that! 'E's a dead beat, 'im."

She was tired of feeling hungry and sleeping in cold places, or dealing with men who'd give her somewhere warm where she could sleep – at a price. She said that she'd telephoned her dad. He told her that he missed her and was sorry that they'd argued. He wanted her to come home where she belonged. I felt a strange wave of sadness when I heard her say that. I needed a drink.

"But I dun 'av any money," said Alice, "so I can't gerra ticket."

Tomorrow Mr Brant would be coming. I'd bought whisky again with the garage's takings. That meant the money in the safe would be short. I didn't want to have another meeting, with Mr Brant glaring and saying he'd take action if I didn't keep the cash records right.

"Can I come to Liverpool with you?" I asked Alice. "I can buy the tickets and we'll travel there together I only need a bed for a bit. Just until –" and I wished it could be true – "until I can sort myself out."

Chapter Six

The city is burning

When I see she has a gun, I'm terrified. I've no idea at all why I'm involved with the woman, or why I must do as she says. How did I get caught up in this?

It must be because I'm not a proper person. I feel like a heap of crumpled clothes with nobody inside. Others make shapes that I must fit myself around.

Darkness is gathering. Something very bad is going to happen. There's no way to stop it. I drink my fear away. I drown the little moments of thinking as quickly as I can.

***

Alice and I didn't buy ourselves tickets to Liverpool. Instead we hitched a lift on a lorry. Her dad opened the door, and when he saw her standing there, he cried.

Alice's home was very small. All its paint was peeling and the wallpaper hung down in curls. Her five younger brothers always seemed to be fighting and screaming. The first day I was there, a man in a suit knocked on the door and said that he'd come for his payment. Alice's mother gave him cash from a tin on the shelf and I could see in her face how much she hated him. Inside her cardigan sleeves, she was clenching her fists all the time that she spoke.

"Bloody vulture," she said, as she shut the door behind him.

I couldn't bear to stay in the noisy, crowded house. I walked into the middle of Liverpool, looking for a drink. I'd started to learn where to go – the pubs and the clubs and the places where I'd meet the other drifters like me, and maybe get word of a place where I could sleep.

That was how my life in Liverpool began. I went from one place to another, drinking heavily and getting into trouble. I stayed in squats and with people I drank with in bars, sometimes for a night, and sometimes for longer. The city's a jumble of pictures in my head, just broken bits and pieces. I drank and I drank. I knew that I was falling. The dark drunken spaces opened up and there are many days I barely remember.

***

I met a girl called Margaret who worked on the streets selling sex. She and her friends used a squat to store their clothes. There were holes in the roof and you could see the sky above you when you stood in the kitchen. They said they needed someone who could try to keep it tidy in exchange for booze and cigarettes. It was hard to keep on finding places to stay, and scary to sleep in the open. I quickly moved in.

The weeks in the squat turned into months. I was forgetting how to keep track of time. The girls smoked spliffs so I tried one, and then I wanted more, finding that drugs were another way to drift through the days without breaking the surface.

There was only one time when they brought a man into the house – I walked in on two of them with him in the kitchen. He was wearing just a blindfold and they'd tied him to a chair. They had long black whips in their hands. They were beating him and he was shouting and moaning. I was drinking so I didn't feel afraid – I just stood in the doorway, dumbfounded. All I could think of was that perhaps the man might be hurt.

"Uh – uh – do you need – shall I call an ambulance?" I said.

"Nick – just get out!" the girls both hissed. Afterwards they told me that the beating was what the client wanted. They laughed and laughed at the astonished expression on my face.

In Liverpool, drink was still my friend. Most of the time, it kept me safe from nightmares. But at other times, things would fall apart. I kept on getting arrested.

Picked up unconscious in a shopping precinct: fined five pounds.

Involved in a fight outside a pub, although I'd no idea at all how it started: to Risley on remand then fined five pounds.

Once I was picked up for dancing with a shop window dummy outside Littlewoods in Liverpool town centre. I never knew where the dummy came from. Drunk and disorderly: fined five pounds and a night in the cells.

I learned that if I kicked a policeman it was straight down the nick, which wasn't so bad on a cold rainy night, so I did that quite a few times. The list of fines I'd never have the money to pay kept on getting longer.

***

Outside in the streets of Liverpool, things are tense. It's the mid 1970s - the city feels restless and on edge. Arguments go on about race and poverty and justice. Sometimes at night I hear the sounds of breaking glass and shouting. Crowds gather outside the local police station following someone's arrest. Very soon, on some hot summer night, the anger here is going to blow up.

And I'm scared that the last little threads of my life are breaking. I'm left with only scattered events that don't tell a story. I'm not a proper person. I'm here and I'm alive, but somehow – I'm not. It frightens me, the way that time goes by without my noticing. The feeling of crazy inside me keeps on growing, even faster than my list of unpaid fines.

But underneath I know there's a much bigger fear. I don't want to think about the past, or remember. When I sense my memories stirring, I get drunk.

It's all there is to do.

One day, the noise outside the door grows louder. A crowd of people surges down the street. Sirens are wailing. I stand watching with a bottle of whisky in my hand. The sky turns amber with the glow of a fire close by.

From down by my feet comes a tiny miaow. There's a kitten crouching on the ground. It's huddled and shivering – I think it must be sick. It can't be more than a week or two old. I put the bottle down, then kneel by the kitten and cup it in my hands.

Hidden by the wall that runs along the edge of the pavement, I cradle the kitten in the folds of my shirt. The flames are so near that I can catch the sound of crackling. Feet pound close by. Sparks drift and glow in the darkening sky. I drink from the bottle and the shouts and yells and sirens start to seem unreal and far away. Then it grows quiet. The incident is under control. The big explosion that I'm sure is going to happen in these streets isn't ready just yet.

I lean against the wall and pass out. When I wake, it's cold and black and silent and the kitten is dead.

***

While I was inside on remand for one of my drinking offences, I met Billy. As soon as I saw her, I was scared of her. But still, I couldn't stay away.

She was big and tough and butch. Everybody said she was a gangster and that when she went out robbing, she used guns. I thought it was a story just to frighten people, although she didn't need a gun to frighten me.

She told me she was planning a heist at a garage. When she found out that I'd been a garage manager, she said I had to help. I didn't want to commit such a serious crime, not just because I was frightened but because it was wrong. In the moments when I could think clearly, I was shocked at the point I was coming to. But it didn't seem to matter how I felt. On the outside, Billy said, I must meet up with her and help her do the job.

The garage that she wanted to rob was close to Penny Lane. When I saw that she had really brought a gun, I was terrified. She smashed her way in as the place was closing for the night. The sound of breaking glass was like a bomb going off. I was trembling so much that it was hard to think straight. There was one young attendant on the till cashing up. When he saw us burst through the door, his eyes bulged with terror.

"Behave yourself," I told him, "or else she'll shoot us both!"

He looked so very frightened that I told him I was sorry. I said that the gun was just a bluff and that all Billy wanted was the cash. As my arm brushed against the lad, he flinched. Billy grabbed the money from the till and yelled that we needed to leave. I muttered one last time that I was sorry and I ran.

The days that followed were a long dark blank. I couldn't bear to think of what I'd done. What was happening in my life? I drank and drank to push the horror of the garage heist away. Then we were arrested. The garage attendant had given our descriptions. Billy and I were both known to the police. Off again to "grisly Risley", as its inmates all called it, on remand awaiting trial. I'd already lost count of how many times I'd been inside.

I'd got to know a couple of the screws. I liked Miss Betts, who was kindly and wanted to help me, telling me to try to make sure that I never came back to Risley after this. "Do your time if you're sentenced, but then make something of your life, Nicholls," she said to me. "Try very hard. Find something better than this."

It was months before my case came to court. The garage attendant told the judge and jury I'd been nice to him and how I'd said I was sorry. He was sure that the heist hadn't been my idea. So the judge sent Billy down for quite a long time but didn't sentence me. He told me that the best thing would be to leave Liverpool and go somewhere else, away from the people who had drawn me into crime.

***

Drifting. I move on and then move on again from city to city. It's an easy thing to do when you feel you come from nowhere and there isn't any place that you truly belong. Sometimes I'm afraid, but so long as I can drink I can just about keep my fear under control.

I don't always know where I am, or how long I've been there. The seasons change but I don't watch the months or even watch the years. I've stopped counting them. I've no idea at all how much time is going by.

***

I ended up in Manchester, visited the clubs and then moved into a squat. In a gay bar, John's, I beat a big Greek man in an ouzo drinking contest. He seemed to be doing alright until he suddenly keeled over and passed out on the floor. I could see how surprised the watchers were that I could take more booze than a man twice my size and still be standing on my feet. I tried not to think about just how much drink that really was.

And at John's, I met Mo – tall, blonde, glamorous and absolutely hard as nails.

She dealt in stolen goods and often was in trouble with the law. She looked very different from Billy – more feminine, softer. But she only seemed soft till you looked her in the eye. Her mother helped look after her children – five of them, by five different men. Some of the dads were policemen. Her mother wasn't well and Mo was getting worried about how she was coping with the kids. She needed to make better arrangements – and when she said that, she was looking straight at me.

She handed me a note with her address in Ancoats. She smiled, but this was an order. Next day I left the squat and went to find her.

***

At Mo's flat, it was chaos. Sam, Ferdy, Angela, Peter and Tommy, her children, ran wild. Sam was the eldest – he was fourteen – and Tommy was the little one, just five years old. All of them constantly fought with each other. In the back bedroom, their grandmother was sick and when Mo was not around, there was no one at all to keep order. As soon as I arrived, I wanted to get away.

But I didn't, because Mo overwhelmed me. Face to face with her, I found that I had no will at all. Like a plant growing sideways near a light, I bent myself around her, though it's hard to explain how it happened. It was the same when she said that she wanted to go to bed with me. I didn't understand how anybody could ever want that. But I did what she said because it seemed there was no room to do anything else but obey.

I did anything she told me to do. I did it when I felt that it was wrong. I did it when I hated it and only wanted to stop. I did it when it filled me with panic and I had to keep on drinking down my terror. I seemed to have no choice about anything that happened. My body, my life and my decisions felt like somebody else's, as if all I could do was go picking up the pieces after everything around me had got broken.

***

Mo also told me that she wanted me to shoplift. She was a professional who stole things to order. Six folded three-piece suits fitted neatly inside the shoplifting bag she took out with her, and it still looked as though there was almost nothing in it. She took her older kids along to teach them what to do and we had a big row about it. It was the one time I was ever really brave with her – I told her that she shouldn't be treating them like that. She should teach them right from wrong, I said to her, not turn them into criminals like me. Her children had done nothing to deserve it.

She was furious. She may have looked soft but she beat me up and left me in the street. I was covered in blood with a face like a watermelon, eyes swollen shut. The police picked me up and took me to hospital.

"How many did this, then, luv?"

"A gang," I said to them. "A great big gang. There was nine or ten of them at least." Then I went back to Mo's flat in Ancoats. Where else could I go? She put me in hospital three more times. Her anger was terrible.

Mo said that I must learn to drive. She taught me. Now I could take the children where they needed to go, or help move goods that she had robbed. We drove into the centre of the city, or sometimes to Stockport for the day, to go shoplifting. My job was to wait in the car and she told me that if she didn't come back – if she had been picked up by police – then I must take the car home and stay put.

Once in Stockport that actually happened – I waited hours but Mo didn't come back. She must have been arrested. I set off alone in the car but I'd no idea at all where I was going. I ended up driving on the moors and got totally lost. All I could see were flocks of sheep. Then it got dark and I was more and more confused and desperate for a drink.

Inside, there was a part of me that knew just how mad this all was. I saw it that night as I drove round and round on the narrow moor roads. Why did I feel I had no choice? Why not walk away – just leave all this behind me and go somewhere else? Surely if Mo hurt me, she wasn't worth all that I was giving. It was like a glimpse of truth from the corner of my eye. But the idea of leaving her still filled me with dread. I needed to be with her, and if she didn't give me a home, where would I go? There was nowhere but the streets with their endless uncertainty and fear. I was desperate to please her and the angrier she was, the harder I felt that I must try to make things right.

The worst day of all was the day I had to steal the tantalus set

– a little wooden cabinet with three glass decanters inside. The tantalus was fitted with a brand new alarm, but Mo knew how to get that off. Then she distracted the assistant while I had to carry it out of the shop.

I was shaking. The tantalus rattled really loudly as I trembled. Every time it clattered, I was waiting for a hand to descend on my shoulder. I was certain every second I was going to be arrested. When I got to the car outside, I was drenched in sweat. Mo told me not to be so stupid.

But I was really frightened. I said that I wanted to try to get a job and not keep on committing crimes. She wasn't too impressed with my help by then, or with my shoplifting skills, so she told me I could do what I wanted, so long as I looked after her children.

***

Hardest of all was deciding what to feed them. I never wanted much food, so it was strange to keep on thinking of mealtimes. I didn't have a clue how to make any dishes, so I gave the children things I could heat up in the oven, or sent Sam or Ferdy to the chippy. I quite often felt sick when I smelled their food, or got it on my hands. Eating meant having a body – and I didn't want to have one, or at least I ignored it as much as I could. But the children never did – they were always saying they were hungry.

Then Mo was arrested again, and remanded in custody in Risley. Now I was alone with the kids, so finding a job was impossible.

I drove them to see her on visiting days, constantly fighting and shouting in the car. I was driving drunk, which I knew was dangerous. Now Mo was gone, there was almost no money. In the kitchen was a huge fridge-freezer that she'd stolen – it still had the label from the shop stuck on it. The fridge had nothing inside. In the back room was Mo's sick mother, who needed more and more looking after.

Sam would lash out in fits of rage like Mo's. It happened more and more and I was worried all the time that he would seriously hurt one of the others. One day I heard a shriek from the kitchen. He'd stabbed his brother Ferdy with a very long knife. The blade had run right through the side of Ferdy's leg, close to his thigh. Now he was pinned to the seat of a chair.

All the others were screaming, except Sam who was white-faced and frozen with shock. Ferdy half-fainted. Mayhem. I remembered army medical training: the knife must stay in the wound or he'd bleed a whole lot more. I rang 999. They told me that there was an ambulance strike, but to take him straight to the hospital. There was no way to get him off the chair, so Sam and I lifted Ferdy and the chair, and carried him out to Mo's Vauxhall Viva, where we slid him in sideways along the back seat with the chair. By now he was whimpering and seemed to be awake. I drove us to the hospital even though I knew I wasn't sober.

All the way there, I was panicking in case the doctors asked us how Ferdy had been stabbed. If I couldn't answer – if police or social services started interfering in Mo's family – I knew that I was dead, without any doubt at all. But I needn't have worried. Ferdy stuck up for his brother. He explained it had all been an accident when they were messing around. Nobody grassed in Mo's world, and everybody knew it. The kids knew it too.

When I brought the children back to the flat, I was completely exhausted. They were wired, shrieking, impossible to quiet or control. I wanted to run. *Something terrible is coming*, sighed the quiet little voice in my head. *I should get away before it happens, whatever it is.*

I drown the voice out. I can't go anywhere. If I dare to leave her children, Mo will come after me and beat me – even kill me. But I know that's not the reason that I stay. I stay because she wills me to do so.

What another person wants is an order and I must obey, however I may feel. It's as if I live with giants a hundred feet tall and I vanish in between them. I don't choose anything about my own life. The one time I really tried to change, when I left to join the army, I failed, and I'm far too scared to try again. I've no idea at all what choosing feels like.

***

More and more now, my fear from the past was rising up, cutting through the whisky and the vodka and the spliffs. Even when I drank myself unconscious, I woke up far too quickly, jittering with fright. Leaving Mo's house by myself for more than just a few minutes made me panic, and walking down the road to the off-licence, I flattened my back to the wall if a car horn blared or a bird flew low overhead. Once when I got to the shops, I knocked down a pyramid of tinned pink salmon. The tins capsized with a great metallic roar. The shopkeeper swore at me and told me to get out. I couldn't stop shaking.

Everything is going to fall apart, the voice in my head kept repeating. *All of this will shatter all around you. It will be very, very bad and it's going to happen soon.*

***

In the Dickens Club in Manchester, I met a gay sailor called George. He didn't have anywhere to stay so I invited him to come to live with us. When Mo was in prison, I thought George could help me look after the children.

When George moved in, he brought a whole crate of whisky. Sometimes he'd get drunk and pass out. But when he was sober he would cook for the kids, and mind them, so then I could leave them for a while. I'd go down to the Royal Oak where I'd sometimes play darts.

Mo's family had to have money. Now I had help, I decided to try to get a job and I was taken on as a catering manager at the Littlewoods catalogue depot. Most days I turned up there drunk.

The staff on shift would lock me in a store room and leave me there to sleep it off, though no one told the management what was going on. When Mo was released, she was furious I'd started the job and at first about George too, until she realised how having him around could be a help. But she didn't like my job at Littlewoods at all. She accused me of fancying the women at the depot, and in any case, what was I doing with a job? Wasn't there enough for me to get on with at home? She seemed to have forgotten that she'd told me I could work if I wanted. Her rage put me in hospital again.

I lost the job by causing an explosion: I turned on some gas jets in the kitchen, then answered the phone. The gas built up but I forgot I'd left them on and when the phone call was finished I came back and lit the flame. There was a terrible bang. The kitchen was completely smashed up and I was fired. In any case, Mo wouldn't have allowed me to work there much longer.

***

There was just one little bit of my life that seemed to be mine, and that was my drawing. I'd started to make some cartoons. First of all, I copied what I saw in the *Manchester Evening News*, just doodling away a few odd minutes here and there to distract me from the worry and the chaos all around. Then I grew more confident, and started to do drawings of my own. Seeing them made me remember the times I'd drawn before, and how much I had liked it, and I felt a little pang of regret. But perhaps, even now, it might not be too late.

Again and again I picked up a pencil. Each time, it brought me a moment of quiet and calm. It made me feel I mattered, too, just a little bit. I didn't let Mo see, in case she was angry. Then one day I had an idea. I wondered if the cartoons I'd drawn might be good enough to go in the paper.

Once I'd had the thought, it wouldn't go away, even though it frightened me too. The address of the *Evening News*'s editor was printed on the letters page. To send a picture in seemed impossible at first, but each time the idea came back, it made me feel excited. When I went and dropped the letter in the post box, I felt sick and very scared, but just for a moment, I realised that I felt happy too. Just maybe, I might be in the local paper. And now I had a secret from Mo.

The art editor wrote me a reply. He said he really liked my cartoon and asked me if I could do others. Eventually I sent in quite a few and the *Evening News* printed them. It gave me another idea. The Dickens Club was being redecorated. I told them I would paint them a mural. I worked on the wall for days, outlining figures that were life-sized and dancing. I used streaks of fluorescent paint all the way across so that now, when the club lights flashed, my wall of dancers came to life. It looked just as if they were moving. I was drunk but I was happy when I painted the mural. It was wonderful, exciting, uplifting. I didn't want to stop.

When Mo found out that I'd been painting and drawing, she was angry. It was easier after she found out that the *Evening News* would pay me. When my cheques arrived, she took them. But still we didn't have enough money.

Crumpled on the floor of the bedroom at Mo's, I still had Fazil's waistcoat, black with red and white brocade around the edges. I loved its colour and its soft, shining fabric, patterned all over with birds and leaves and flowers. Its beautiful colours shone brightly in the dirty, messy flat with its glaring lights overhead.

"You wear this, you will feel happy! Nicky No Socks is a friend here! We are always happy when you work here for us!"

I sold my friend's gift to a man that Mo knew, and went out to buy us some food. But as soon as I left the house, I was gripped with panic. The street seemed very wide and exposed to the sky. I felt dizzy in its big windy space. Then when I made it to the shops, I'd no idea what I ought to buy. To think about eating and to make a decision seemed impossible. My heart was hammering and I was soaked in sweat. I wondered if I was going mad. More than anything, I needed a drink.

I leaned against the wall. People were staring. I knew that if I stayed there looking strange, somebody would order me to leave.

A drink a drink a drink to make the panic go away.

I bought vodka with the money that I got for Fazil's waistcoat, and drank it outside in the car park.

***

Next day, the booze ran out again.

In Mo's flat, the inky smears of mould on the walls were growing bigger. There was nothing in the fridge. The children kept fighting with each other and the bin had overflowed. When I tried to empty it, stinking brownish liquid dripped on the floor. I must have a drink.

George was nowhere to be seen. I was scared to leave the kids. Mo would be murderously angry if she ever found out. But I couldn't stay here. A drink a drink a drink. I gave Sam some of the leftover money to buy chips and I headed for the Royal Oak.

Chapter Seven

They'll execute
me now, thank God

Flash! A bloated purple face from a nightmare.

Flash! Her mouth hanging open, dried yellowed crusts around her lips. Swollen tongue poking right out. Vomit on the front of her dark red blouse. The whole room stinks.

Flash! A mop of bright blonde hair with pewter streaks.

Flash! Her staring grey eyes streaked with red, like markings on a map.

Flash! A heavy brown trail of blood down her neck from just below her ear. Another smell too — the faintly sweet reek of a corpse.

She's propped against a pile of pillows. I stretch out my hand in disbelief. When I touch her, she slowly topples sideways and lies there staring up.

She's dead.

It's 2am on Saturday October 25th, 1980. I see all this like flickers of lightning. I'll never stop seeing it. I'll never stop screaming, though I can't make a sound.

***

I see her as soon as she comes through the door of the Royal Oak. She stands out: a stranger, not a regular, bright bottle-blonde, dressed in a dark red blouse and tight flared trousers with a shiny narrow belt. A party girl, but when you look closer, the blondeness has grey metallic-looking roots. Her face powder cakes in the up-and-down lines above her mouth.

The friend she has with her is younger. The two of them go over to the bar and stand there laughing and smoking, drinking gin and orange and eyeing the place up. They'll soon have company in here.

I'm drinking, fading in and out. I'm talking but I don't know what I'm saying. The two blonde women at the bar are right up in my face, friendly, out to have a good time. Andrea and Teresa. Andrea drinks heavily – I notice this. I notice she's keeping up with me.

Andrea invites me back to her place, just a few friends to have more drinks. I need to get back to Mo's children, but I push the thought away. Andrea says that her place isn't far. I don't have to go for very long. Smudgy car headlights swing by as we walk. We're crossing a very wide road. I see traffic lights above me, big balls of light that are changing from green to red.

Then a blurry gap, a jump in time.

I know I shouldn't be here at the house. I must get back to Mo's children. I should never have left them on their own. I drink. If I stop drinking even for a moment, my skin crawls with unease. She'll kill me if she finds out what I've done.

I drink more. I drink my way to black.

***

It's much later on. The music's still playing. There are still a few people around. I need to find the toilet very soon. Surely it has to be upstairs. But where are the stairs?

I search along the hall. It's pitch dark. I stick my arm right out to the side, to guide me with a finger on the wall. I can feel the raised pattern in the paper. Round the corner there's a door. It must be the bathroom – but when I push it open, I fall straight down two steps and out the back. It's bright outside and now I see the house is very low. The roof starts just above the ground floor window. I don't think it has an upstairs.

I go back inside. The toilet must be somewhere off the hall. There's another door – it's open just a crack. The lights are very low but there's a glow from inside. But when I push the door, it's still not the bathroom, just a bedroom. There's a big heap of clothes on the bed. The light is coming in from a streetlamp right outside the window.

Something glints in the middle of the bed, like the flash of an eye. I realise it's not clothes – it's a woman, leant up sideways against a pile of pillows. I can see the whitish gleam of her tumbled bright blonde hair. It's Andrea.

"Sorry –" I say "– where's the –"

Then I catch the hot taint of vomit. It makes my nose burn. I take two more steps forward. The block of white light from the window falls fully on her face.

***

Flash! Ring for an ambulance, or call the police.

My legs won't hold me up. My hands shake violently. There must be a phone. There's a socket on the floor. I crawl along, following the wire. It runs up the leg of a big curved dressing table. I pull it and the phone crashes down on my head. I moan out loud with fright. When I hold the receiver to my ear, there's no dialling tone anyway.

Flash! I'm dragging myself along the hall. My face is only inches off the ground. The palms of my hands press down on the grit in the carpet, like crawling on gravel.

Flash! I see her bulging grey and red eyes. My whole body judders. I suck in air in rattling gasps.

I reach the kitchen door. I let out a shout which is more of a croak: "Andrea's dead! In the bedroom!"

The sound of bottles tinkling over. Some people leave by the kitchen door; others run past me down the hall. The music cuts out. In less than a minute, there's nobody there.

Flash! Outside on the pavement, searching for a phone. There's a box on the far side of the road. As I dial 999, I clutch my arms tightly round my chest and squeeze my eyes closed.

Where am I? The ambulance people will be asking. There's a road sign on a wall right there. The glass wall of the box is cold against my forehead. I stare through a tiny pane at the dark open door of the bungalow across the street.

***

Flash! The light this time is blue. Police cars, men in uniform. Loud voices. I'm crouching on the step at the front. There's no one here now but the policemen, walking through the rooms and talking on their radios. I hear the spit and hiss.

Flash! I see the horror-face in purple and white with her bright hair hanging down. I want to stop the pictures but I think they've burned into my eyes.

A policeman pulls me roughly to my feet.

"Did you do this?"

What happened to Andrea in the black, blurry spaces? I can't remember anything. I don't know where she went or who was with her. I don't know.

I say, "I'm the only one here."

***

Flash! I am arresting you on suspicion of murder. You have the right to remain silent. Anything you say can and will be used against you in a court of law. You have the right to a lawyer. If you cannot afford one, one will be provided for you.

On suspicion of murder.

Of murder.

Everything goes black.

***

Flash! A small plain room with a table and three chairs. Two police-men opposite. No windows. The younger policeman is jabbing with his finger.

"We all know you did this. Quicker and easier just to confess now."

Murder. Suspicion of murder.

I don't know how Andrea died. There were gaps that night. There have always been spaces where I don't know what happened. But I didn't –

"Just – confess – now – luv – eh? Much easier for all us. And 'specially easier for you."

I don't know what happened. But it couldn't have been murder. I have to have a drink.

"You want a fag, luv?"

"Yes."

He holds out the cigarette, and when I start to take it, he draws his hand away. I put my hand out further but he pulls his further still. He breaks the cigarette in half, throws it on the floor and then he laughs.

Flash! One policeman slaps my face, over and over and hard. The other has my wrists in a grip like bone on bone, tightly in the small of my back.

Flash! They drag me by the arm next door, into the tiny little toilet. They push me to the ground on my knees, then force my head forwards, right down the pan.

"Why don't you just tell us that you strangled her? Tell us that you murdered her?"

I didn't. I don't know. I don't remember. I must have a drink.

He flushes. Sheets of water wrap around my face. It shoots down my nose. When the flush stops, I gasp in half a breath of air and give a bubbling scream of panic.

"*Tell us what you did and then we'll stop.*"

I don't know. I don't know what happened. I can't remember anything at all.

He flushes again. Then he pushes me down on the floor and kicks me in the back.

***

I don't know how long I've been held at the police station.

There's a lawyer. He's telling them that I should be admitted to a hospital, not kept here. Then later on, he's not there any more.

Flash! A photo of Andrea's dead face. They put it on the table in front of me.

"Look at this!"

They took it before they moved her body. She's slumped over sideways on the bed. They pin me in my seat and push my head down very close to the table. I try not to look, but one of the policemen spreads his fingers right across my eye sockets, forcing my lids to open.

Flash! Now there's a second photo, this one taken much closer up.

"You remember this! You did this!"

I can't look. I don't know. I can't remember.

"Nobody knows where you are, luv. And if they did, do you think they'd care?"

He's right. Nobody knows.

"You know we'll come and get you, any time we want? If you get off this rap, we'll still bring you in. We can question you as long as we want, whenever we want. Don't you be thinking you can ever get away with what you've done. So tell us!"

Darkness and confusion. I can't answer any of their questions.

"Nobody knows where you are and nobody cares. You know what that means, luv? It means we can do whatever we want. If you're never seen again, it's just one less piss-head waster we've got to take the trouble to dry out."

No one would care if I was never seen again. I wouldn't care myself.

***

Flash! This time the young policeman's standing right behind me with his mouth pressed to the side of my head. His breath feels very hot. His stubble rubs my neck.

"You're one of the them dykes, aren't you, luv?"

The other policeman lets out a loud raucous laugh.

"You know what your lot need, don't you?"

"You'd give it to this one?" says the other, and this time both of them laugh. "Bloody hell mate, but this one's a butch. You must be desperate, haha!"

"Oh, I'd give it to her proper. Your lot need a bloody good fucking – isn't that right? Well, I'm the one to give it you."

Flash! I'm climbing up the stairs in London, higher and higher, losing count of just how far I've come. The man in the smart white shirt and waistcoat opens the door at the top. He gives me his strange little smile.

I walk into the room. On the great big bed lies Andrea, staring, her slack lips all speckled with vomit. I turn around and scream. The man shuts the door and walks towards me.

"There's a little room next door all ready for us, isn't there? We keep it all special. Shall we go in there, luv?"

No God no.

No.

"Or you could tell us what you did. Tell us that you killed her and I'll leave you alone."

I remember now. I'll remember anything you say. Yes, I did it. But please don't take me in there. Please don't take me up the stairs.

***

If I pleaded guilty, the charge would be reduced to manslaughter. That meant it wasn't a pre-meditated killing, so the sentence would be lighter. I signed my confession without reading it. Then they put me on suicide watch, with the cell door left open. Every few minutes, someone looked in to make sure that I was still alive.

Except that I wasn't. I was breathing, for the moment. That was all.

***

I was remanded in custody at Risley once again.

Flash! I recognised Miss Betts' anxious face.

"I'm extremely surprised about this, to say the least," she said to me. "I find the situation very hard to believe."

"Why, miss?"

"I'm surprised that you appear to be involved in such a serious crime. I think that – whatever happened here – it needs to be properly investigated. I think you had probably had a great deal to drink and don't remember what you were doing. Were you put under pressure to confess?"

You know we'll come and get you, any time we want? If you get off this rap, we'll still bring you in.

That's what the policemen told me. They can do whatever they like.

"No, miss."

"You weren't – encouraged to say that you had done this? Tell me the truth."

"No, miss."

"Are you sure about that?"

"Yes, miss."

"But Nicholls – she gave her head a very sharp shake – "this is completely unlike you. It doesn't seem in character, even if you're drinking. I don't at all accept that you're a violent person."

I don't know. I don't know what happened. I can't remember. But I'm never going back for more questioning. Anything but that. Guilty to a murder charge – anything. But please not that.

***

Flash! It's my trial. I'm climbing up a narrow winding staircase. I almost trip and fall. At the top is a big gloomy room full of heavy dark wood. I'm standing in the dock. I see Manchester Crown Court Number One like a picture in a mist. Nothing seems real.

A judge is on the bench. Higher to my left, rows of seats and faces I recognise. One of them is Mo, with a woman I don't know sitting there alongside her. Mo turns her head very slightly and looks straight at me. Her face holds total rage. Down on the right, I see the two policemen who took my confession.

The darts team from the Royal Oak starts waving and calling. "Good luck, Nick! You didn't do it, Nick! You tell 'em!"

Silence in court!

The judge asks me how I will plead. I shiver.

A plea of not guilty, my solicitor said, means longer on remand in Risley, and then a trial by jury. Every single day, the police can come and get me, any time they want. And what if – just what if – the jury lets me go? I know for sure that Mo wants me dead, because I left her children. She'll find me.

My choice is fear or safety. I need to go to prison.

"Guilty."

There's a mutter and buzz in the court. My barrister steps forward and speaks quietly, only to the judge. The judge shuffles papers, then he frowns.

"I'm sorry that your plea leaves me very little choice. I'm forced to give you the minimum term of imprisonment. However, I will send you somewhere where I hope you can get help. Three years. Take her down."

I stumble on the narrow little stairs. At the bottom, a policeman stands on duty. As I step past, he pushes his face right up to mine.

"Fuckin' three years for bloody murder," he says. "It's fuckin' disgustin'."

***

I leave court in the back of a van. They're taking me to Risley to wait for my transfer. I'm not on remand any more.

We march along a corridor, one prison guard in front of me and one right behind. I think that I'm not going to do those three years. I must have been sentenced to death. They're taking me somewhere to kill me.

A heavy metal door. The guard knocks sharply. When it opens, I wonder if it's going to be a noose or an axe or a gun. They'll execute me now, thank God, and all of this will stop.

But it's just another cell. I faint and fall to the ground.

Chapter Eight

The lady in the garden

Four months now since I'd arrived to start my sentence.

From the dock in the courtroom I was taken back to Risley, then from Risley to here, Her Majesty's Prison, Askham Grange. Gripped by endless waves of panic, beating its wings in my chest. I must have a drink. A drink a drink a drink.

Flash! Again and again I see a bloated purple face from a nightmare. Staring grey eyes streaked with red. A brownish trail of blood down her neck. I smell the corpse-smell.

Flash! I remember the day that I peeped round the door of the smart front room of the house by the fire station. I saw teapots and china and cake. And that day I saw something else, something I have drowned so deep and far down that it was almost lost to memory till now. Something I cannot bear to see.

It's a small dark-haired boy who is crouching on the floor. He's naked, facing away from me. There are brownish smears on his thin white backside and down the side of his leg to his knee. The soles of his feet are pink and clean. When he sees me watching him, he covers his face with his fists so that I won't see him cry. Behind the child are three naked men. Their long, white bodies are matted with thick black hair. The little boy's blood is smeared across their thighs. The blood smell is everywhere.

I feel as if the past has broken through. The memories I've been running away from for so long are filling up the everyday world. There's no escaping from them now. I see the little boy's bewildered torment in black, white and red on my eyelids whenever I close my eyes.

As the sleepless weeks went by, thick dark stripes began to criss-cross my vision. I knew I must be seeing things that weren't really there, but it was hard now to tell what was real. It was as though I saw the world from inside a cage. Then sometimes the cage bars moved, like terrible stick men marching, and I heard their pounding feet.

Among the endless days and nights, in the prison's visiting room one afternoon, Mo came to see me. She ended everything between us – except that it was far worse than finished. She said our relationship – the only security and anchor I had, the one thing that held me to the world – had never existed at all.

"It was nothing but sex," Mo told me. "Just think – you've been around for 35 years and that's the only thing you're actually good for. Forget about the kids – you left them alone. I should kill you for that. Forget the whole thing – just do your time then go somewhere else. You're no good to us."

All the time she spoke, I felt that I was falling. Down and down and down. Mo didn't say goodbye – she just left me sitting there. Then I found I couldn't stand up. A screw came to help me, but I couldn't move at all. I couldn't see anything but black. No one could prise away my fingers from the chair's wooden bars.

"Don't keep on pulling at her hands," said a voice in the dark. "She's too frightened. She can't let go."

They picked up the chair with me in it and carried me to the prison hospital.

***

The Askham prison nurses are kind. They tell me that I'm having a breakdown and that they must give me medicine. It's strong, and for the first time in weeks, I find the long silent blanks of sleep.

Not a Proper Child

Christmas is coming. In the daytime, I walk round the grange and find out a bit about how the place works. Although it's a prison, it's open, which means that they talk about "rooms" and not "cells" here: prisoners hold keys and can come and go until lockdown at night. Most people work, some here on site doing cleaning, gardening, laundry. Women who will soon be released leave Askham completely on weekdays and travel by bus to do their jobs in York.

I can't work yet. I can't communicate with anyone. Moment by moment, I struggle with endless waves of fear. When terror rears up out of nowhere, the nurses have told me to breathe very slowly. They say I should remember that the things I'm afraid of are nightmares. It's just that they come while I'm awake.

I can't eat at all. The idea seems strange and remote. I start to trade my meals with the others in the dining room: they'll give me roll-ups if I pass them my trays of unwanted food. Then the screws tell me I'm on food watch, which means that they think I might deliberately starve myself. They're supposed to keep an eye to make sure that I don't, but still, they aren't always looking. I even trade Christmas dinner for something to smoke: three roll-ups for turkey, two for the roast potatoes. Sprouts are only worth one. Nobody really likes sprouts.

One morning in the hospital, I start to do a drawing on a cereal box. Then I draw on magazine covers. I draw on a packet of Rizlas. One of the nurses asks if I'd like a drawing pad. Paper's not really allowed in here, she says, but I think we can make an exception. All of us can see how drawing keeps you calm.

***

The night I arrived, the oak-panelled hall of the grange with its carvings round arched windows filled with multi-coloured glass had seemed like just one more mad mistake. Surely I'd been sent to a prison, not to live in a stately home.

Askham was built by grandees who lived up to their name: their sprawling mansion was certainly grand. It had black and white beams and a large formal garden. The road through the village, Askham Richard, led right to its high front gate.

The weeks went by and slowly Mo faded from my thoughts.

There was quietness around me. They let me leave the hospital, back to a room to share with four other women. I was given a job in the laundry.

The early days of 1981. The wind grew less biting. I saw the first blossoms. It was spring.

***

I saw her first in a long line of others in the dining room, holding her tray against her chest like a shield. She was dressed in a plain blouse and trousers that she'd tucked into knee-high boots. Her head bent so far forward that she was nearly stooping. Her long dark hair concealed the side of her face.

"New girl's just come in," said someone at my table, and pointed.

"Yeah – that one's the drug dealer."

"Drug dealer? Her?"

"That's what I heard. Only got 'ere yesterday. Drugs charge – high security. Been inside a while."

She'd picked up her dinner now, and tentatively looked around the hall to find herself a seat. With her still, gentle face, she didn't look at all like a drug dealer.

There was a wolf whistle – the standard response to a new arrival in the dining room at Askham. Then there was another. Someone on the next table laughed. The girl dipped her head even further, then found a place to sit at the far end of the room.

"Don't she look posh? Too posh to be in 'ere!"

"Well – that's the more fool her, then."

I couldn't see her now for the other people seated in the way, but when she rose to leave, she pushed her hair right back. It flowed smoothly across her slight shoulders, and rippled as she moved. I saw her face in profile, her serious expression and her pretty little snub of a nose.

Pale-faced and graceful, a poem in boots, I watched her step out of the dining room's spotlight and vanish down the corridor.

***

"Hi there."

Breakfast next morning. I looked up. The girl with long dark hair was standing right over me.

"Hi."

She had pale grey eyes with dark smokey specks in them. Her black hair was parted in the centre above her schoolgirl's face. She'd bitten her nails very badly and her skin was indoors pale and dry, like parchment. Her anxious smile lit up her face.

"Please can I sit with you?"

"Uh – yes. Yes, of course."

"It was really quiet, last night," she said to me. The tone in her voice was almost wonder. "It kept me awake. Where I was before, at night it's so noisy."

I remembered the shouts and cries of prisoners, echoing.

"Yes."

"And this morning I heard the dawn chorus. You know – the birds singing? And there's a garden!"

"Um – there are gardening jobs," I told her. "If you want to work outdoors, you can put in for one."

"I'd love that. I've really missed being outside."

She started to eat, and I sipped my tea.

"Better food in here," she said. "The milk's almost cold and my Rice Krispies aren't too stale to actually snap, crackle and pop."

I realised I'd joined in her grin.

"What's your name?" she said. "Do you have a job here?"

"I'm Nicky. I work in the laundry. It's warm in cold weather."

"I'm Caroline Beech. Carrie. We do our own washing here, don't we? It'll be so strange just to do normal things. You think you've not changed while you've been inside, but you have. Having the doors not locked – walking straight through without needing a screw with a key. That's unusual to me now. I keep just standing there waiting to be let out." She sighed.

"You have to book a laundry time," I said. "You come down with your clothes and use the machine and the dryer. I can help if you get stuck."

"Thanks."

I wanted us to carry on talking.

"The first time I did a big wash for the baby unit," I told her, "I did it wrong and dyed all the nappies blue."

"What, even the ones for the girls?"

Caroline Beech made me smile. And it was true – when I got the laundry job, the first thing I did was mess it up: piles and piles of blue towelling squares and Mr Norris, the laundry supervisor, rolling his eyes. As Carrie laughed, I felt a bit better about all those blue nappies.

"Listen," she said, "thanks so much. I'm sure I'll catch on once I'm used to it."

"If you want any help, you know – you can ask. It's not so bad here really."

"Thank you. I will. I don't think it's so bad here either."

***

One morning, the governor of Askham had come along to see me in hospital. I'd heard that people liked him, and even the ones who said they didn't showed him respect. He didn't come to visit prisoners normally: you had to go and book an appointment if you wanted to talk to the governor. So everyone stared when he walked down the ward and sat himself in a chair next to me.

Mr Whitty was stocky and short. He looked like a boxer. His sparkly blue eyes met mine.

"So. Nicholls. I hear you've been having a pretty bad time."

I couldn't think of anything to say.

"But you seem to be starting to feel better. That's good."

"Yes, sir."

"I've also been told you've been doing some drawings."

"I know I'm not supposed to have paper."

He tilted his head.

"Well, let's say just for now that we'll turn a blind eye."

"Thank you sir."

"You enjoy drawing, don't you? They tell me you're good — did you know that?"

I didn't know how to respond to his praise.

"Uhhhh…"

"Can you please show me that drawing pad?"

It was lying on the table. He flipped through its pages.

"Hmmm. I like some of these," said Mr Whitty. "Ever had art lessons, Nicholls?"

"No, sir."

"Right then - I'd like you to practise your drawing."

"What do you mean, practise, sir?"

"When they discharge you from the hospital, you'll need a prison job. I'm going to send you to the laundry. While that washing goes round, I want to see you drawing some pictures. If you can do this now, without lessons – just think what you could do if you worked at it."

He put the sketch pad back into my hands.

"And don't you worry about your drawing paper – no one's going to take it off you. When you've filled up the pad, just ask for another one."

"Yes, sir."

"Make an appointment to see me in a month and bring what you've done along with you, then I'll decide if it's ready to go into the Tate."

"The Tate, sir?"

"Big London art gallery. Ever so smart. Where people go to see proper artists. I want you to be an artist, Nicholls – whether you think you're one or not. So we're going to get you practising."

***

"Whitty lets you have paper, then?" said Moira.

"Yes."

"You know it's against prison rules?"

"I know. He said he was turning a blind eye."

I was drawing whenever I could. I'd started to decorate the letters that the women in my room wrote to send home to their children. I drew little creatures on the envelopes: a bumble bee, a snail. When people saw them, I started to get more requests.

"I like Whitty."

I liked him too. "So do I," I said.

"Did you know it was him who took the numbers off the babies?"

"What numbers?"

"Before he came, the babies in the unit all had their mums' prison numbers on their cots. Whitty stopped it."

"Why?"

"He said that babies aren't prisoners."

When I thought about that, it seemed a wonderful thing to have done.

***

I forgot to make the appointment to see him. I'd started my job in the laundry. Mr Norris kept on telling me to go into the towel room and saying they could manage without me. On the pile of towels, I'd find sketch pads and packs of coloured pencils.

In the long grey blur of days, I found I had started to see colours once again. They shocked me with their brightness. I kept on drawing, just like Mr Whitty had told me. Mr Norris hardly ever came in to interrupt.

Then Mr Whitty stopped me in the hall.

"You were supposed to come to see me in my office, you toe-rag!"

Sitting at his desk, he riffled through my drawing pad: cartoon characters, sketches of women working in the garden, a study of the front of the grange. He looked closely, then up at me again, peering over his reading glasses.

"Kilmarnock the snail? What's that about, then?"

"Moira asked if I could do a funny birthday card to send to her daughter. I did a drawing of a snail and some other people liked it too, so then I did some other cards with him on and then we gave him a name. He has a tartan shell."

Those words were the most I'd said in weeks. My voice sounded strange and echoey in my own ears.

"And why Kilmarnock?"

"It's where Moira's from."

"Oh. Well, that makes sense then."

"He's a cartoon character," I said. "For children. But adults like him too."

Mr Whitty pushed his chair back from his desk.

"A little bird told me you've been writing songs as well – is that true?"

"Ummm – yes, sir."

"Is there no end to your talents, Nicholls?"

I didn't understand what he meant.

"I'm teasing you," he said. "I'm impressed."

"Oh."

"Tell me about your songs."

"Er – I write the words – the lyrics – and sometimes when I'm writing them, I think of the tunes as well."

"What are they called, then, some of these songs?"

"Um – one is called, er, Nobody Can Call My Baby A Bastard."

"Nobody Can Call – I see." The governor looked down at the desk and rubbed his hand across his mouth. I realised that behind the hand, he was smiling.

"That title wasn't mine though," I explained. "One of the other girls wrote it but I finished it for her."

"Are there any that you wrote yourself?"

"Er – one's called Whisky."

"I see. And what's that one about?"

"Ah - it's about how drinking whisky always gets you into trouble."

"Is that what happens to you, Nicholls?"

"Yes, sir. I think drinking vodka is better. Not so much goes wrong when I drink that."

"You think a different drink might solve the problem?"

"What problem, sir?"

Mr Whitty frowned. "Any other songs?"

"Yes, sir. There's Silent Christmas. And, erm, Rock Bottom. Right now I'm doing one called Footsteps."

"Well, sometime soon I'd like you to sing some of those for me. Maybe get some of the others to sing with you. And I want to see more of that chappie Kilmarnock as well."

"Yes, sir."

"Keep practising, Nicholls. We'll have you hanging in the Tate yet. Or if they're too hoity-toity to have you, it'll have to be Top Of The Pops."

***

There was plenty of alcohol inside Askham Grange. There was plenty of all sorts of things. We bartered in chocolate and tobacco, bought with our wages from work round the prison.

Moira showed me the strings running down from the bushes near the edge of the duckpond into the water. One end of each string was tied to a sturdy branch and the other to a bottle. Our supplies of drink lay safely on the bottom, keeping nice and cool in the mud. They came from the girls who worked in York, and sometimes former inmates who'd pass them to us over the wall.

There was blonde Lebanese hashish, arriving in blocks and broken up to chew since nowhere was safe enough to smoke it. Sometimes we'd get red Leb too, which was darker and stronger. Red Leb was something to rely on. On difficult days, it smoothed my thoughts away. I started to trade, making sure that I got a good price.

Whisky, though, did seem like bad news. From Bicester to Bradford to Liverpool to Manchester, I could see that wherever there was whisky, chaos would follow close behind.

"Stick to vodka," said Moira. "You'll keep a clearer head."

***

"Nicholls?" said the screw.

"Yes, Miss?"

"You're joining a group on Sunday afternoons."

"On Sunday?"

"Yes. There's an AA group that meets here. Mr Whitty wants you to attend."

"Why?"

"He says you might learn something useful. It's in the Education Unit, 3 o'clock Sunday afternoons. Don't be late."

I was puzzled. Why did Mr Whitty want me to train as a mechanic? Up to now, he'd said that he thought I was an artist.

Still – working with engines paid good money. And everyone in Askham kept on about how to get work and what to do in the future. It would be good to have an answer to their questions. Sunday was a funny day for lessons, but weekdays at Askham were busy. By now I'd had a sharp prison haircut, trimmed in my room by a hidden pair of nail scissors. I spiked up my hair and rolled my sleeves to the elbow, ready to become a mechanic.

The instructor was a woman in a greenish dress and jacket. Perhaps she kept her spanner in her handbag. There were two other women sitting with her in the Sunday quiet. The class was well-attended, with nine or ten prisoners. I took my seat uncertainly.

Green Jacket cleared her throat.

"Shall we begin, ladies?"

"My name is Evelyn, and I'm an alcoholic. I'd like to welcome everyone to this meeting of Alcoholics Anonymous."

Not the Automobile Association. Nothing to do with cars at all.

"Hello Evelyn!" said everyone else in the room.

"This is Angela," – she nodded to the lady next to her – "who has over ten years in recovery. She's come to talk to us today about her experiences in those ten years of sobriety, so welcome to Angela. But before we hear her, let's all introduce ourselves to the meeting."

Angela pushed a stray strand of hair behind her ear and said calmly, "Hello, my name's Angela, and I'm an alcoholic."

Her neighbour seemed to know the ropes too. "Hi, my name's Amanda and I –"

Awkwardly I got to my feet. I couldn't see the need to waste my time with this. I headed for the door.

It was locked. I turned the knob harder, then shook it. I realised that I was locked in. The first slow beats of the panic wings stirred in my chest. I tried to take a breath, but a heavy weight seemed to be pressing me down. I felt an airless lightening in my fingers and my toes.

Askham didn't feel like a prison. You could always open the doors. You were even allowed to go outside. But now I was locked in this room. I tried again to get out, throwing all my weight against the door.

They have locked me in.

I heard heavy footsteps coming up behind me and spun round

in panic. But there was nobody there – just the circle of women in their chairs.

"Uh – um – this is a mistake."

"Can you please sit down?" Evelyn said.

All of them were watching me. Panting, I pressed my back against the door.

"Please sit down," said Evelyn again, "and we'll come to you in a moment."

"I'm not an alcoholic," I said hoarsely. "I didn't -"

"If you would just like to listen in this meeting, that's quite acceptable."

"But *I'm not an alcoholic* so I don't –"

Angela turned her gaze calmly towards me and said, "Please sit down and just listen, just for today."

I trusted them! I believed them when they said that they wouldn't lock me in.

The youngest of the women got up from her chair and held out a packet of Embassy. Real cigarettes – not prison roll-ups.

"Want one?"

A proper cigarette was a reason to stay. I tried to breathe more slowly like the nurses had told me.

The lighter clicked in her fingers. I took a long drag. Then I sat down for my first ever AA meeting.

***

Once, I tried to run away from the house by the fire station.

It's summertime. The front door's been left open. Now, instead of shadows in the silent brown hall, a long slab of light lies over the threshold. It exposes the smeary floorboards with their scuffs of feet and the palm grease on the handle of the door. Sunshine makes the house feel dirty. People are passing on the pavement outside. They can't see me in the darkness of the hall.

Then I realise – there's a chance to get away. Although I'm scared to do it, the room upstairs frightens me much, much more. As I get to my feet, my legs tremble, but I walk outside and then I start to run. I don't know where I am or where I'm going, but as I run I feel as though my feet are growing lighter, until they seem to barely touch the ground.

Down the path I run, and onto the pavement. At once heavy footsteps behind me shake the ground, or perhaps it's just my heart, which is pounding half out of my chest. I see the London street in vivid colour with black shiny cabs passing by. I see a green van that's parked by the kerb. There's the bright summer sky and a pile of high white cloud, and a woman in a bright pink dress who reaches out her hand towards me. I run faster still. She's speaking but I can't hear what she says, only the crash of the footsteps charging at my heels. I run and I run.

I don't know where to go, so I end up running straight into the fire station, under the high brick arches and inside. There's a man in black uniform standing by a fire engine: its hose isn't stowed away, but lying in a pile on the ground by his feet. Maybe he's mending it. I dash right up to him, so fast that I almost fall into the heap of hose. I'm taking great juddery breaths and I can't talk.

"Whoops a daisy!" the man says, holding up his arms to halt me. "We don't want you tripping and hurting yourself! Where did you come from then, missy?"

Then I hear real footsteps approaching. Right behind me is the man from the house, out in the street in his crisp white shirt-sleeves and waistcoat. He's been running too: he's red in the face and blowing. He gives me a sharp little smile and holds out his hand.

"Oh, you are a naughty little girl," says the fireman, 'to run away from your grandfather like that!"

"She's a very a naughty little girl," the man replies. "You just come along now!" He grabs my wrist tightly and I have to go with him.

The man in the crisp white shirt keeps on smiling all the way back. His grip is the hold of bone on bone. Still with a smile, he drags me through the big front door.

***

April in Askham grew warm. By early May, it was properly hot. It was lovely to leave the stuffy laundry and walk in the garden. I went out at morning break to have a cigarette, and again after lunch for as long as I could stay.

Summer lunchtimes were the best time of all. The grange lay in golden light with all its windows open. I walked down to the duck pond, where mothers who picked up their babies from the mother-and-baby unit took them to play in the sunshine. The babies laughed at the ducks. The prisoners' stash of bottles lay hidden in the cool brown ooze. When one day's break was close to ending, I was walking back to the house and saw Carrie sitting there among the flowers.

She'd kicked off her shoes, stretching herself out with her legs slightly bent up in front of her. Her bare toes were deep in the grass. Her arms flowed out behind her with the palms of her hands pressed flat to the earth. Her head had dropped back dreamily, hair drifting, face turned up to the sun. Her eyes were closed.

She was graceful. Beautiful. I stood still and watched her and grew warm and very happy. And then I felt shy and afraid, all in a dizzy, muddled moment.

I found myself walking towards her across the grass.

"Hi, Carrie."

She opened her eyes and peered up at me, shielding her gaze with an arm that was speckled in sunshine.

"Hi there! Nice to see you. Isn't it lovely out here?"

"Yes."

"The mums take their babies down to the duckpond after they've had their lunch."

"Yes, I know."

"Would you like to sit down?"

"I've got work in a minute."

"Me too. I'm on the gardening team now. But we've got a bit of time. Are you still laundering?"

"Yes."

Awkwardly I sat down next to her. What should I do with my legs and my arms?

"I was in the laundry yesterday but I didn't see you. Perhaps you were round the back. It's ever so hot there in summer!"

"It's the dryers. It's better in wintertime. The house gets cold, but not the laundry. I don't feel the cold so much, but all the others do. They're always moaning about it."

Carrie smiled. "I'm very lucky, then. I'd never complain about my job here. I'd still love working in the garden, even if there was a thunderstorm."

She leaned forwards and wrapped her warm arms round her knees, so close that I caught the salty scent of her skin. She had long, pretty feet. Her face grew serious.

"Lucky. I just said I was lucky. It's funny. I never thought I'd say that again, or ever even think it at all."

For a moment she seemed to be so sad that I didn't know how to reply.

"Where's your room?" I asked her.

"Right up the back. I'm on my own right now, so it gets a bit lonely sometimes." She grimaced. "But better than sharing with someone when you just can't get along."

"Did that happen to you before?"

"Oh, yes. In high security. It was terrible, Nicky. It was like the end of my life. You could almost wish for that. At night, sometimes. Just your thoughts, in the dark. Girls screaming. Such terrible thoughts."

I looked straight into her eyes.

"I know," I said to her. "I've been in Risley."

"High security is such a bad place. It's – it's bad beyond bad. Too bad to describe. And sometimes – they send people down and it's just not fair. What if you didn't – "

I knew the rule of prison was never, never to ask. You don't say what you've done, or even what you claim you didn't do. You never ask anyone else to tell you. You don't ever talk about any of that.

She knew the prison rule too. She stopped, then said only:

" – so are you okay now? You were ill, weren't you? You were in the hospital. Are you feeling better?"

Around us were women walking slowly across the grass, reluctant to leave the early summer garden. I wanted to stay here too.

"I'm – um – I'm okay now. There are five of us sharing in our room and they're alright, except for Jen. She's –" I hesitated.

"Is Jen the very big one? The tall girl with the really wide neck? Like a sumo wrestler's?"

"Yes." I was frightened of Jen, but Carrie made me giggle.

"Yeah – I've seen her. She's a bit – um – she's pretty intimidating."

"She beats people up sometimes. She –" I stopped. I didn't want to start telling tales.

"Does she scare you? She'd certainly scare me!"

"A bit."

Carrie jumped up. "I have to get back to gardening."

She held out her hands. Without thinking, I took them. She pulled me right on to my feet.

"Nick – I'll see you later, ok?"

"See you later."

The lady in the garden gave a smile and walked away.

***

"Nicholls!"

"Yes, Miss."

"Would you be planning to move rooms?"

I'd been stopped on the stairs by a screw.

"Er – no, Miss."

"You sure? There's a request come in for you to move."

"A request, miss?"

"A request from Beech."

"From Carrie?"

"Yep. She filled out the form. She said that you're in a big share and you'd like to move rooms. There's a space up in hers. She's on her own in a two-bed. She says the two of you have been getting along."

"Carrie said that? Um – well, yes. Yes, we've been chatting at breakfast and on breaks."

"She seems like a very nice girl. Very bright."

"Yes. Yes, she is."

"So if you'd like the share – shall I put you down to be transferred up there?"

"Er – yes. That would be – yes. Thank you, Miss."

***

Carrie was educated but she wasn't intimidating. She knew things, but she didn't put you down. She explained if you asked, to make sure you understood for the future. She didn't want attention for herself – she was just very kind. Also, she could be silent, but not in a way that was awkward. Carrie's quietness made a space to rest.

When she saw me pull my sheet and blanket down off the bed and make a pile on the floor to sleep instead, she looked at me hard for a moment but didn't ask questions. It took me weeks to find out she was a doctor.

"You're a *doctor?* You're Dr Beech?"

"Yes." Carrie laughed in the dark. It was after lights out one night in that first early summer. The room was stuffy and warm. "Yes. I thought you knew I'm a doctor. There's not many secrets in here!"

But I'd never imagined that I'd talk to a doctor in the way I could talk to Carrie.

"A doctor who can do operations? Why didn't you say?"

For a moment she didn't answer, but I already knew. The prison bullies would rip Dr Beech to pieces.

"Well, I can't do operations because I'm not trained to do that. I can do other things."

"But that's good. You can be a doctor again when you get out.

You have a proper job, a career."

Then there was a very long pause.

"I don't know, Nick. I have a drugs conviction – a serious one. It will be on my record for the rest of my life. I don't know what I'm going to do about working. I don't know what I'll be allowed to do."

You never ask about the crime. To think of the past is to focus on all that has been lost. That was the prison rule. I stayed silent.

"I would so love to carry on," she said. She turned over restlessly in bed. "I miss it very much. I always wanted to be a doctor, when I was a little girl. It was such an adventure, going to medical school. There are more and more girls going now. If you're lucky, that is. If you have the opportunities I did."

"Why did you want to be a doctor?"

"It seemed like a good thing to do with your life. To have a purpose for yourself, and to make other people's lives better."

Carrie sighed the deepest, saddest sigh that I had ever heard.

"All I could think about – when I was arrested – were my plants. That sounds really silly, I know. But it seemed a bit unreal. I mean – I understood how serious it was. It was going to be prison. I knew I wouldn't be seeing my plants again for such a long time. But at the same time, it didn't seem possible that such a terrible thing could be happening to me."

I thought of Carrie, captive in the dark. Carrie who loved to be lying on the grass in the sunshine, feet and hands to the earth as though she were a plant herself, drawing up water and life. Her smiling face turned like a blossom to the light. The scent of her skin and her hair. Carrie, the lady in the garden.

I felt another person's suffering, sudden and sharp – a harsh ache that grew in my chest. Carrie's pain was mine, as though I'd burst through my skin and joined with her. I'd never known this feeling existed. How beautiful and terrible to live like this, not just as one person, but as many. To be open to the agony of others, because you'd travelled far beyond yourself. It hurt, but I saw that it was wonderful. My hands clenched on the sheets.

"I did sell drugs," said Carrie, softly and suddenly, as though she was releasing a great torrent of words that had been trapped deep inside her. "I made acid – LSD – and I sold it, and so did some other people that I knew. But it wasn't about the money."

It was hard to tell now if anyone was meant to hear her speaking. She twisted around in her bed.

"The whole thing just got out of hand. I was never trying to get rich. The cash was a great big problem. And I know that might sound like I'm lying – but it's true! It just made more problems, like money always does. It wasn't why I did what I did"

There was a very long silence.

"I believe you, Caz, about the money."

"Thank you."

"But – what was it about, then?"

She let out a long shaky breath. "It'll just sound silly if I tell you."

"No, it won't. It won't sound silly."

"What I wanted," said Carrie, "was to make the world better for people. To help them be more alive, so they're not so obsessed with things that don't matter – you know, material things. And I thought, when I was young, I really thought that there are drugs we can take which help our minds get bigger, so that our stuff looks smaller. Drugs that help us see what's really important."

"You think that LSD can do that?"

I wondered if Carrie would mind me asking questions. But she wouldn't be angry if you said the wrong thing to her. She'd understand what you meant to say, even if it wasn't what you said.

She didn't speak for what seemed like a very long time.

"Yes. Maybe. Oh – I don't know. I'm not sure any more." She gave a sharp sigh, as though she was annoyed with herself for not knowing the answer to the question. "When I was young, I thought LSD was the answer to a whole lot of things. And I think now – I think now – I don't know what I think now. I think I was very naive. I didn't understand that I would just look like a criminal. And then – when they arrested us – my friends and me – the way the police were behaving – I realised they thought that we were dangerous – like gangsters. And I was just shocked."

Her mattress squeaked and creaked. She was sitting up now, gripping her arms around her knees.

"And then – I was in high security. I'd been sentenced for years. I was all by myself, I was terrified. It was the most unbelievable nightmare."

I wanted to tell her that I hurt for her. I wanted her never to feel sad or frightened or lonely.

"So I'm guilty. I know you're not supposed to say that, inside. But it's still quite hard for me to believe it. Because – it didn't feel as if I was plotting. Or committing a terrible crime. I truly believed that what I was doing was going to help people."

"I understand now, Carrie," I whispered. But I don't know if she heard.

"I still miss everything so much. I miss the house where I lived and the sound of the rain on the roof. I miss my job. I loved taking care of my patients. It's like – it's like my whole world just exploded and the pieces are still flying through the air and I don't know where they're all going to land."

There was even more creaking and rustling. She sounded as though she was pulling her whole bed to bits.

"Sorry, Nick. I'll stop. I don't want to bring us both down."

"That's okay."

Footsteps passed by in the corridor outside.

"At least here the screws don't come peering in all the time. They give you some privacy."

"You miss being a doctor, don't you?"

"Yes. Yes, I do. I miss it ever so much. It was more than just a job to me. It was something I really did love. I'm sorry – I'm talking too much and you need to rest. I must let you get some sleep."

"It's okay. I don't sleep well anyway."

"But I must let you try. Night night, Nicky."

"Good night, Caz."

I heard her breathing slow down as she drifted off to sleep. I lay awake as I always did. As she was speaking, I'd had an idea. I tried to work out how to put it into practice.

***

"Is she coming yet?" I asked.

"What?" said Moira.

"I said *is she coming?*"

"Yes! I can see her feet! She's coming up the stairs! Shit, Nick, you'd better go and hide!"

"Let me in your room then!"

I slid around the half-open door of the room next door to mine and Carrie's, and flattened myself up against the wall.

"Do you think she'll mind that you've done this? What if she goes nuts?"

"She won't!" I hissed. "She never goes nuts! SHHHHH!"

"Well if she *does,* just you tell her I had nothing to do with it! It was all —"

"SHHHHHH!!!"

I heard Carrie's footsteps on the second flight of stairs. Our room was on the top floor of Askham. Only a few slept up here: all the climbing put people off. But I didn't mind, and neither did Carrie. It was good to have quiet.

Except that today, it wasn't quiet. Outside the door there were voices. Two or three women were sitting on the staircase. A line of half a dozen straggled down the passageway. The first was right outside our door.

"Sorry. Sorry." I heard Carrie wriggling along, treading on somebody's toe. "I'm so sorry." Then her footsteps stopped.

"I'm sorry – can I help you?" said her puzzled voice. "You're not waiting here for me, are you?"

"She said – Nick said – there was a doctor we could see. She told us we could make appointments."

"Sorry? Nicky made doctor's appointments?"

"She had a sheet of paper, and she made appointments for us all to see the doctor starting at two o'clock. You can't get seen in the hospital for weeks."

"How many appointments did she make?"

"She's got the sheet. She told us what time to come up here. Are you the doctor?"

"How many appointments did she make? Nicky? Where's Nicky?"

"She's – er – she's outside somewhere. She said she'd be back later. Where's the doctor?"

"*Nicky!*"

Now I heard another voice, sounding rather cross.

"Nicky said you're a doctor and that if we had anything we were worried about, you might be able to help. It's either a roll-up or half a bar of chocolate to see the doctor."

"*You paid her in roll-ups to see a doctor?*"

"Yes. So where's the doctor then?"

"Ah. Um. Goodness. How many appointments did she make?"

I heard the footsteps of another new arrival at the end of the corridor.

"Is this where we see the doctor? Nicky said –"

The line shuffled forward.

"Please," said Moira. "It won't take you long."

Then Carrie spoke in a very different voice. She sounded determined.

"Alright. Okay. You're all here, and you were told – right. Look – everybody – I'll be as quick as I can and if I can't see everyone today we can do some more tomorrow at the same time. Is that okay?"

"Nicky said she's got another sheet for tomorrow. All the sheets got full."

"*All* the sheets got – right. Okay. Well, let's get started, then. Can you sit on the floor out here while you wait? And I'll be as quick as I can."

***

"Nicky?"

"Ye-es?"

"You shouldn't have done that without asking me."

"If I'd asked you, you'd have said no."

Silence in the dark.

"Yes, you're right. I would. You know why that is."

"Yes, of course I know. If people find out you're a doctor in prison, they pick on you."

"They pick on you so much. In Durham first of all, Nick, it was very bad. It was the worst, worst time. I was brand new inside and I didn't know what to do and all the time I'd say the wrong things. I was so lonely and scared, and they were so horrible to me. The things they said, the threats. I was so desperate then, Nick."

"I'm sorry, Caz."

"It wasn't your fault."

"But it was good today, though, wasn't it?"

"That's what I wanted to say to you. Yes, it was good today. They were worried about some things and maybe now they're a bit less worried. Maybe they'll take better care of themselves."

"You're a very good doctor, Caz. You made… their lives better today. Just talking to you helped them. In the dining room after, they were saying so. They liked you."

"I'm glad you did it, Nicky. I was angry – but I'm not any more. It was the right thing to do."

"And *we* have lots of sweeties and rollies!"

Before I even said it, I knew how much she'd laugh. The warm sound rippled round the room.

"Okay! Those too. I'd have stopped you if I'd known, but now I'm glad I didn't."

"They won't pick on you now, Caz."

A longer silence.

"No. I don't think they will. Thanks for making it better for me, Nicky."

***

It wasn't just drink and hashish that were smuggled inside. A good prison trader must keep up to date.

"What's this?" I asked.

There were three of us in the towel room, examining a brand new box from the shoplifters in York.

"It says it's a Walkman."

"What's a Walkman?"

"You play music on it. Look – you put a tape in. Then you can carry it round with you. It's got headphones."

"That's really good!"

"My brother's got one. It's the latest thing. He loves it. Music while you walk about!"

I picked the Walkman up and examined it. I was wondering how much we should charge. "I bet those headphones make a racket," I said.

The door swung open and we all looked over our shoulders. It was Carrie, with mud from the garden on her hands.

"Hi Caz – mind the clean towels! Don't touch them!"

"Sorry!" Crestfallen for a moment, then: "It's break time. Can you come outside?"

"In a minute. Look at this."

"It's a Walkman," said Carrie, looking round for something that she could wipe her hands on. "Where on earth did you get – ah, ok, well. Yeah – my mum told me about these."

"Caz – you could play your music tapes on this at night and nobody would hear. You could play them after lights out."

"Oooh," said Carrie. She smiled. "I could, too. That's really good!"

Now I was thinking even harder.

"And we can start to lend this thing around. Four rollies or a full bar of chocolate to use it. More if you want to keep it overnight."

"That's a lot to charge."

"But it's ever so good. They'll pay for this for sure!"

Carrie put her hands on her hips. Flecks of soil sprinkled the towel room floor. "You and your deals. You're a right little capitalist, aren't you, Nicky Nicholls? A proper capitalist *pig*."

I knew she was laughing and I laughed right back.

"And *you're* dropping dirt in my laundry! Get outside!"

***

"Have you loaned it out yet, Nick?"

"Loaned what out?"

"The Walkman."

"Tomorrow."

"I think you should keep it for a bit, and listen to some music."

"I've not got any music."

"But I do. Look – the new stuff my mum sent me came through today."

Carrie's little Casio cassette player sat on the windowsill in our room. She loved to listen to her tapes in the evenings before we had to put the lights out. But everything brought in for prisoners had to be checked by the screws and it could take a long time. Today there had been a delivery: there on the sill was a pile of new tapes.

"What is it?"

"Indian stuff, mostly. Ravi Shankar's that top one. You'd like that."

"But I like rollies better! Let's lend it out!"

Carrie smiled a little.

"You sleep really badly, Nick. I think it might be good to do something at night that would help you to feel calm."

"Sometimes I sleep."

I caught up in the daytime in dozes. Or sometimes if I got really high on Lebanese, I'd find myself wiped out for while.

"Not properly, though," said Carrie. "I can't remember you sleeping really well. Or staying asleep long, if you do drop off. Anyway – I was thinking. Some of my new tapes are for relaxing. My mum brought them in for me. You know – like meditation."

I'd started to fidget, but Carrie was firm.

"What I think is that you start to go to sleep but you're too scared to stay that way. Something wakes you up. I think you've learned to do it. You make yourself wake up to stop your dreams."

I'm eight years old on a summer's day down by the river. I see Uncle Vernon up to his knees in the water, holding Dog underneath. Dog is frantically clawing and scrabbling with all four legs but I can't see his head because it's below the surface.

I cry out in panic. I'm too scared of Uncle Vernon to run into the river to try to save Dog, so I stand on the bank screaming as loud as I can with my hands by my sides. Screaming and screaming: "No! No! Stop!"

When I try to go to sleep, I see it over and over. How did Carrie know?

"Caz – do I talk in my sleep?"

"Not exactly talk. It's not clear words. It's like listening to a little girl sometimes. I think the little girl wants to cry but she wasn't allowed to."

I didn't want Carrie to say any more.

"I think that perhaps you have bad memories from a long time ago, Nick. Things that are locked up in your head. I think – if you really fall asleep – you're afraid they'll come out."

I really, really wanted her to stop.

"Anyway – relaxation tapes might help you. Get you in a nice place where you can dream about nicer things."

"But what if there aren't nicer things?" Even to me, my growl sounded rough and ungrateful.

Carrie smiled a sad little smile.

"Sweetheart, maybe you're right. Maybe there honestly aren't. I think it's been very hard for you, in the past. I don't think you've told me everything – and that's okay. You can take your time to deal with it."

I loved the way she talked. She could make even bad things sound hopeful.

"Anyway – I'm a doctor! And the doctor told you to relax. So that's an order!"

I saw that Dr Beech could be flinty.

"I'm going to prescribe it to you."

"Prescribe it?"

"Yes. You have to do your relaxation if Dr Beech said that you do."

"What would you prescribe?"

"Have you got some paper left, and something I can write with?"

My drawing pad lived in a bedside table drawer. She ripped out a sheet.

"Right," said Carrie. She smiled and she started to scribble. "So. This is my prescription pad. Because I'm a doctor I have really awful writing so you'll have to read it carefully. I'm going to put your name and the date and I'm going to prescribe that this afternoon when you finish work, before we go down to dinner, you have to go outside on your own and sit under the beech tree. When you get there, you have to listen to one side of this tape on the Walkman. This one here."

"Ravi Sha –" I stumbled over the word.

"Yes. Ravi Shankar."

"Then what do I have to do?"

"Nothing else. We're just going to give it a try. It might help to calm things down. I think you'd sleep better if you were more peaceful inside."

***

She leads me out to the garden, holding the Walkman in her hand.

"Right then, let's sit down here under the beech tree."

"Okay."

"I'll get the tape started, then I'm going to leave you to relax."

"Okay…"

She stops and looks at me.

"It's worth a try, Nicky."

"But —"

"But what?"

"I don't like going to sleep."

"I know."

"Anyway, I can't."

"I know, Nicky."

"Look —" I draw a long breath then my words come out all in a rush. "You don't know, Caz. There are things you — there are things I can't — I —"

Things it's impossible to think of. Words I would rather die than speak. Carrie, you don't know this.

"I do know a few things, Nicky. Sometimes you say some words in the night, when you doze. I know it was bad, your past. Actually, I think it was really, really bad. I think it was worse than you'll say."

I look at the ground.

"There's a terrible line in a Shakespeare play, about murdering sleep. I think that happened to you. Somebody murdered your sleep. They made it too frightening for you to rest or to dream."

Murdered my sleep. That's right. She does understand.

"You don't have to tell me. You don't have to say anything. But if you did ever want to tell – Nick, I would believe you. However bad it was. I know that you are truthful."

Her grey eyes look straight into mine. I never imagined that anyone could be so beautiful.

"Anyway – this is the tape, so let's try!"

I stretch myself awkwardly down on the grass. She fiddles about with the Walkman. Once the earphones are fixed to my ears, she stands up.

"I'm off. Just press play when you're ready. See – that button on the top."

"Okay."

"See you soon. See you in the dining room."

She's gone. The late afternoon glows around me.

If you told me, Nick, I would believe you. However bad it was. I know that you are truthful.

Because she has said this, I will give her my trust. I hit play.

***

I am in a beautiful dream. I go climbing with Dog up the slag heaps in Stoke on a warm afternoon. Up and up we go, so high we can see over everything. Sometimes the dirt slides away from my feet as I'm scrambling up and I keep tight-hold of the piece of string I hold Dog by and he pulls me and I pull him and we make it to the top. He licks my nose when I sit down next to him. I hug him close. I can see over all the rooftops from here, and over the pottery chimneys, standing like bottles of black medicine.

I think that Carrie's here too. Her whispering voice fills my dream. Sleep well, sweetheart.

And far, far away on the distant horizon, I can see the hills where I'll go with Dog one day, to run and play in the sunshine.

***

At midnight I push away the blankets and climb to my feet. I stumble across the room. It's three long steps, then my knees bump the edge of Carrie's mattress.

I don't quite know what I'll do when I get there. I just know I can't stay where I am. I know that this moment holds everything, future and past. Whatever wrong there's been, the awful things have led me here to this. They have led me to something that cannot be wrong.

It's a longing to give – to empty myself, knowing that even if I do, I still won't find myself empty. Carrie will fill me with light. I reach for the thing I fear most. Except I know now it's the thing I have longed for without ceasing, before I ever knew its name.

I kneel clumsily down on the bed above Carrie. I stretch out my hand, finding her shoulder first of all. I move my fingers up along the curve of her neck. I clumsily caress her cheek.

I hear Carrie draw in her breath. For a second I wait for the slap, the rough arm shoving me away. For Carrie to recoil. But she doesn't.

"Nicky," says Carrie. "Oh, Nicky."

And now I am certain.

I lean downwards, blind in the dark. I push strands of hair from Carrie's face and kiss her on the mouth, so clumsily our teeth clash together. Carrie parts her lips to answer the kiss.

"Nick. Nicky. It's okay, sweetheart, it's okay."

She pulls off her t-shirt in a single stretch upwards. She captures my hand to place it on her breast.

"Nicky – you're a really good person. I knew that the moment I saw you. It's going to be okay, Nicky."

Then there is warmth, light, blessing.

Chapter Nine

Hangover love

I wake up each and every morning
With your face spinning round in my head
No courage to face another day
I think I would rather be dead.
(Hangover Love, by Nicky Nicholls)

"I've got some good news for you, toe-rag!"

"What is it, Mr Whitty?"

It's autumn 1981. The days are growing cooler. Outside the governor's office window, leaves reddened. They looked as I'd seen them for the very first time, almost a year and a lifetime ago. An anniversary inside.

"I've had a letter." Mr Whitty unfurled it with a flourish. "A *very* interesting letter. AHEM! A-he-he-he-HEM!"

"You're making me nervous, sir."

He smiled.

"'Dear Mr Whitty'," he read aloud. "'Thank you for HMP Askham Grange's entries to the national prison service's Koestler Awards for creative work in the arts by detainees and offenders. Standards have been higher than ever this year... real challenge for the judges to decide on a shortlist... blah blah... blah blah...

looking for artistic originality, creativity and skill... blah... Here we go... the judges have been delighted and impressed by the standard of so many of the entries...' Sounds pretty good, this, doesn't it?"

"Yes, sir."

"But they have decided, toe-rag. They've decided to shortlist you!"

"What do you mean, sir?"

"A shortlist, Nicholls, means a list of the best entries to the competition. The ones the judges want to look at more closely before they decide on the winners."

"The best entries, sir?"

"You entered the Koestler Awards in two categories – one in music, and one in art."

Mr Whitty paused.

"You do remember this, don't you? The Koestler Awards? The national prizes for prisoners, to help people show their talents. Askham decided that we would enter you."

"Yes, sir. Of course. I'm just a bit – I'm just – I'm surprised."

"And can you remember what you entered?"

"Erm..."

"I can remember very clearly, toe-rag. But I want *you* to be proud as well."

Actually, I did remember entering. Carrie had nagged me to do it. Mr Whitty had nagged me and Moira had nagged me as well. Eventually I entered, just so they would all stop talking.

"It was the song 'Footsteps' for the music prize and the book of drawings for the art one."

"Ah, good. Well done. Yes – you entered your cartoon book. The 'Women in Prison' drawings."

"Yes."

"Now, don't you go saying you're surprised about being on the shortlist. I'm not surprised. Your entries were very good."

"Er… sir?"

"Yes, Nicholls?"

"What does a shortlist mean exactly, sir?"

"It means we all have to wait a bit longer while the judges have a think. Then we'll hear if you've won anything."

I felt pleased. Sort of. It didn't seem that much to do with me. I knew who else would be pleased about it, though, and I did feel glad about that.

"How long will that be, sir?"

"I'm not sure. I'll try to find out for you."

"Thank you, sir."

Mr Whitty looked at me closely.

"You know that this means you're good, don't you? It's not just the girls who queue up in the laundry and ask you to decorate their letters to their kids who like what you draw. Proper artists like your work. Educated types. Competition judges. People who go to that Tate Gallery I was telling you about."

As I looked at the letter in Mr Whitty's hands, the outside world reached into Askham Grange. Up to this moment, I'd not known how much I wanted to stay safe inside. A jolt of homesickness hit early. It made my chest hurt.

"Are you okay, Nicholls?"

"Yes, sir. It's all just a bit of a shock."

"I can imagine," said Mr Whitty. He pressed his lips together. "I think I can imagine. You have a chat about all of this with Beech and see how you feel then. Go and tell her now – I'm sure she'll be delighted for you."

"Yes, sir."

"And Nicholls?"

Already I'd half turned away.

"Well done, toe-rag. I'm proud of you."

***

But what will happen when these Koestler Award judges — nameless, unimaginable, terrifying — discover that I'm not a proper child? What will they say when they find out I'm not a real person at all?

I know that Mr Whitty is kind. He doesn't mean for bad things to happen. But I'm frightened by this talk of awards and shortlists and prizes.

A drink a drink a drink until his words mean nothing at all.

***

The five of us never named the Askham prison band. It just formed around us until nobody remembered whose idea it was to start.

We sang the songs I wrote in the laundry: 'Whisky' was our first, rather tentative try-out. Then I heard Estelle singing late one evening, her smokey voice floating through the silent corridors of Askham Grange. Next morning I searched till I found her and asked if she'd like to join in.

Estelle was a promising singer, then violence scattered her life. She was sentenced for murder. You didn't ever ask about that. Something for Estelle now was what mattered. She sang and played piano and guitar.

Lena worked in the laundry, and that's where we got talking. She was a singer as well. Then there was Jane who loved clocks. The clocks were my idea after someone said they missed the sound of a clock ticking at home. I heard a chorus of agreement. Now — *there* was a great chance to trade. I mentioned clocks to the girls who went shoplifting in York. A couple found their way to Askham Grange. Then I charged two roll-ups to have one in your room for the night. It was ever so popular.

"It's reassuring to listen to a clock," said Jane. "Just like listening to your heart." We always called them heartbeat clocks after that.

Then there was Carrie, bringing her voice, her harmonica and her beauty along with the tiny little Casio keyboard her mother had given her. Anyone who wanted to could bash the tambourine.

The neglected Askham piano at first struck so sourly off-key that it was no use at all; the Casio had to suffice. Then, as the band caught on and the others heard our music, everyone agreed to pay a penny from their wages to bring in a tuner to fix the piano. And everyone did.

Our line-up: a forger, a murderer – a maybe-manslaughter rap – a shoplifter and a drug-dealer. Carrie had a way of completing things.

***

Mr Whitty was right behind us. We played for the prisoners first, then he fixed up charity gigs in local pubs, raising money for Victim Support and children with Down's Syndrome. I heard that not all the screws saw it his way; for charity or not, they said, "open prison" shouldn't mean going out at night. But Mr Whitty, just like always, went on doing what he thought it right to do.

He even let us play in the quiet evening hours, as shadows gathered in the grange. It kept the screws happy: there were far fewer arguments in the television room. The music rose up through the stairwells and corridors, spinning its dreams in space. I knew that the women were listening: I felt it in the air. Next morning, they wouldn't say a word.

Sometimes I watched the others as they sang and played: Estelle, with tears in her eyes; Jane who was counting the days until she next saw her children; Lena, lost in her world of unknown thought.

And Carrie. She loved to dress up and gig, grey eyes flashing as she faced an audience. She shook her dark hair back from her face and smiled. You stir my soul alive – and now I began to write songs for her. Some days it seemed as if the words and music flowed from my fingers, two new songs or three, then I'd pester Estelle to play them on the piano straightaway. Estelle rolled her eyes and would sometimes oblige. Carrie, the whisper in my mind.

More and more, I understood that this beautiful girl who met love without fear had always been free. Whatever had happened and whatever might come – the lady in the garden was a spirit unchained.

***

One day the front gate of Askham will open and I will be free to go. Outside into the early morning chill and down the lane to the pond. Past the Rose and Crown beside the village green, and on and on to – nowhere. One day, they will send me away from the place that is now my home.

At first the thought drowns me in panic. I kick and gasp to keep my head above water. A drink a drink a drink. But more and more my sadness just flows by like a slow wave passing. I have learned to be sad in the same way that Carrie is sad; somehow this makes her feel closer.

The answer to this problem isn't just to drink it away. Perhaps I can find a solution. Perhaps I can find a way to stay in Askham Grange.

Then I have an idea. I'm going to be needing a tape recorder. Luckily, I know just the girls who can get one for me.

***

"Afternoon, toe-rag."

"Good afternoon, sir."

"And what can I be doing for you today?"

"I've got something for you, sir."

"What's that, Nicholls?"

"Before I give you this, sir –" I cleared my throat "– before I do – I was the only one who knew anything about it. It's important to tell you that no one else had any idea."

Mr Whitty frowned and placed the tips of all his fingers together, making a steeple.

"Hmm. This is starting to sound serious."

"It is, sir. It's very serious."

"What have you been up to, toe-rag?"

I held a cassette tape tightly in my hand.

"I know it's illegal to do this in prison, but I taped our band. I recorded us singing. It's very important and I want you to listen to it."

"I've already heard the band play, Nicholls."

"These are new songs, sir, and I taped them. *I made an illegal prison recording.*"

"And where did you get a tape recorder, Nicholls?"

"I found it, sir."

"You found it?"

"Yes, sir."

"So I expect you'll be taking it back to where you found it."

"I will, sir."

"You obviously know you are forbidden to make recordings in this prison? It's a serious disciplinary offence."

"I do know that, sir. A serious offence. Two years on top of your sentence is what you can get for making a recording in prison."

"Er – yes. That's absolutely correct. Two years it is. You're very well informed."

"And that's two years on top of my existing sentence. That's why I didn't tell the others. No one else knew but me."

"No one else had any idea they were being recorded?"

"I did the recording. They didn't know anything about it, sir."

Mr Whitty leaned back in his seat and folded his arms.

"So you are confessing to making a secret, illegal recording?"

"Yes, sir. I'm confessing to that and now I'd like you to listen to the illegal recording that I made. Here you are, sir." I held out the tape.

He took it and put it on his desk.

"Go on then – you have to tell me, Nicholls. Satisfy my curiosity. How did you do it?"

"How did I tape them, sir?"

"How did you tape them *without them knowing*?"

"I hid the recorder, sir."

"You hid it." Mr Whitty rubbed his nose with the back of his hand. "Where exactly did you hide it?"

"I hid it inside the piano, and I pushed the cable in between the guitar case and the piano stool and I put Carrie's cardigan by the power socket where it was plugged in."

"You thought it through carefully, then."

"Yes, sir. I knew it was a serious offence."

"And how did you stop it and start it?"

"I did that before they came in."

"Didn't it make a noise? I mean – didn't the tape recorder click on and off?"

"I coughed, sir."

"You coughed?"

"If I thought I heard it click, sir, I coughed or I said something, or I played a bit louder. They didn't know it was there so there's a bit of background noise at the end and there's us talking before we got started."

"I imagine you were telling them to get on with it so the tape wasn't being used up."

"Yes, sir."

"So this recording - this is all your greatest hits, is it?"

"It's the songs we like the best, sir, and some new ones. But they didn't know, the others. No one had any idea. So no one should get the extra two years here but me, sir. I – ."

"Alright, Nicholls. Alright. I believe you. You're entirely capable of getting up to this with no one to give you a hand."

We both looked down at the tape cassette lying on the desk.

"So you want me to listen to this illegal recording?"

"I thought you would be interested, sir."

"And I certainly am. I love your songs, Nicholls," said Mr Whitty.

"What, sir?"

"I said I love your songs. Love them. I'm pleased they've been recorded and I'd like some other people to hear them."

This wasn't at all what I'd expected. I cleared my throat.

"*I do realise, sir, that what I've done is a serious disciplinary offence.*"

"Yes, yes. Will you leave this here with me?" He picked up the tape. "This is – I'd like to send this round, to some people I know who might be interested. I think you're very good at what you're doing with the band and I'd like my friends to hear what you've written."

"Erm… okay, sir." Not being able to get into trouble was not how it usually went.

"There are five of you, aren't there? In the band?"

"Yes, sir. But the taping was only done by me, so the extra two years –"

"I understand what you're saying, Nicholls."

Mr Whitty put the tape in the drawer of his desk.

"I'll take good care of this, don't you worry."

"Um… okay, sir. Thank you, sir."

"Is that all?"

"Ahhh, yes. Yes."

"Thank you, Nicholls. That's it, then. You can go now."

"Oh. Yes. Okay." I took a reluctant step away.

"Oh – and Nicholls?"

He must be angry with me now. Surely, he must.

"Yes, sir?"

"About that tape recorder you found…"

"I'll take that back right now, sir. Straight away."

"Right now and straightaway sound good, Nicholls. That sounds very good indeed."

***

"And now I've had three absconders, toe-rag."

"Three, sir?"

Mr Whitty was standing by the window in his office, looking

out at the bright new snowfall lit up by rare sun: a brief pause in the December blizzards when the roads could be cleared and the pathways dug again across the grange's lawns. My second Askham Christmas was approaching.

"They wanted to see their families."

"They – um – I think they miss their children, sir."

"I know that they do. And you're going to say that's under-standable with Christmas coming. And it *is* understandable. But this is a prison, and you know and I know that absconding can't be allowed."

I made no reply.

"So we fetched them back, which is what we had to do. But now comes the interesting part – do you know what they said?"

"No, sir."

"They said it was the song, Nicholls, that made them abscond. Your song."

"Which one, sir?"

Mr Whitty turned to face me. "I think you know which song."

He was right – I knew.

"It makes Estelle cry when she sings it, sir."

"That song makes everybody cry." He lowered his head, then he sighed. "It makes us all cry because it's beautiful. It makes you think about what love is and what Christmas means."

Somehow I'd not been expecting him to say that.

"But it's no good, Nicholls. I can't have you lot singing a song that makes prisoners abscond. Think about it. Try explaining that to the Home Secretary."

I looked at the snow outside, the white altered world in the window.

"I'm banning it," said Mr Whitty. "You can only play it in the summer."

"We can only play 'Silent Christmas' in the summer?"

"Yes. Ridiculous as I know it sounds, that's my decision.

Sometimes – a thing can be too beautiful. It can be too much."

Too beautiful. Too much. Yes, I could understand that.

"Yes, sir."

"Can I leave it to you to tell the others? The song mustn't be played again this year. There'll be penalties for all of you if it is."

"Yes, sir. Will that be all, sir?"

"Actually, Nicholls, no. There's something else."

"What's that, sir?"

"I've arranged a lawyer for you. Don't look so horrified – this time you didn't do anything wrong!"

"Sir, why do I need – ?"

"To protect you, Nicholls."

"Protect me from what, sir?"

"I've thought for a long time now, Nicholls, that protection from yourself is what you need the most, if I'm honest. But as well as that, you need to be protected from people who aren't to be trusted. There's plenty who'd scam you soon as they look at you. Yes, I know – you've been round some lowdown places and there's plenty of tricks that you'd see coming. But you wouldn't see them all. I want you protected by law against things you might not see."

"What would that be, sir?" I was only half understanding him.

"Do you know what copyright is, Nicholls?"

"No, sir."

"It means that you register something – and this has legal force – so it's recorded at a place called the Copyright Office so then everybody knows that it's yours. Like an idea, or words, or an image. Then no one else can say they thought of it, or make money out of it. Only the person who created it can."

"Okay, sir."

"Do you understand what I'm saying?"

"I think so, sir."

"I've contacted a lawyer and he's drawing up some paperwork. He's going to come in here with a contract you can sign. Then your ideas – your cartoon characters, the music you've written – will be protected and recorded officially as yours."

"Errr – thank you, sir."

"One day you'll thank me, Nicholls – even if you don't understand it now. I don't want anyone taking things away from you. If you've got the brains to have an idea, or create something – and I think you do – I want the person who benefits from that to be you."

"Thank you, sir."

"Ask Beech to explain copyright to you."

"I will do, sir."

Mr Whitty straightened the papers on his desk and cleared his throat.

"You're going out on work placement soon, aren't you, Nicholls?"

"Yes, sir."

"Well – think of this as something else for your release. You're just over halfway through your sentence already. A copyright's a big achievement – it's something you'll have in the outside world that you can use to help you. Work placement's the same. It helps you start to get ready for release. You don't look very happy about it."

I tried not to think about leaving Askham. Although I kept on trying to break rules, no one would extend my time inside. Even Mr Whitty was telling me: I wasn't wanted here. One day my sentence would end. A drink a drink a drink.

"We'll both be moving on in the end – did you know that? I'll be leaving too – I'm going to a new job down south in a few weeks' time. It's going to be different for us both."

He was watching me, as he often did. But thoughts of the future and change were so strange and so remote that no words could reach around them.

"I'll miss this place, in some ways," he said.

And I am missing it already. My body aches with desolation.

"Try to work hard on your placement, Nicholls. Get some experience you can use – a good reference, maybe – something to help you get started. We can set you up with a nice job you'll enjoy. How about working in a charity shop?"

"Thank you, sir."

"I don't think you believe me."

"I do believe you, sir."

"But before we do all that – you speak to the lawyer and you sign the dotted line and get that copyright. Your art and your music should make money for you and not for some toe-rag."

"I thought it was me who was the toe-rag, sir."

He smiled then.

"You did, did you? Well, maybe you are, but believe me, there's lowlifes out there a whole lot lower than you are, Nicholls. Let's try to keep you safe, shall we?"

***

"*What the hell, Nick?*"

From very far away, I could hear Carrie shouting.

I lifted my head from my pillow but then quickly laid it down. The whole room was spinning.

"Ummm?"

"Nicky – what on earth happened? What did you do?"

She stood in the doorway with her hands on her waist. She was out of breath from running upstairs and her face was very flushed. I rolled away and turned my face back towards the wall.

"They just told me downstairs. They said they had to bring you back from York early because you'd been *drinking*. Why were you drinking on your work placement?"

My head hurt. My eyes hurt. More than all of that, Carrie's disapproval hurt.

"I can't... can't now... can't talk. Sor... Caz."

Carrie pressed her fingers to her forehead.

"Well – okay. Okay. You sleep it off. We don't have to talk about it now."

"Whaddidey say?"

"What did they say? You mean downstairs?"

"Mmmmnn."

"They said the van had to go and pick you up from the charity shop because you were breaking things and smashing up the window."

"Wasn't," I mumbled. "Dancin'. I was dancin' in the window!"

"It's not funny, Nick."

Carrie took my work placement seriously. She talked about the future. I could see she didn't think that a proper person would behave like this. Her judgment made me raw and afraid.

"They were hiding, they said – the other people there, the shop manager. They were scared of you. Nicky – look. We can't talk about this now because I'm angry and you're still really drunk and that would be stupid. Later on."

But I felt far too scorched to let her come close.

"Go 'way" I muttered. "S'none of your business."

I heard Carrie taking a breath.

"No, you're right. You're quite right. It isn't."

"So jus' go 'way an' lemme go sleep."

Carrie closed the door very softly behind her.

***

My job had begun at half past nine on Monday morning.

Mr Whitty kept his promise. They found me work in a charity shop in Bridge Street in the middle of York. The prison van dropped me for my very first day. I was feeling very frightened so I made sure I was high.

Bridge Street was a curve of uneven-looking buildings close to the river. In my blonde Leb haze, I saw black and white tiles in its entrance. Its big cheerful window was gleaming and the Ouse twinkled twenty yards distant. Everything was sparkles and light.

The manager had very long hair and a worried expression. She told me that while serving the customers was the best part of the job, you worked up to that. First of all, you must sort the donations. She said this in the way that you'd say something written down in great big letters.

She took me round the back into a great big room where a table was piled high with all sorts of things. Clothes and books and records, bracelets and earrings, beads and bags and crockery and hats. The donations.

There were so many categories: things for sale here, things that might sell somewhere else but not here, things that weren't suitable for selling at all because they were too broken or too stained or too old, things that needed mending in order to be sold and things that were so good that the shop window was the place for them. Then, if they didn't sell in a fortnight, you took them out of there and sent them somewhere else. Heaven knows how anyone could ever keep track of it all.

But somehow, those donations had all come together in this massive, muddlesome pile. My job was to sort it all out. It wasn't clear at all where to start, or how I would ever tell the difference between them.

The morning dragged on. I needed very badly to have another smoke. Or a drink. A drink a drink a drink. The piles of donations were getting mixed up with one another. The manager kept coming in and moving things around. Each time she seemed to be crosser. At lunchtime I was sent outside to buy myself a sandwich.

The screw in charge of work placements gave me some money: this will be enough, she'd said. I didn't know how much lunch cost in any case. In my rising anxiety about the day ahead, and chewing blonde Leb, I'd not looked too closely at the little bag of coins. The money was heavy in my pocket; there was no way to carry it that felt right. The idea of spending it seemed strange. I tipped a few coins into my hand in the van and examined them: some were five-sided, unfamiliar, and seemed to be far too small. Perhaps they were foreign coins she'd given me by mistake.

I peered into the window of the bakery a few doors along from the charity shop. It contained some things you might eat for lunch. But I wasn't hungry. A pile of bread rolls – but they all had salad in. I'd never liked salad. Alongside the rolls, there were slices of what looked like cake. Next to all of that I saw a sign. I couldn't read the word and I didn't know why it had an X in it.

"Can I have a gattux, please?"

"Have a what, love?"

The man behind the counter seemed annoyed.

"A gattux."

"What are you talking about, love?" Behind me, where I couldn't see, someone in the shop began to titter.

I stood there in front of the unreadable sign, holding my impossible money. Soon I'd have to go back to work. They were angry with me there as well.

Something inside me began to give way. A fissure of fright grew in seconds to an avalanche of panic. I was dizzy. I turned from the man and reached for the door handle. Then I was outside. Two doors away I saw Bridge Food and Wine. A drink a drink a drink. It wasn't a decision. I knew it couldn't wait. I must make the awful panic stop.

Now I was inside Bridge Food and Wine, looking at the labels on the bottles. I picked up two and held out the senseless money. The coins had all grown hot: my hands were a big metallic stink.

"Is that the right amount to buy these?"

I knew I sounded hoarse.

"It's too much, love." The man behind the counter had greying hair, a fraying cardigan. "These are 20ps."

"20ps? These things?"

"20 pence pieces." He stared at me. "You only need five to make a pound."

"But I didn't know there were –"

New coins. Different currency. No one had told me there were 20ps now. There never used to be any.

I pushed the money into his hands. Some of the 20ps fell on the counter and a couple bounced further, down to the ground. The shopkeeper started to complain but now I had the wine I couldn't hear what he said. I knew that very soon, I could make all this stop.

I held the bottles tightly. I clambered down a steep flight of steps to the river. The cobbles of Queens Staith pressed hard on my feet. The bridge had a low wide arch of honey-coloured slabs with a pattern like sunrise. The earth beneath the arches was damp. Then I couldn't walk any more.

I knew how to drink from a bottle when you didn't have an opener – that and how to knock the crinkly metal top off a beer. A tinkle of glass, then I drew out the cork with half the neck intact to fit my mouth. So long as you drank from the smooth unbroken edge, you'd be fine. At last I could lean against the cool pale stone and drink.

By the time the bottles was both empty, the crackling roar of panic in my head had gone far away.

Later I went back to the shop. The manager started to say something. Then she changed her mind. She didn't seem so angry now, either. There was a black jump in time, and now a whole crowd of people had gathered on the outside of the big pane of glass at the front.

They were laughing and pointing. I could hear cheers and whistles. Around me was a whole lot of mess. I was standing in the window on something that seemed to be broken. Also I was wearing a hat. Then I saw blue lights flashing.

***

"*You were waving a broken bottle,*" said Carrie.

It was next day. All through the night she had been angry. Hours of awkward silence in the presence of a stranger.

"They were frightened of you – that was why they hid. They phoned 999. They thought you were going to hurt them."

"I wouldn't have hurt them."

"Well I know that and you know that, because I know you. But they don't! You went off on your lunch break to buy yourself a sandwich and came back with blood on your face waving a broken bottle and shouting – well, apparently you were shouting something rude about what they should do with the donations."

But the same things made us both giggle. Carrie bent her head. I knew when she was trying not to laugh.

"Come on, Caz – you know that sounds quite funny. She was potty about those donations, the manager – she banged on and on."

When Carrie looked up, her smile filled the room. But then she grew grave once more.

"Why did you have blood on your face?"

"I cut myself drinking from the bottle."

She nodded.

"Nicky – we have to take this seriously. I thought you were going to AA."

I flinched.

Carrie, don't leave me.

Long, long ago, I was so frightened, running along the pavement, taken away from my home. I hear those smart heels clicking and rapping. I look up into my mother's face and see there only her terror.

Shut up, she tells me. Just. Shut. Up.

"Nick?"

I gripped my forearms tightly, feeling my bones through my skin.

"Nick, I'm not trying to be critical of you. I know it's really hard. I know you have a problem with booze. But this was a decent job, something that could really help you. If you found it too hard to go there without drinking, I think that AA might help. You do still go, don't you?"

Do not cry when I hurt you. If you cry, I will hurt you more. A beautiful, twisted, raging face above me. What had I done? And what can I ever do to make this pain stop?

"Look – Nick. I'm saying this because I care what happens to you. I think that if you went to AA meetings more often, you –"

Sometimes I really did go. I went because Mr Whitty said that I must. The people in the group were very kind and I heard what they were saying. Mr Whitty would invite other AA groups from outside to meet in the dining hall at Askham: there was even a gathering one Sunday with members from all across Yorkshire. The place was packed and the prison band played.

I talked a little bit in that AA meeting, describing the times when I'd been homeless and the dreadful night in Manchester that brought me to the Grange. The night that Andrea died. I don't know what happened, I told them. Truly – I was drinking and I just don't remember. The people there seemed to understand.

But they want me to give up drinking. And I can't.

When the present and past possess the same space, you must make it stop, or else you will die. And for that you need a drink. A drink a drink a drink. There are moments when unless you are drinking, you can't exist alive.

Carrie, you are beautiful and true. You are true to yourself in everything you do. Your beauty makes me afraid. But I don't know how to be like you.

And still she was trying to help me.

"– you might find that it makes a difference, Nick. There are other people who feel the same as you in the meetings. They have the same problems as you. No one blames you. I don't blame you. Never think –"

You are dirty. Dirty. You are not a proper child. I can still hear the words in my mind.

Now Carrie's mouth is lipsticked and twisted and raging. I shrink back and squeeze my eyes tight shut. When I open them, I see her real face: her solemn grey gaze and her worried frown.

"Nick, sweetheart, are you OK?"

I want to hold you, Carrie. I want to love you. I want to wrap you up in me. I'll do whatever you ask.

It took me a moment to realise that I hadn't really said those words to her out loud.

"Nick, if you want me to leave you alone then I will. I can't do anything apart from advise you. That's all I'm trying to do. But sometimes if you care about someone, you have to say things they don't like."

You bitch. You dirty little bitch.

But this time my words came out aloud. Carrie got to her feet in that brisk way people do when they say with their whole body: right, enough of this.

"There's no need to talk to me like that, Nicky. I'll leave you on your own. I didn't mean to upset you – I was trying to help."

Carrie had cried when she heard a song I wrote for her. *Would You?* it was called. *"Is there ever such a friendship? So full of loving too. I know that I could be that way – I would do it, love, for you."*

Except that in real life, I didn't think I could. How would I ever be like that – be loving, and gentle, and good? I am not a proper woman, not a proper lover, not a proper friend. I am not a proper person at all. Proper is just too hard a thing to be.

***

"You wanted to see me, sir?"

When I was summoned to Mr Whitty's office, he often had a half-smile, even if he mostly tried to hide it. Not today. Today he looked serious.

"Yes, Nicholls."

There were quite a few things that I could have done wrong. I wondered which one of them had got me into trouble this time. I didn't want to give myself away, so I waited.

Mr Whitty looked up at me, then down at the desk.

"I want to tell you something, Nicholls, before I leave Askham.

To share something with you."

"Okay, sir."

"This might come as a shock."

"What is it, sir?"

"It's about your conviction."

To think about that was unbearable. I didn't want to hear. It must have shown in my face, because then he went on, "I know this is difficult for you. But it's important. There's some information that I want you to hear."

I stared at the floor.

"I made enquiries, Nicholls, about the night that you were arrested. About the lady that you –" and then he laid the palms of his hands very flat on the desk "– the lady who died that night."

"Andrea," I said.

"Do you remember her?"

"Yes, sir. A little." Andrea had seemed a nice person. For a split second, her dead face appeared between me and the governor's office. Then I squeezed my eyes shut. A drink a drink a drink.

"I made some enquiries, Nicholls. The reason for her death was not clear."

An endless silence before he went on.

"It was so unclear that three postmortems were done. They decided in the end that the likeliest cause was choking."

I was unable to speak. But I understood.

"Other causes may have been possible. But. But. The likeliest explanation is usually the right one. I thought that you should know."

"What do you think happened to Andrea, sir?" Until I uttered the words, I didn't think I dared.

Mr Whitty raised his head. His blue eyes looked straight into mine.

"I think that Andrea choked to death, Nicky. I have thought so for quite a long time."

He's telling me he doesn't think I killed her. I knew that by tomorrow, this moment would no longer seem real.

"Thank you, sir," I whispered.

He gave a long, slow nod of his head.

"You had often been in trouble, and then there you were at the scene. This sort of thing is wrong, but –"

He didn't continue.

Thank you, sir. Thank you. I will never forget you.

"Accept the things you cannot change, Nicholls, but change the things you can. When your sentence is over, in the future – I hope you can go well."

***

When Mr Whitty left his job as governor of Askham, we threw him a party. The party in the prison was reported in the paper, with pictures of me and the band all costumed up and singing. The farewell concert was our gift to him. We wanted to say thank you.

When he saw the way we'd set up the stage, he raised both his eyebrows.

"And how did you get a microphone in here, toe-rag?"

"I found it, sir."

"Well, tomorrow you'd better take it back to where you found it."

The concert was fun. I sat on his knee in a bright pink wig. I was very, very drunk and there'd been plenty of blonde Leb with Carrie before we came down here to play. The band regaled the governor with 'Hey, big spender'. Mrs Whitty looked on tolerantly.

"The minute you walked" – bang crash – "through the door..."

A man of distinction. I wanted to spend more time with him. Now the future was all loss, all endings. A drink a drink a drink.

No one went to bed when they were meant to that night: it was late and there was still the sound of voices in the hall. There was even someone outside in the garden, shouting and running about. Mr Whitty and his wife had gone home a while back, and the screws were sorting things out now, telling us to go upstairs and that the party was finished. The band was packing up.

"Got any vodka?"

"No, Nick, not here" answered Carrie.

"Where, then?"

"*Not here*. Let's put this stuff away and move the chairs back."

"Where is it?"

"I said it's not here! Will you give me a hand?"

"If it's upstairs I'll fetch —"

Nobody had any vodka. All of us were sad and disgruntled and cross with each other. A good night tonight, but now it was over. Tomorrow was the future and change.

A drink a drink a drink.

"Nicky, for God's sake, just pass me — where did she go?"

"She's in the hall."

Carrie came after me with long, tense strides.

"Nick — can you give us a hand, please?"

"Let's have another dr —"

"No — let's *not* have another drink. Let's just tidy up and call it a night."

"You tidy up."

"Oh, this is silly. Go upstairs, then, and leave it to us."

My chest was aching hard from forcing down tears. I needed to make the feeling stop.

"I just want a drink. We can —"

"We've all had enough now, Nick. We need to get to sleep," said Carrie.

"I want a drink."

"Nick, I know you're sad about Mr Whitty. We're all sad. But you can't just pour drink on everything."

"I don't pour drink on everything."

"Actually — you do. You don't try to solve things. You just jump straight into a bottle."

"I don't jump –"

"Yes, you do, Nick, and it's no good. It doesn't make anything better."

I stared at the ground.

"It's that horrible look," said Carrie. "That scary, addicted look you get – like booze is the only thing you care about. You have to do something about it or else I –"

It's not a decision. It's something that just happens. Wine is the reason. Vodka is the reason. Whisky is the reason. There is the drink and there's no way round it. You have to drink to make the pain stop.

Then I lashed back.

"Or else you what? You what? Anyway – you're the one who's really addicted!"

"No, I'm not, Nicky."

"Yes you are! You're just as bad as me and you know it and I don't yack on at you. I don't do all this 'no more, you've had enough you've had enough!' Have I ever said that – have I once?"

"Okay, Nick, no, no you haven't, but then I'm not an –"

"Oh – oh I see, I see! You're not a what, Caz? You're not a what?"

"Nick. Nicky." She's angry now but she's trying to be calm. Still, the lady in the garden can catch on fire. Her grey eyes are flashing.

"Nicky, for God's sake. Let's not argue now."

"Oh let's not argue let's not argue – you started it! You started it when you started telling me what to do."

"I'm not telling you what to do! Although somebody damn well should. But anyway, I didn't."

"Oh, somebody should? What you mean is you should!"

"Nick – you have a problem with this – with drinking. A bloody big problem, actually. You know you do."

"I have no more of a problem with drinking than you do with drugs!"

"No – that's not true."

"That is so true! That is just so true! You want to have drugs all the time and I've never tried to stop you – I've never started lecturing you!"

"Well, yes. Yes, I do use them, I do, but the difference is that I choose when. I don't do drugs because I have to. I do it because I decide to and I think it can sometimes make things better for me. I'm in control of that. But you –"

"How are you in control? You got sent to prison! You can't be a doctor anymore! Drugs don't make things better for you! Drugs make you just the same as me!"

The moment I said it, I was sorry. Carrie bowed her head. I felt the hurt go through her, as though I was inside her skin. Carrie's regret. Carrie's loss. Carrie's tears. I could feel her pain that wasn't mine at all, but still it could break me in bits. Living like this fills me with fear.

A proper person would know what to do now. A proper lover would be able to comfort her. But I am not – and I will never be – a proper child. I want to love you, Carrie, but I don't know how. So I hurt you instead. And then I leave you crying alone.

***

I'm standing outside Askham Grange. It's early in the morning. They have let me go. The birds are singing. I know what I'm going to do next.

In my pocket is the £20 they issue to everyone the day you leave prison. First I need a bus into York. I have to get to the shops.

For the last two weeks I've been living in Askham's release hostel. It's a building in the grounds of the grange where prisoners are helped to prepare for return to the world outside. You lose skills in prison, the hostel manager tells us. You lose independence. Above all, you lose structure: when it's provided, you forget how to make it for yourself. We're going to help you to find it again.

I wasn't really listening. My head was far too full of my unspoken words.

I didn't say goodbye to Carrie. The terror of it all became too great. Saying things can make them come true. So since it wasn't said, there's been no goodbye.

The first York bus comes round the corner and I climb on board. It's full of the early office workers, bound for the city – people who do this normal thing every normal day and head home when the day is done. People who never lost structure, who never looked down past their feet and saw they were standing on nothing.

I never said goodbye to the lady in the garden. I couldn't. How would I know what words to use? I'm not proper. I don't know how to do the proper thing. Instead I just drifted into silence. When our silence had become too hard to break, I left her.

"If you have had a relationship here," said the hostel manager, "or a special friend, during your time in prison – we do understand. But it's best if prison friendships come to an end. You're making a fresh start now. You don't want to be reminded of the past."

Reminded? This place is with me forever. I broke as many rules as I could: rules about drinking and rules about being on time and rules about borrowing things from the Education Department. An extra week here and an extra week there, but then they got wise. Then they wouldn't give me any more time in Askham no matter what I did.

"It's best for you to put the past behind you. Make up your mind that you'll never come back. Try hard to get your family on track. Give your children time to settle down. Keeping in touch with people from here might seem important now, but it won't help you do all of that."

I moved to the hostel and never said a word about going. But now I just think every day, every minute of the day, of Carrie walking in through our door, seeing that my clothes were gone. My drawing pads and coloured pens. My leaky old shoes.

I crushed the sheets of paper that we'd made into origami shapes and arranged on the windowsill. I threw them in the bin. But pieces of crumpled paper aren't an ending. I never could have made a real end.

The bus from Askham Richard stops near York's old city walls. There are lavatories opposite the bus stop, next to a flight of stone steps which will soon be crowded with tourists. I cross the road and search. In a small hardware store I find it: clothesline. I'm the very first customer that day.

Inside the lavatory cubicle, I tie the clothesline in a loop. A collar knot – a hangman's knot. That's what we called it in the army.

I climb up on the seat. I wind the clothesline tightly round the cistern, testing to make sure it's secure. Carefully I test its strength. I'm thin and light, but still the knot and noose and pipe will need to hold. It's quiet and early still; the pavement outside is getting busier. But people on their way to the office don't stop in public lavatories. My plan can only go wrong if someone comes in. At this hour, it's not very likely to happen.

It's going to work.

I've wanted heaven since I was eight years old. Heaven – my heaven – is to be with Dog. Or to sail along bright jewelled reefs with beautiful blue turtles. Later on, I found a different kind of heaven, and that was with Carrie. But I broke it. I spoiled it. Of course I did. I am not a proper child.

Carrie, I'm afraid to be without you. I don't want to live when each day is nothing but your absence. If I had been better, if I was worth anything at all, I wouldn't have let you down.

There's nothing at all for me now but the space between what is and the things that ought to be. The worst thing that dying can do is to close that space.

I remember the peace and the stillness of death from long, long ago in a house in North London. It never, ever frightened me. I stand on the seat with the noose in position. Then I step forward, wanting nothing at all.

It seems like a long time later that I realise I'm lying on a cold tiled floor. A man in uniform is bending above me. He has a worried frown. I see jags of darkness and light. There's a terrible pain in my throat.

I hear a sobbing voice above me. "Oh my God! I just walked in, and I heard this strangling sound –"

And another voice replies, "Best that you did, love. You found her in time and saved her life."

But it isn't for the best. I couldn't even die. It turns out that I'm not a proper suicide either.

***

I was admitted to hospital in York. But apart from a ring of raw flesh around my neck and a very sore throat, I hadn't been hurt. I'd been hanging in the toilet for just a few seconds when a woman on her way to the office popped in because she just couldn't wait. She saw the straining clothes line and quickly fetched help.

I spent nearly a week in hospital. The doctor told me sternly that now I had come out of prison, it was time to try and start a new life. Don't go harking back or thinking that it's hopeless. Anyway, your friend down in London – what's her name? Yes, Gail – is going to help you. Give you a place where you can stay until you sort yourself out.

Gail was a friend of Estelle's who lived in Crawley. She offered me a room as a favour to Estelle and I'd nowhere else to go. When the doctors let me out, I boarded the train from York to King's Cross.

***

As the train to London moves off, I remember my beautiful Dolly. Where is she? Quickly I check everywhere, but Dolly's not stuffed in my coat pocket, or in the string bag, or in my mother's hand. She wouldn't fit into her black shiny handbag. I look all round the carriage, turning my head back and forth, catching my breath. Dolly's left behind.

I want Dolly with me and my eyes fill up with tears. I don't want her to be all alone and frightened.

My mother doesn't say a word. One look and I don't cry out loud for Dolly any more. I don't make a sound. The train tears forwards. My home is left far, far behind me.

***

I sat at the bar on the train and kept ordering Black Russians. I didn't know exactly what they were. They gave you money for travel and £20 in cash when you were let out of prison. When I boarded the train, I'd still got most of it left. By the time the train's bar closed ("There's no vodka left, love – don't you think you've had enough?") I'd spent the whole lot.

***

Estelle's friend came all the way to meet me at King's Cross station.

Gail told me that she knew coming out of prison was hard. She'd helped another woman, a little while ago, and seen her struggle at first hand. The simplest things become an effort of will. To decide what to eat and then prepare your food. To structure the shapeless days you drift through when there's no one there to tell you what to do. She offered me a room and time. She was very kind, and I was truly grateful for her kindness. But when you can't fill up your emptiness, Gail, the emptiness fills up on you.

I wanted to tell her I had nothing to give her. That would save her waiting for the big disappointment I was surely going to be. The progress I knew she was hoping for – the normal life restored, to see that what she'd done had really helped me – I couldn't give her anything like that. I'd only had silence for Carrie, in the end. We drifted apart as though a rift had opened up that no words could ever heal. I knew that I had hurt her and I wanted to tell her I was sorry, but how could I begin? Carrie, deserving everything good – what goodness had she found in me?

A drink a drink a drink and there's nothing left of memory. When I can forget her, Carrie will be gone. But I can't quite work out how to do it. Carrie, for always the whisper in my mind.

***

Within a short time, Gail helped me to move out of her spare bedroom to a place of my own in Crawley. She made all the arrangements for a furnished flat just down the road, even paying my deposit and for three months' rent. She said she'd be popping round to make sure that things were okay. She wanted to help me start a new life – but I knew she also wanted me to leave, and I didn't blame her.

At first I couldn't sleep, for a long stretch of time. Then came a block of days I found myself so stunned that I could barely wake. I didn't feel hungry, though while it was still light I went down to the shops to rob wine. After dark, I was terrified to step outside the door. Sometimes, even in daylight, I would panic on the way to the corner of the street.

Once or twice Gail gave me money and asked me to bring back groceries: milk, bread, biscuits. But shopping made me anxious and the lists would slip my mind. I'd buy drink instead. I could tell that she thought I wasn't trying very hard. She helped me move house in the long, hot summer. The sun glowed orange through the curtains in my new furnished flat. Then there were lightning storms, and one day even a flurry of hail.

Then Gail came round to see me in the new place like she'd said, and one day she brought me a letter. It was addressed to me at Askham Grange, then that address crossed out and Gail's had been written underneath. The date was weeks ago. When I opened it, I barely understood what it said, so I gave it to her and asked her to explain.

When she read it, she seemed to be terribly excited.

"Nicky – this is from a record company! It says that they'd like you to come to their office, to talk about publishing your songs. It says – um – it says something about an award — it says the Koestler Awards for art and music – and your songs were very good and then somebody sent them a tape of your music. This is amazing, Nicky! I didn't know that you could write songs!"

I barely remembered the Koestler Awards. It all seemed like a dream and I stared at her blankly.

"You'll have to ring them up. You can use my phone, don't worry. Tell them that you're sorry that it's taken such a long time to reply. I'm sure they'll still want you to come for a meeting."

***

Gail was worried that I didn't seem to know what was going on around me. You need to know what day it is, she said to me – it's good to know what's happening and keep track of time. Why don't I come round and cook us both dinner and then we can watch the news on TV? She cooked in my unused kitchen and we sat and had our dinner on trays.

A picture of Brighton came up on the screen. A reporter was standing there in shirtsleeves. He was speaking but at first I couldn't make out what he said. I saw bright summer sky just behind him: a pile of vivid cloud up above and the pier with its amusements. There were people on the beach in the sun.

Then I noticed what he was saying. A six year old boy had been sexually attacked. The reporter told the viewers that the child had been kidnapped by three men: they had grabbed him off the street. We sat there in the living room listening, trays of food on our knees. There were potatoes and carrots and peas. What a shocking crime, Gail said to me. How could anyone do such a terrible thing? It's unbelievable, really.

I can believe it. I stared at the screen.

I realise the reporter knows everything, whatever his pretended horror. He is staring into the room and I can see now that his eyes are mad and cold. The rape of the child is happening right now. Nothing can stop it. Panic wings lash in my body, like an injured bird struggling to be free.

There's black, white and red before my eyes, and then there's only darkness. I can't see the room any more.

***

What happened? I heard a yell of rage, a hiss and a crack and the sound of splintering glass. A woman's voice shrieked. On the floor lay two upturned trays next to two broken plates and a splatter of carrots and peas. There was a smell of burning; the coffee table had fallen on its side amidst the china rubble. Gail had backed into a corner, her face in her hands.

The black, spider-webbed TV screen had a hammer sticking out of it: the hammer that was kept in the kitchen drawer.

"Nicky! For God's sake! What are you doing?" Gail could barely get out the words. "Nicky!"

I was certain that the men who raped this child were in my flat. They must be hiding somewhere. I desperately searched for a weapon. There was a big copper warming pan hanging in the hall. As I grabbed it, I smashed the picture that hung alongside. I backed up the hallway, holding the pan up before me. I heard the crunch of broken glass as I strode.

I was panting so hard that I grew dizzy. Where are those men now? They

might be right behind me. I spun around and round, gouging the wall with the
pan in my hands as I swung it to keep them away.

***

In terror, Gail rang the police. She thought that I was going to attack her. When the officers came, I still believed that the men who'd assaulted the boy were hiding somewhere. I fought the policemen with the warming pan. A little crowd gathered outside. I could hear people cheering.

Later on, they took me to hospital. It was hard to explain what had happened – that I wasn't violent, just frightened, and how it felt to me when the past and the present folded in on one another. I had no way of knowing which was real.

They gave me medication and I slept.

***

In my deep drugged sleep, I dream about the best day of my life – a day in
Askham Grange, back when the Grange was my home.

In my memory, I'm in the laundry, drawing. There's a pile of paper on
the table, and all my pens and crayons, and a stack of requests that I need
to get done: things people want me to decorate for them. Birthday cards,
passed-your-driving-test cards, congratulations to somebody who's had a
baby. They've had a little girl.

"Nicky! Nicky Nicky Nicky!"

The sound of footsteps outside, and the door crashes open.

"NICKY!" It's Carrie, running like the wind.

Her face is pink and her eyes are shining. Her hair's all over the place. Her
shoes are dirty too, but I've no time to shoo her away because in one single
second I've been crushed in a massive hug. Carrie's ice-cold cheek is up against
mine, smelling of autumn roses.

"Nicky, you won! You won! Mr Whitty just got the letter!"

"Won what?"

Carrie giggles with excitement. She's been shouting: the door opens. Lena comes in.

"What did Nicky win?"

"She won the Koestler Awards! She won both! She got two first prizes!"

Again Carrie's arms are around me, Carrie's face close up and laughing, our foreheads pressed together.

"Sweetheart, well done! I'm so pleased for you! I'm so proud of you!"

"Nicky won!" yells Lena. Then in a lower voice, "what did she win, again? First prize in what?"

"Not one first prize! Two first prizes! The Koestler Awards – the first prize in both categories! Nicky is the best artist AND the best songwriter in the whole competition!"

Carrie hugs Lena as well. She's practically dancing.

"Crap!" shouts Lena. "That's bloody amazing!"

"Wow," I say. I can't help thinking that 'wow' is probably not the response Carrie was looking for.

"I know! It IS bloody amazing! Mr Whitty said I could come and tell you – actually I just started jumping about and he said I'd better tell you before I exploded. He wants to see you. He wants to say well done!"

The noise is making people look round the door. There's even more shouting.

"Nicky won a prize!" "Nicky won two prizes!" "Crap!" "Well done, Nicky!"

Now I'm being hugged by everyone at once, which normally I wouldn't like at all. But this is what it's like to be real. When I find out how to be real, it's properly beautiful.

Chapter Ten

Nicky from Nashville

"Here she is! It's Nicky Nicholls!"

Several people break into applause. Someone even bangs on the table with his hand.

I'm not quite sure what's going on. But after Gail gave me the letter, I rang up the record company just like she said. Now it's the day of the meeting and I'm here in a producer's office, right in the middle of London.

***

It was shabby and grey round Victoria station. There was a line of black cabs, and beyond it the bright red buses in Victoria Street. I could hear a siren, or maybe an ambulance. Its wailing rise and fall sounded strange, just like a soundtrack from a film. It wasn't the English nee-naw sound I knew. It merged with the howl of the city.

I was very, very high from smoking spliffs. These days they seemed to be the only thing which stopped my stomach ache from doubling me up. Sometimes I had to reach out for the wall to keep me steady. It had rained while I was on the train to Victoria from Crawley and my shoes had cardboard linings. They were wet now, and one of the soles kept flapping and slapping on the ground. I stopped to look around me and the stream of marching people right behind tut-tutted, then swooped either side and strode on towards the blue-lit entrance to the Underground.

I was searching for an office nearby. Then I caught a glimpse of an odd-looking figure in a shop window. It was me, but with a strange, round lump on my hip. That must be my roll-ups, stuffed into a Rizla pack to make them easier to carry. I was sure that the bulge would make a bad impression at my meeting, but I couldn't throw my rollies away.

I saw a broken Dunhill box lying on the kerb. I picked it up, then slowly transferred my rollies into it, careful not to drop them in the puddles. My ticket back to Crawley went safely in as well. The packet was silver and red, so now the rollies looked much smarter. There was lots more tutting all around me while I stood there fumbling, and nearly a collision with a woman rushing by.

The traffic moved giddily. I found the place I wanted easily enough. Inside, the place was lit as brightly as a stage with a shiny high reception desk, and two women in black uniforms seated behind. Both of them looked up as I approached, and both of them immediately frowned. I knew I must look shabby and not like the sort of visitor they normally greeted. A great chandelier hung above them and the sparkles it scattered in the hallway made me blink. I stuttered when I spoke.

I had been high every day since the doctor had told me that I had to stop drinking, the last time I was taken to hospital. Each time I was arrested – always for being drunk and disorderly – they sent me to detox to dry out, which meant that they kept me on a ward and sometimes gave me medicine to try to reduce my craving for booze. I'd shake and hallucinate, and sometimes I'd be very, very sick. The worst of it would last a few days – then they'd let me go and as soon as I got out, I'd drink again. I lost count of the number of times I went through this. I'd also lost count of all the D and D fines that I knew I'd never pay. But this doctor had a much more serious face. He drew a big black ring on my belly.

"Can you see the swelling? This circle shows the size of your liver. You need to stop drinking. Your liver is damaged. It's important to listen – do you understand? If you continue to drink like this, you could die very soon."

Yes, I understood that I could die. But just beyond the drink, my memories were waiting. I didn't know how to explain this to the doctor. So I decided on spliffs in the daytime, and to keep my drinking only for the night. But the pain in my stomach still wouldn't go away. The skin where he'd drawn the big black circle was often too tender to be touched.

Numbed out, zoned out, spliffed up, with more and more short-outs in my head. Time would slow right down so that one moment lasted far too long: an echoey word was extended or somebody's expression froze. Then there'd be a bump as I skipped back up to normal speed, but a few seconds missing and no way to be sure what had happened. My ears felt dull and blocked. It made the world noisy and muffled, like listening to a continual buffeting wind.

I managed to stammer out my name. The receptionists looked at each other, then both of them got up. I was steered by the arm across the hallway to a lift. On another, higher floor I was led into a room where a group of very smart-looking people sat round a table. It seemed as though everyone was waiting for me.

One of the receptionists announced:

"Here she is – it's Nicky Nicholls!" It was followed by echoey applause.

"Brava! Brava!" cried a theatrical-looking man with curly dark hair, waving his arms excitedly: he even banged the table with his hand.

There were more gaps and jumps in my head, then I found myself sitting in an office with a man and a woman on the far side of a desk. Another man was seated at my side. I could see the gloss and gleam of success on all three: both the men in pinstripes, the woman with her shoulder pads jutting and collar-length icy blonde hair. They all wore wide shiny smiles. Behind them on the wall were framed certificates, dozens running all the way from ceiling to floor with gold and silver circles. The lights gleamed off the metal, shimmering like mist in the room.

The man alongside me said his name was Gerry Forrester: a quick, weak shake of a hand and a single glance at me. I clearly didn't interest him much.

Somebody had made me a coffee; I could see a china cup on the desk. I didn't like coffee but it seemed polite to drink it, so I stretched out my hands. If I bent too far forward, it would wake up the ache at the top of my stomach. I found I was too dizzy to reach as far as the cup, and now my belly hurt. I needed a spliff for the pain.

"Nicky! Welcome."

The two behind the desk beamed even wider.

"We're all so very grateful that you've found the time to be with us today."

A pause, but I didn't know what I should say in reply.

"You were brought to our attention because of the music prize you won during your impris – ah – your time staying in… er – er –" – he glanced down quickly at a paper on his desk – "in Askham Grange! You remember this, of course. You won a Koestler Award for music – for your songwriting. Marvellous songs – and all written while you were – well, yes – marvellous."

Somehow, by a process so strange that I could scarcely imagine it, the music I had given Mr Whitty – the illegal prison tape, when I had tried to break the rules and stay safe inside Askham – had passed through the hands of many strangers and reached the headquarters of Norse Records.

"So! Well then – this is a very exciting opportunity for you. We think that you're a genuine songwriting talent – a real new find. Norse Records is keen to release your songs. We have drawn up a contract."

He clearly expected a positive response. I said, "Okay." There was another short pause.

After that – a whole lot of legal talk. My stomach was hurting more and more. I hazed right out. Coming and going, I only caught scraps of what they said.

Set for success – and 'Footsteps' – well, now, that's an amazing song – they'd thought I was heading for the big time the moment they'd heard it. And 'Child of 1945' – so terribly moving. Lucky that you entered the Koestler Awards – your big break – rescued from the scrap heap, really, weren't you? – the Performing Rights Society – great opportunities ahead and people love a turnaround story, after all – so in the end it all helps sales. Just as well your prison governor – now who was he again ? –

"Mr Whitty," I said clearly. "Mr Joe Whitty."

The mention of Mr Whitty's name in all this glitter-talk seemed to be the one solid thing, as though he was here in the room for a moment, his calm blue eyes regarding me. Mr Whitty, who'd done everything to help me that he possibly could do. *I'm proud of you, toe-rag.*

– Yes, well – it was lucky for you that Whitty was smart and he saw your potential – got you a very big break – and of course you'll be working with Gerry here who's *a really great guy* and who's going to be your manager –

Gerry was still sitting at my side. He'd said nothing further to me, after his first sideways glance.

I signed the long contract Pinstripe placed on the desk without reading it. Time kept freezing and then jumping. A drink a spliff a drink. Just the titles of my songs stood out in the blur of the text. 'Footsteps'. 'Hangover Love'. 'Silent Christmas'. 'Whisky'. 'Silver Dream'. 'Would You?' 'Space Age Ecstasy'. 'Child of 1945'. The songs of my love for Carrie. Something about royalties from these sales.

"So you – er – well – you'll be needing some new gear, by the look of you, Nicky, eh? Haha! A coat, definitely – because, um, it's cold today and I can see that you aren't wearing one – and, er – your shoes – maybe some new shoes…? I'm sure we'll be able to help you out!"

The three of them all laughed politely at this.

"So we'll be in touch soon – we have your address I think? Yes, it's… er… Crawley now, isn't it? – nice part of the world – and good luck producing the next lot of songs which we absolutely can't wait to hear! – so exciting – you must be excited too – such a great story, so moving – good times ahead – Gerry will take your details so that he can find out how you're getting on –"

I found myself outside in the corridor. My stomach hurt so much that it was difficult to stay standing up.

A drink a spliff a drink.

Gerry Forrester walked me all the way back to the gleaming reception desk down in the hall.

"So – Nicky. Ring me when the next lot of stuff is ready – you know – your new songs. Here's how to get hold of me." He handed me a Norse Records business card. "Very good to meet you at last."

I wasn't sure exactly what had happened. I felt certain that I should ask him questions. But he seemed so sure of himself, so intimidating. What if he was angry with me?

As I stood there confused, my new manager turned on his heel and stepped briskly back inside.

***

Back to Crawley. Back to chaos. I hadn't paid the rent in months.

I spent a lot of time at the pub across the road, the Charcoal Burner, where I made new friends. My friends began to drift towards the flat, first of all staying overnight, but then they stayed for longer. No one paid anything, and slowly the place became a squat.

At first, Gail kept coming round to visit. She tried to tidy up but the mess grew worse and worse. When she was there, I pretended to be sober, except I kept forgetting. Anyway, I think she always knew that I wasn't. I didn't want to see Gail any more. No job, drunk or high all day and living in a rancid heap of fag butts and empties seemed a very poor return for her kindness and her help. When I knew she was coming, I would hide all the empties in the washing machine.

Spliffs in the daytime and booze all through the night seemed to stop my endless stomach ache from getting any worse. What bothered me more and more nowadays was vertigo, the way that things kept tilting up and down and side to side. The flat was like a crazy place with sloping, tipping floors, and when I went outside, the pavement was doing just the same.

Threatening letters about rent and bills started landing on the mat. I could see I needed money so I worked in a garage for a while – it was something that I knew from my days in Bradford, and it put some cash in my pocket. Garage shops had changed – they were starting to sell not just petrol and cigarettes but food. Sometimes they were even selling wine. They sent me on a training course to learn about that, but when the day came round, it went by in a spliffed-up blank. I came to my senses in a classroom full of people in a smart hotel in Horley where I found that we were learning about product management. I had no idea what had been said. Still, the teacher told me that I'd passed.

At the garage, they went on about my shoes: no trainers on the job, and anyway, that pair you've got on is falling apart. My manager told me sternly to buy myself some new ones. You have a wage, he said – wear something decent to work.

But I can't afford to spend any money on shoes. Money is for drink. Drink my way through chaos. Drink my way through hopelessness. Drink my way through all that remains in the mist and the haze of memories. Memories that might still come back if

I let them. But I've learned how to lock them down tight. That's all that matters. Forget about shoes.

In any case, I only kept the job a few months. I often wasn't sure what time it was. I turned up for work at the garage in the late afternoon once too often, and got fired. New shoes would have been a waste of money.

***

D and D for drinking in the street. Sent for a mental assessment. Warlingham hospital for detox. Netherne hospital in Hooley, Surrey: same again, but there they used a different drug to make it easier to come off drink. I had a very bad reaction to this drug. I was screaming, throwing tables – hurling them so high up in the air that they were hitting the ceiling.

Riding the detox roundabout, all the way to nowhere.

***

I was more and more ashamed to face Gail. But she kept on ringing at the door, so I hid. Then the next day or the day after that, she came right back and rang the bell again.

I'd always been a drifter, so I drifted out of Crawley. I'd heard about another squat in Thornton Heath, Croydon, just a few miles to the north. Harcourt Road was five minutes from the hospital in one direction and five minutes from the crematorium in the other. There were seven or eight others in the squat – it was hard to be sure. People came and went. I didn't know who any of them were. The place smelled of spliffs, spills of stale booze and drains.

But Gail must have talked to the people in the flat back in Crawley. She found out where I'd gone. She came all the way to Harcourt Road and put a little note through the letterbox. She told me to make sure I stayed in touch, that she'd done what she could now but that if in the future I wanted to find work again and to sort myself out, to remember that she was my friend and she would help me.

If I could feel anything, I would have cried at Gail's kindness. Standing alone in the hallway, I whispered a thank you and hoped she understood. Then a drink a spliff a drink, and after that, nothing.

***

Once again, I lose track of the months and eventually of years. I don't have any markers to show me.

A big fight in the Harcourt Road squat scares me badly. I don't know how it starts, all the shoving and shouting, fists flying and threats. Somebody calls the police. They give me another D and D, and yet another night in the cells. After that, I don't go back. Harcourt Road seems too dangerous.

I hear about another squat in Avondale Road, South Croydon, and move there. This one doesn't have electric power either. But at least I'll have a roof.

I know that time is passing. It's passing me by. So perhaps I should sort myself out.

***

One night came a moment when things suddenly seemed clear. Before another drink to block the pain, I thought about Carrie. I closed my eyes, and heard her voice speaking.

"… a decent job, Nick – it could help you… for your CV… something that would help your future… If you find it too hard to go to work without drinking, I think that AA might help…"

I looked round my smelly, gloomy squat. If Carrie saw me here, I knew that she wouldn't be angry. I knew that she would cry. And I was also certain of the next thing she would say: she'd tell me to do something about it. She'd tell me I should try very hard to make things better. Carrie would tell me that I should get a job, and try to stop drinking.

I remembered how steely she could be, the way she squared her shoulders, the down-to-business glint in her eye. Carrie always dealt with things – she never tried to shove them away. She'd say what needed saying, face up to the problem, always try to do the right thing. I decided I would do what Carrie said.

I found out the date by looking at the papers. It was autumn 1984. I realised that soon I would be 40. In two months, yet another Christmas would be here and everyone would start posting cards. There was plenty of work in the Post Office. I got a job down in Croydon and then I joined AA.

***

There are men in the sorting office, right next to East Croydon station. Now that I'm going to meetings of AA and trying not to drink, I'm frightened to be close to them. I tell myself firmly and slowly in my head to stay very calm and to go on taking long, deep breaths.

Some of the men work right behind me, walking about across the room. They call to each other and sometimes they make jokes. I'm scared of their voices, their footsteps, their shadows, the dreadful looming height of them. I know that if they grabbed me, even the ones who don't look tough or have enormous muscles, they would still be quite quietly, relentlessly, ever so much stronger than I.

If one of them bumps into me, horror shivers all around my body. I shake with it. Somebody asks me if I'm cold. I say no. Inside, I freeze in fear. I remember a hand taking hold of my wrist like the touch of bone on bone. The worker at the table just along from me gives me a look and I realise that I've probably said something aloud that sounds strange.

But still, I'm very fast at sorting letters. That's because I see the letter-shapes, bright and clear and perfect. I'm not slowed down by reading,

I'm just seeing – dancing through the patterns without missing a beat – and I start off quickly then find that I get quicker. And quicker. It's as if I've discovered I can run through a maze. In a couple of weeks, they tell me I'm the fastest in the room, in the depot, in south London – a champion of sorters. On my very best days, the ink on the envelopes, the loops and lines and swirls of people's pens, even take my mind off how much I need a drink.

But not for very long.

I don't want to lose my job at the depot. I know that if I drink again, I'll do so. But I'm terribly afraid of having dreams, so at night I smoke spliff after spliff. They keep pictures of the past very tiny in my mind, as if they're far away, at the wrong end of a telescope. Still, every day gets harder and harder. All I can think of is how much I need to have a drink. A drink a drink a drink.

Carrie would tell me to keep on. Mr Whitty would be proud of me for trying. Although it's difficult to know what day it is sometimes, or when it's the weekend, or what time the AA meetings are – as much as I can, I try to keep going to AA.

***

But I kept on confusing day and night. The streetlights outside looked the same in the dusk as they did when dawn was coming. I spliffed all through the night, then couldn't leave the house without another, so sometimes when I thought that I'd left enough time to get the bus to the depot in George Street, I found that time jumped forwards and half the working day was gone. I was cautioned for getting in late.

When I finished my shifts at the depot, I felt so exhausted that sometimes I would sit down on the pavement. I couldn't get the bus back to the squat until I'd rested, and sometimes as I sat there, I'd find that commuters passing by tossed coins into my lap. There were flurries of snow in the air. If I didn't get up, I knew that somebody would contact the police.

***

Gail still forwarded my post. One day, a letter from Norse Records landed on the mat.

It came from Gerry Forrester, saying he was sorry it had taken him so long to get in touch. He was wanting to meet up with me to give me some exciting news. And he was dying to hear about the great new songs I must be writing. How about a coffee and a catch-up really soon?

I rang him. He asked where we should meet. I didn't want to go to the gold and silver office. He said he'd come to Croydon and we met at a coffee place nearby. It was a very cold day, and I sat at a table in the corner keeping warm while I waited. Christmas was close and carols were playing in the cafe. A bent little tree with coloured baubles sat alongside the ketchup. When he arrived, I noticed the warm softness of his scarf and the drape of his long navy coat, hanging in the way clothes do that cost an awful lot of money. He paid for a coffee and a tea, and he joined me.

"So – Nicky. It's been a long while! Great to see you looking so – really great to see you! Just – great. What are you doing these days?"

"I got a job. I'm a postie."

"A postie?"

"A postman. Woman. I sort the post. There's lots of extra post coming up to Christmas so they take on more staff."

"Oh. Oh, I see. Well – that's very interesting. That's good."

Gerry stirred his coffee.

"Actually – I've some very exciting news for you. Norse released some of your songs. We chose 'Silent Christmas'. A good time of year for it, haha! Very seasonal. A lot of people like it."

"Does it make them cry?" I asked him.

But I don't think that Gerry understood.

***

Mr Whitty is standing by the window in his office at Askham, looking out at the bright new snowfall lit up by rare December sun.

"That song makes everybody cry. It makes us all cry because it's beautiful. It makes you think about what love is and what Christmas means."

Somehow I'd not been expecting him to say that.

"Sometimes – a thing can be too beautiful. It can be too much."

Too beautiful. Too much. I think of Carrie. Yes, I understand.

In a cafe in Croydon, my heart aches for the beauty I have lost. It aches so much that I can scarcely breathe.

***

"Anyway – the song did very well! Then we released 'Child of 1945'. A singer called Dave Vernon did the recording. And that did even better!"

"Did it?"

"Not just here in Britain. It did pretty well in the States."

He paused and I thought that he expected me to speak.

"Oh. Good."

"You underst – Nicky, do you understand this? I said the song sold well in America. That's very big news."

"Right."

"It's a successful record in the country music charts."

I didn't know what to say to that.

"A big hit!" said Gerry.

"What do you mean – a hit?"

"I mean the record didn't just sell well. It did better than that. It's made it into the country music charts, you know – in Nashville. That's in Tennessee. The heart of country music!"

"You mean – it's in the Top Forty?"

"Better than that, even."

"Top Twenty? Ten?" It all seemed unreal.

"It's number one, Nicky. A number one hit record. Many congratulations to you from all of us at Norse Records!"

"Well," I said. "Well, I like country."

"Of course you do!"

Gerry Forrester sipped his coffee. I stared into my tea. When I looked up, he was holding a small plastic bag in his hand.

"I thought – we thought at the office – that you might like a copy of it."

"That's my record?"

"Not just 'a record'! This is your number one hit single! Here's 'Child of 1945' on vinyl."

"This is for me?"

"We're very proud of you. You're a big musical talent."

I took the vinyl single out of the bag. The sleeve was black and white, with a picture of the dark-haired singer.

"Thanks."

"So here's the thing – you're going to be doing a press interview!"

"What kind of interview?"

"We've contacted the *Croydon Advertiser* – told them all about your success. It's a great story! Local – ah – postwoman making it big in the country music charts! They'd like to talk to you and to Dave."

"Dave?"

"The singer, Dave Vernon! It's Dave who sings your big hit song. He's a wonderful talent and *such a great guy* and –"

"Okay."

"So – erm – if I write down where you need to go on this – er – on this napkin here –" Gerry Forrester grabbed one from the pile by the salt and pepper shakers – "can you be sure to come along? It's tomorrow. It's at 3pm – just down the road."

"Yes, okay."

" – and – ah… Nicky – listen, this is very important – the reporter will ask you about your music and how you wrote it – listen carefully – so what we need here is a positive story – something upbeat and Christmassy. A feel-good interview, to make sure we sell more records. You know – 'tis the season to be – ah – jolly. Do you understand?"

"Yes."

Gerry looked as if he didn't believe me.

"You'll make sure to keep it very light?"

"Yes."

"Right-oh. So – ah – till tomorrow!" He got to his feet.

"Till tomorrow."

After he left, I realised that he'd never mentioned money. Perhaps I should have asked him, but somehow I felt sure that his answers would make everything just the way he said it was, even if I thought something else. He was always so confident – how could I argue?

So now I'm Nicky from Nashville. I walked through Croydon in the cold winter wind. The plastic bag was in my hand, but I couldn't play the record. I didn't own a record player. Anyway, the squat didn't have electricity.

***

I had no idea at all what to say to the man from the *Croydon Advertiser*. The more I thought about the interview, the more I started to panic.

What if the reporter started asking me questions? He would do. It's his job. It's what reporters do. What if he asked about my childhood? What if he could guess where I came from? Or what if he'd already found out? Found out the truth about my life in Fletcher Road. My mother and my grandfather. If that happened, I would die of shame.

I smoked and smoked. But instead of fading out and drifting far away, I grew more and more panicked and afraid. What if he decided he would write all about me in the *Croydon Advertiser*? I longed to have a drink to make the terror of the thought go away.

A drink a drink a drink.

By the time I reached the newspaper's office, I was trembling with fear. Dave Vernon and Gerry Forrester were already there waiting. Dave Vernon seemed nice, but he was confident and loud: he must have talked to people from the media before. He chatted and laughed, and Gerry Forrester kept on laughing too. The camera was flashing. The reporter made his notes in squiggles.

"So – well – and what about you, Nicky?"

Last night I decided that I'll say something interesting. Definitely more interesting than working in the post office. If it sounds interesting, he'll write it down and then he might stop asking questions.

"My father was a Native American chief," I said. I wished that it was true. Native Americans were noble and beautiful – I'd always liked looking at pictures of them in magazines. How wonderful if I could be as dignified as they seemed to be.

"Wow!" The reporter's pencil flew. "How did that happen, then?"

"He came – ah – he came over here to England during the war and met my mother."

"So you certainly have an exciting background!"

"Yes."

"I can see you're proud of him."

"Yes. Very proud. I didn't – I didn't know my father very long, but I do remember him quite clearly. He was a very noble man. The Native American people have a wonderful tradition."

Twenty minutes later in the lift, Gerry Forrester asked:

"Er... Nicky – about the Indian chief – is that really – er...? Is your father a – er...?"

I wanted the story to be real. I wished so fiercely that just for one moment, it seemed as if it was.

"Yes," I said. "Yes, it's true. He is."

The lift door opened but Gerry Forrester stood still. For a moment he stared at me hard. And then he turned away with a shrug.

Over his shoulder he called out, "Always a pleasure! Great to see you and – I'm glad things are going – ah – yes – do get in touch when you've written more material. We're all very excited about that."

"Yes. I will. I'll be in touch."

"Great. Great. Well – I look forward to it. Very good to see you."

He pushed the door open and disappeared out into the street. His last words flew away in the roar of the South Croydon traffic. They sounded a bit like "It's been fun!"

The piece about me appeared in the *Croydon Advertiser* on 25th September 1985. There was another, all about my song, in the music paper, the *New Musical Express*. It mentioned my father and my Native American heritage. Dave Vernon repeated it too, in an interview he did on the BBC World Service. The story I made up that day in Croydon travelled all around the world.

***

The effort of not drinking was so great by now that any other effort wore me out. Every day there was only one choice: to drink or not to drink. Everything else hung on that. Every single time it got harder.

But I must keep on trying. I have to. For Carrie's sake, for Mr Whitty's sake, I must do this.

I know that I should telephone Norse Records. I should find out what's happening, and ask them for my money. I should find someone with a record player so that I can listen to my number one hit. Perhaps I should even write more songs. But I can't do anything at all. Every shred of energy I have must go into trying not to drink.

***

Dear Miss Nicholls, You are invited to be the special guest of Norse Records at a party to be held on December...

Another letter lying on the filthy hall carpet, covered in footprints.

I didn't understand what it meant. What party, and why was I invited? I rang Gerry Forrester.

"Nicky! Always a pleasure."

I asked him about the party.

"It's tomorrow. Can you do tomorrow?"

"Yes."

"Ahh. Hmm. Well, then. Yes. Yes, very well. We shall – ah – we shall send a car."

"Send a car where?"

"We will send a car to your home. The car will collect you, and take you to the party."

***

At 5pm next day, a car drew up outside.

The journey seemed long. I kept on blanking out. I was high, to try to stop the pain in my stomach from burning right through me.

We left London's outskirts on a motorway. Daylight was fading. Then a jump in time and a very grand hotel. A huge shining room with a big stage at one end. A Christmas tree that towered to the ceiling, covered in a rainbow blur of lights. A murmuring crowd in long dresses and black bow ties. Tables laid for dinner. White cloths flowing down to the floor and the silvery sparkle of cutlery. A live band playing. Everyone is laughing and chatting and mingling. I've no idea at all what I should try to do or say.

In the centre of each table is an island of bottles. I instantly know that I will drink. It's impossible to stay here any other way. A drink a drink a drink.

I lift a glass from one of the trays that the waiters are handing round the room. I drink the wine in one long swig. It takes me two or three seconds. I pick up another. The waiter stares hard at me and then he moves on. I haze right out.

Flash! Gerry Forrester comes up to me, shakes my hand and claps me on the back.

Flash! I see Pinstripe and the woman from Norse Records, nodding and smiling.

Flash! A different man approaches me, waving his arms: he has dark curling hair and deep brown eyes. I've seen him somewhere once, but I can't remember where.

"Brava!" he cries. "Brava to our great songwriter!" It's the man who was banging on the table at the Norse Records office in Victoria.

My wine glass is empty and he finds me another. I empty it again. I can't hear much of what he's saying. He has a nice smile. But then he glances side to side, leaning in towards me. He speaks in a low and urgent voice.

"– but, Nicoletta darling – your clothes – I think your life is hard for you, no? You own the rights to your beautiful music, bellissima, yes? What payments have been made to you?"

I'm not sure what to say, so I hesitate. The man's face fills with consternation.

"My darling, you are saying that you have received no – ?"

Then a friend passing by in the crush of people grabs his arm and starts talking. As soon as the man looks away, I duck out of sight, stop a waiter with a tray, and pick up another glass of wine. The misery, anger and confusion that I feel are overwhelming. I drink to make them stop.

A blank after that.

***

When everyone had eaten and people were smoking, a lady in a beautiful blue dress with a microphone stepped onto the stage. I was very drunk by now, far away and floating. The lady started to sing.

The song she sang was 'Child of 1945'. I had no idea at all what to do. When the music ended, there was very loud clapping. Blue Dress clapped too, and looked around.

"… and I understand that the writer of that beautiful song, Miss Nicky Nicholls, is with us here tonight. Nicky Nicholls – can you make yourself known?"

I slumped in my seat in horror.

"Just to remind everyone here tonight," continued Blue Dress, "of how successful this song has become this year. It's made the charts across Europe, in Germany, in Switzerland, Italy and Spain. It's a popular feature on radio and –"

There was even more applause. Gerry Forrester started trying to raise up my arm. I pulled it down as hard as I could.

"Nicky Nicholls?!" trilled the lady in blue, "Nicky?! I'm sure you're out there somewhere!"

Gerry shouted loudly, "Here she is, ladies and gents!" and tried some more pulling on my arm. I pulled back even harder. Perhaps I'd have to kick him to make him stop. People around us smiled uncertainly as we tussled.

Then a loud voice rang out from the table next door.

"Stand up, woman – it's a great song!"

I saw a little man in a big bow tie with longish dark curls and a grin. A warm and proper grin. He rose to his feet and nodded towards me, raising his hands to applaud. When he started clapping me, everybody else clapped too. He had a nice face. I managed to stand up like he said, and tried to smile back.

"That's Dudley Moore!" hissed Gerry. "Dudley Moore!"

Blue Dress up on stage went on talking. Now Dudley Moore was standing by my chair.

"When they've done with all this taradiddle, Miss Nicholls," he said, and he rolled his eyes and gestured all around, "I'd be delighted if you'd join me in the VIP room as my guest." Gerry Forrester stared.

People did as Dudley Moore told them – and they did it very quickly. I was shown straight into the VIP room. The waiters rushed to bring us champagne. And it turned out he also played a mean game of snooker. He asked me lots of questions, all about my music, and ordered us even more champagne. He was easy to talk to and told funny jokes. No one gaped in here, or made me feel uneasy. I'd thought the VIP room might be scary, but it wasn't.

"And very well done to you, Miss Nicholls," he said. "It's been a real pleasure. The very best of luck for the future."

It was starting to grow light as the car drove me back towards London. Dudley Moore made a good memory. His smile reached all the way to his eyes.

***

In the New Year, the post office asked me to stay on, but not just working in the sorting office. Now I'd be out in the streets, doing a delivery round as well.

This job was harder. I carried heavy post bags, and there was lots of walking. Sometimes it was hard to get the work done in the allocated time. I had to go slow because the pavements were slippery. Then there were gates to be unfastened, angry dogs, and letter boxes snapping at my fingers. One day I tripped and put my foot right through the ice on someone's pond.

I thought that I'd rather drive a van, like some of the delivery team did. I told them in the office I could drive, and my supervisor asked for my licence. I never knew I needed a licence. But they helped me fill the form out, and I proudly passed my test first time in Croydon town centre.

I was drinking again, so I had to be careful not to do so in the daytime. I didn't want to lose another job. But at night there was whisky, even more than before. The pain below my ribs came and went. And now there was a new kind of pain crouching lower in my belly, griping and grinding. Sometimes it was painful to pee. Even when I had the van to drive, and wasn't carrying sacks of heavy post up the hills of South Croydon, I was often so exhausted that I wanted to lie down on the ground.

My supervisor gave me a caution for my lateness. Then he had to give me a second one. He said that I'd been a good worker but this had to be my final warning. I was very scared of losing my job. That night I drank and drank just to keep the fear away. The next day I turned up at lunchtime and was fired.

There was trouble in the squat in Avondale Road and I left. This time the only thing to do was sleep rough in the middle of Croydon. The buildings loomed up high in the modern town centre, where long straight roads made canyons for the wind. It was hard to find shelter in the big concrete spaces. I was terrified to stay there, so I walked away from the wide roads and underpasses, looking for houses with gardens. At least there'd be bushes to shelter in, a porch sometimes, or best of all a shed that wasn't locked. Out in the open in the dark, jumping at the tiniest sound, ten minutes' sleep could last ten days.

Perhaps I could sleep in a van. There were lots of jobs around and I still knew people I could ask. I worked on deliveries for several firms. Then at night I parked the van in the quieter streets of South Croydon and lay on a blanket in the back.

Somebody reported me for sleeping in the van. Police picked me up. I resisted arrest. I was sent for a mental assessment.

They gave me a little plastic basket in the ward where I went to be assessed. They said that I should put all my things in it. I didn't have very many things. I stood looking down at my entire life in that tiny little basket. For a moment fear rose inside me like it had in the old days when the panic waves still came and I had to keep still although I wanted to scream. A drink a drink a drink to force it down.

This time they also gave me tablets: they told me that anti-depressants might help me. I couldn't understand what that meant because I didn't feel sad when I was drinking. I only felt an endless nothing. How could any tablets change that? The day I left the unit, I lost them.

***

Picked up again by police. Detox. But this time it was much, much worse. It wasn't just the sickness and the trembling and the longing for a drink. This time I entered a void.

Needing to drink like I need to breathe air. A craving so total that there's no space around it, not the tiniest sliver. I have no thoughts. I have no reason. I am empty. I am nothing but my need. A drink a drink a drink. This can only be ended by ending myself.

I can hear my mother's voice speaking. "Do not cry when I hurt you. If you cry, I will hurt you more." Again and again I see the smart, quiet man in a crisp white shirt, walking towards me with his strange little smile. Panic. Terror. My body's drenched in sweat. I'm shaking so hard that I can't stand up.

I'd never known a detox as difficult as this. I wondered if the antidepressants might have made things even worse. But I also blamed *them*. I blamed the ones who told me that somehow not to drink was the answer. *You must stop drinking. You must sort yourself out.* For so long I'd been told this, and put through a cycle of help that didn't help me and solutions that went nowhere.

These people didn't know what they were asking me to do. They were telling me that I must see the past every day, see it and hear it and feel it and remember. They imagined I could do this and somehow go on living. They're wrong. I can't. It's impossible.

***

By now, my stomach ache was constant and dreadful. Some days I couldn't stand up. Nothing seemed to numb it any more. One day I collapsed in the street.

In detox, the nurse suggested that I spoke to a social worker.

"She works for the council. Tell her that you're homeless," she told me. "She might be able to do something – get you on a housing list, maybe. For a proper place – a decent home. Otherwise you'll just keep coming back here."

Nervously, I asked. Was there anything the housing lady could do to help me?

"We don't help criminals," she said.

In and out of hospital. Back again to Warlingham. Detox. They prescribed me a drug called heminevrin, to help relieve the symptoms. The patients all called it "I'm in heaven". But I'm not in heaven. I'm sinking into hell. I can't escape and I don't think I can take much more.

***

Next they tried a different approach. Lifestyle Modification, it was called. They told us that we had to eat healthily, but I felt so ill that I couldn't eat at all. There was exercise out in the garden, but my belly was too sore to bend over. The exercise lady wouldn't have it. Stretches, brisk walks and bunny hops.

"Up and down! Jump *up* and down!" Somebody behind me muttered: "Bunny hopping with the Grim Reaper."

After I'd been hopping for a while, I collapsed. I woke up back in Croydon, in hospital.

***

The doctor is asking me to spread my legs apart. She says that she needs to examine me. I refuse. I scream. I try to get up off the raping bed. I can't.

She seems to understand that I'm frightened. She tells me very calmly that nobody here is going to hurt me. She talks slowly, and gives me lots of time to take it in. My blood tests show a problem. They think I might be ill. The pain in my belly could be serious, she tells me. And it turns out that it is. It's cancer. I need to have a total hysterectomy. She explains what this will mean.

I can tell from the way that she talks about this, in a light, quiet voice that doesn't rise and fall very much, that she thinks I'll be terribly upset. But I'm not. To me, it's good news. I don't try to tell her how I feel. She definitely wouldn't understand.

These are the parts of my body that made me a girl, then a woman, and so they made me weak. These were the parts that were once used to hurt me. I wish I'd never had them in the first place. Now they will be taken away. I don't know who I'll be when they're gone – the woman-bits she talks about while I try not to listen. I don't even want to hear their names. I certainly don't want to keep them.

Whoever I become when they are gone, I won't be the same me any more. I'll be someone else who's different – someone else who's free. Free of all the powerlessness and pain that come from being born a female. To become this new person, no longer forced to be a woman and to suffer, might mean a proper life for me, at last.

***

After the big operation, I was tired and I felt very sore. I had a long deep slash across my stomach. The people at the hospital told me that they'd found a place for me to live: a refuge in Upper Norwood. A few weeks after that, they moved me into sheltered accommodation in Addiscombe, a green, quiet area just outside the centre of Croydon.

Now they wanted me to detox – to totally stop drinking, to go to AA yet again. But when they told me this, I felt ashamed. They were kind and they'd looked after me. But if I tried to do it, I would fail them. I'd always failed before. It's too hard.

"Nicky – I agree with you." Fiona Wilson Carr was a hospital psychologist. "I think it *is* too hard. This really isn't something you can do on your own. If you decide to deal with the problems that you've had, there'll be lots of support here for you."

"And what does that mean?" I didn't want to growl, but it came out that way.

"It means having therapy. Really proper therapy – with doctors and nurses who know how to help. They're trained to help people who've been through terrible things. I don't know what it was, Nicky. But I do know it was bad."

"How? How do you know?"

"I know because of you. You are an intelligent person. Unless something very bad had happened to you, things wouldn't be as hard as they are."

***

Therapy. My therapist's name is Laura Greaves. I realise that she wants me to tell her how I feel, to talk about my past, to tell her things I've never told anyone. Things I can't speak of. To tell her why I'm not a proper child. She's asking me to say the words that make me want to die of shame.

But I won't. And anyway, I can't. My tongue feels like a big, dry log. It blocks my mouth solid. It's impossible to speak.

We sit for 50 minutes. I can't say a word and Laura doesn't either. She doesn't even look at me. She clasps her hands together very still, and keeps her gaze turned down. The silence stretches on until we run out of time. She doesn't seem angry at all. The next session goes just the same. Still she's not angry, even then.

I think she knows it's bad. I really think she does.

Session three. The room is very still. She smiles at me and asks me how I am. I am in pain. I am in so much pain. My pain is unbearable.

Then I remember a face I saw a long time ago, the first time that I was sent to Risley. A prisoner in an orange dress, surrounded by guards. Her mess of stiff blonde hair and her heavy-featured face. I remember how our eyes met and I looked into emptiness. She didn't just feel nothing. What I saw was something worse: there was no one left alive to feel. The angry women threatening to kill her for her crimes didn't know it was already far too late.

I see that the meaning of my pain is that I am still alive. All these years, all this struggle, and I go on living. Because underneath the pain, life is worth holding on to.

That's why I decide to speak. I can only find four words.

"My mother beat me," I say to her.

Chapter Eleven

I'm proud of you, toe-rag

"You might want to come and stay with us. I think we could help you," said Laura Greaves.

She wanted the choice to be mine. So in January 1999, I was one of the first three patients admitted to Purley Women's Service. The new unit was based in a large brick house in a tree-lined street, with eight bedrooms, a communal kitchen, therapy room and garden. It was a residential treatment centre for women recovering from trauma or experiencing serious mental illness.

Everybody there seemed nice. They were so very nice that I was sure they must want something. How could I trust them?

"You're perverts, all of you!" I said to them accusingly. I needed to find out the worst.

***

When I moved in, I wouldn't sleep in my bed. But that was fine. They simply moved a beanbag upstairs so that I could be more comfortable.

Therapists and specialist nurses came to work with us. There was always someone to talk to or just to be with, if it was too hard to talk. We could cook for ourselves in the kitchen, with nurses and carers to help. If we didn't feel up to it or didn't know how, they made our meals. In the mornings, we talked in a group, taking turns to say how we felt or what was happening right now. Nobody was forced to join in – you could sit there and listen. For a long time, I hardly said a word.

Each day we had one-to-one meetings with our specialist carers. We did activities: art, crafts, gardening. In the late afternoons, visitors could come, so long as they'd booked in advance. Evenings were free, but if you were frightened, you'd never be left on your own. A one-to-one could happen any time, sometimes even very late at night.

The house became my sanctuary of sanctuaries. It was here that I found understanding. Every hand reached out. Slowly, slowly, I told them what had happened to me.

Like dropping down a well on the end of a rope, out of the bright busy blur up above, into the darkness and silence and cold – for the very first time, I talked about my childhood. I thought they would beat me because I was dirty. Instead, they just listened, sometimes with tears in their eyes. I saw they were shocked – and yet they believed I was telling the truth.

And slowly, slowly, my words made me real. They helped me to become a proper child.

***

Purley Women's Service had a relaxation room, with cushions and beanbags and low, soft lights. Two of the nurses suggested a massage. I said no. I won't let anybody touch me. Weeks later, I let them massage my hands, but only if two people were there all the time, and if I could draw rings around my wrists. Those lines in biro declared my boundaries. They mustn't go higher. They didn't.

I still found it very hard to eat. I never felt hungry and food seemed strange. One evening in the kitchen, one of the nurses made me toast. I hadn't asked for any; she just quietly put down the plate in front of me. I couldn't swallow a mouthful until everyone had gone. Then I started to cry. I couldn't believe she had given me food. She sat down beside me and smiled.

"Can I have a bit as well, then?"

I wasn't used to cooking or planning for my mealtimes. I'd never been taught, and certainly hadn't been interested so I didn't know what many quite common foods were. When they asked me to wash some lettuce, I did it in warm soapy water. One of my nurses, Connie, took me shopping on the bus: we went up to Surrey Street in Croydon, an old-style open-air fruit and veg market. Stallholders shouted out the prices of the goods. "Best bananas! Get your ripe bananas here!" We shopped, and patiently, Connie taught me what food was what. Together we worked out what I might like to eat.

***

I heard other people's stories. They had been through terrible things. I felt angry for what they'd had to bear. Listening, I saw more and more clearly that what had happened in my childhood was not normal. It had always been dreadful and wrong. I never understood that before.

But when someone remarked that my mother was evil, I was very upset and stormed from the room. I was starting to see that she too had been a victim. Like me, she was abused. If I wasn't to blame for my overwhelming pain, then I thought perhaps neither was she.

***

Drinking had never been my friend. Whatever I might have had, or even tried to reach for – boozing had taken it away. Drink was my deadly enemy. I saw this clearly now. But how could I ever live without it?

I followed the AA programme. From hour to hour, and sometimes from minute to minute, I tried not to run away to hide in a bottle. A group of us held three AA meetings a day. Mostly they took place in the garden, without much structure or plan. We read from the AA book and just shared how we felt.

I was very, very scared. Scared of drinking – and scared of not drinking. I'd agreed to be sober and I knew that if I drank, I'd lose what I had: the hope of remaining here and receiving help. But I was 54 years old, and since I was 18 in the army camp at Bicester, the bottle had been my oblivion. Now it was gone. What would I do when the nightmares came for me?

It's hard to change. It's such a terrible risk. What if I tried to start a new life and still failed? What if I never escaped from hospitals and nurses and care? Fear was everywhere. Fear of everything. Fear of the future and fear of the past. So stay here, stay in the present. Just work out how to live today.

***

I went to my first art therapy. "Draw what you feel," they said to me.

I sat there for 45 minutes. With five left to go, I grabbed my pencil and put a small dot – just the one – right in the middle of the paper. That's all you get. I wanted to know if anyone would hit me if I wouldn't do as I was told.

They didn't. I started to draw and in time to paint, not just on paper but right around the walls and then outside in the garden, until I had covered the fence. I drew a seascape, blue and green with white cresting waves and sailing ships. The garden shed became a stripey beach hut. Inside the house, a giant tiger stalked down the hall. There were Native Americans, Marilyn Monroe and James Dean, and Rudolph the red-nosed reindeer at the wheel of a bright pink Cadillac.

And somewhere along the way, I began to draw me. I drew Nicky. Nicky is a little girl with brown hair in bunches. She looks like a proper child.

***

But still, I could slip back down. Waves of self-hatred rose up and almost overwhelmed me.

When I talked about my mother, I felt dirty. I found that I wanted to scour myself until my skin was raw in the way she had done, to scrape away my worthlessness and everything about me that was wrong. I must have a shower – but one was not enough and I needed another. Suddenly I found I wanted five showers a day – then ten a day, twelve, fifteen. I tried and tried, but still I didn't feel that I was clean.

She takes off my clothes and lifts me into the bath. She pours jugs of water down my legs. She scrubs until I bleed. The salt blood smell rises. The water runs down and makes a brownish puddle at my feet.

The harder she scours, the higher and louder her voice becomes. She's nearly screaming through white lips that scarcely move: "Bitch! Horrible little bitch!"

The nurses came with me. They stood outside the shower to talk to me and help me not to hurt myself again.

***

I rise up, but sometimes fall back.

I'm sitting outside in the garden. There's a huge fallen tree trunk. It must have come down in the storm of '87, says Laura, which did awful damage round here. Ivy has lashed it to the ground. I feel close to the tree – like me, it was torn from its roots and thrown down to be trapped and confined.

It starts to rain. I sit on the trunk. The rain grows harder. I'm soaked through and frozen. That seems right. The outside of me matches the inside now. Guilt. Pain. Remorse.

Then I feel an arm around my shoulders. A nurse drapes a coat across my back and my head. She leads me by the hand towards the house.

***

"Earth Mother", I call her, though not to her face. It's my name for Laura, the woman who runs this place. Earth Mother wanted me to live when I didn't want to live at all. I still don't understand her reasons, or why she would care about me.

I spill out my pain to her. I want her to take it away. The pictures, the voices – when will they leave me? She tells me that it will take time, but I'm angry. I need the pain to stop now. Sometimes it feels like a battle between us – my demands and my fury versus her patient reassurance. She repeats and repeats that the end will come.

***

Is she telling the truth? Is there ever an end? At night, I see pictures. I see all the terror of the past.

A white-shirted man with dark shiny shoes and a strange little smile is standing in my room. I hide my face and tell myself again and again he isn't really there. But my eyes go on seeing him, in nightmares that don't belong to sleep.

Sometimes a small dark-haired boy is crouching on the floor. He's naked, facing away from me. I see brownish smears on his thin white backside and all down the side of his leg to his knee. The soles of his feet are pink and clean. The blood smell is everywhere. He covers his face with his fists so I won't see him cry.

I scream out in panic. Make it stop make it stop make it stop!

The nurse puts the light on and talks gently. She brings a warm drink and plays music that's peaceful and quiet. She stays as long as I need her. Slowly, slowly, the pictures start to fade.

Earth Mother believes me, feeds me, holds me. She cares for the child without a face.

***

I tried to talk about Dog, but I couldn't. I told them that he was my friend – that I loved him. I told them that he died. After that, I could feel myself falling, disconnecting, vanishing into the dark. After the session, I went out into the garden.

I crouched down beside the tree trunk and clung to it. A long time passed. Night came. It grew colder and colder. For so many years I had never felt the cold.

The nurses came outside to find me. I'd frozen to the tree. My hands were stuck to its bark; there was ice on my skin. They fetched insulating blankets and gently tried to warm me, until they could pull me away.

***

There are no short cuts.

As my recovery continued, I returned to my sheltered flat in Addiscombe, and went on with therapy as an outpatient. But sometimes when I talked about my past, the horror was still beyond bearing. I suffered a series of breakdowns.

Feelings I had drowned in alcohol rose up and at times it seemed that they would overwhelm me. I had always turned away from them before, terrified that facing them would be too much. But denying them had never been the answer, and drink had only made things worse. Still, it seemed as if all I could do was splinter into pieces. Would I ever find the strength to rebuild?

I was admitted to hospital 103 times between 1999 and 2005. Sometimes I returned to Purley Women's Service and at other times I was sent to the Bethlem Hospital in Bromley or Purley Hospital. A visit might last just a week or two, or it could last a couple of months. There were times when my journey of hope seemed never-ending.

***

And then one day, I was done.

Done with mental hospitals.

Done with drinking and spliffs and wipe-outs and not knowing what's just happened.

Done with never being safe.

Done with living in squats and with sleeping on the street, with hiding in vans, being frightened, being lonely.

Done with all of it.

Most of all – done with the guilt and the shame which were never really mine. They made me my own abuser.

Earth Mother told me the truth. In the end, I was ready to leave it all behind me and move on.

***

There were so many firsts in my new life and the learning curve goes on.

My first trip to the theatre: going up to London's West End to see The Lion King. My first holiday, in Wales. Meals in a cafe. My first guests at home, and working out what I should offer them. A series of uncertain attempts to make sandwiches. Finding out how to use my first washing machine.

One of my visitors was Gail. I contacted her and she came to Croydon from Crawley to see me. I was able to thank her for the way she'd tried to help me, even though at the time I wasn't able to respond. We are friends to this day.

***

In 2000, I was invited to take part in the Mental Health Testimony Project. I was one of 50 patients and former patients of psychiatric institutions who were interviewed on video, to create an archive of experiences which is now in the British Library. My testimony is number 18.

An American professor, Gail Hornstein, got in touch with me after she saw my video testimony. She was in England on a visiting professorship at the University of London. She visited me in Croydon and interviewed me for her book, *Agnes's Jacket: A Psychologist's Search For The Meanings of Madness*, published by Rodale Press in 2009.

When we first met, I was very apprehensive. I had only just started therapy and distrusted most people. I couldn't believe that what I said could be of value to her. When she sent me a signed copy of her book, I was dumbfounded that she had written a whole chapter about me. In a letter, she told me that she lectured on my story to psychiatry students in Massachusetts.

I began to appreciate that Professor Hornstein is a great ambassador for the mentally ill. Just like Joe Whitty, she saw me not as a bad person trying to be good but a very disturbed person trying to get well. I drew strength from this.

My story now forms part of the national and international record of trauma, mental illness and recovery in the twentieth century. I hope that it can help others on their own journeys to health.

***

Most exciting of all is my work as an artist.

The Bethlem Hospital in Bromley, south London, displays the work of its patients in the Bethlem Gallery there. Paintings I had done while I was in the hospital were exhibited, and later this work was shown at the Novus Art Gallery in central London.

I'd started to visit the city more often, loving its buildings and architecture. One of my favourites is Southwark Cathedral, close to Borough High Street. Its beauty is tucked away, glimpsed from the trains to and from Charing Cross. Just across the road, the gleaming Shard reaches for the sky.

On a visit with a friend, I saw that the cathedral was undergoing restoration. I decided to donate a painting to sell, to help them raise funds. I painted 'Rainy Day In Southwark' and took it along in a carrier bag. When I tried to give it to someone in the cathedral's shop, she insisted on taking me to talk to the manager. The cathedral asked me if I could do more work for them, so that they could use the images on greetings cards. I'd never thought of selling my art like that before, but I was very pleased with the cards when they were printed.

I was offered my first solo exhibition at a cafe in Croydon. When my work was displayed, more offers followed. Before long, my paintings were hanging in galleries, coffee shops and community centres across the town. My cards were sold in hotels and charity shops. I was interviewed by the local papers and invited on the radio.

Selling my work was a big shock at first. If I'm honest, it still feels that way. I was embarrassed when people started to recognise me. I was stopped a few times in Croydon by people asking for my autograph! I was even asked to cut a ribbon at the opening of a bank branch.

So many people have helped me, and I wanted to give something back. So I donate my greetings cards and postcards to several charities, especially those that help the homeless. I have visited and even made friends back in Stoke, and I donate my paintings to charities there too.

I talk at AA meetings – once in front of 2000 people at a conference. I speak in prisons. I spoke at Southwark Cathedral in support of its Robes charity, which helps the homeless.

My very first talk was close to my home, at St Mildred's Church community centre in Addiscombe. I was very nervous. Then, at the end, people started to approach me. Some of them told me about their problems, bad memories and difficult past experiences. They thanked me – and if you can deal with all of this, so can we, they said. That's when I realised that my words could help others.

Telling my story gives me the chance to spread a message of hope to all victims of abuse. Yes, it's hard sometimes, but life can get better.

I wish my prison governor, Joe Whitty, was still here. Sadly, he died in 2013. If he could see me now, I hope he'd say, "I'm proud of you, toe-rag."

***

But it's not quite over. It will never entirely be done. I know that. The night terrors come. Choking in my throat. Panic wings, lashing in my body. Pictures on my eyes.

I painted Dog. First of all, he went on a Christmas card which sold well in Croydon, and later in other paintings. He's been to so many places! One day, I had an idea. I remembered the heartbeat clocks in Askham Grange: how much the girls loved to hear ticking, reminding them of home. Back then, I could get two rollies for the night-time loan of a clock.

These days, I have a clock of my own. So I painted Dog on its face. Dog's clock is by my bed – and yes, I sleep in a bed now, at last. If I'm frightened at night, I look at him and hear the clock ticking. The heartbeat of my first and truest friend is with me, keeping me safe until morning.

Chapter Twelve

Nicky in her own words

These days, I have a ceiling. In squats, you can often look up straight into the sky.

I am a Croydonite! After all those years of struggle and trauma, I have a town, a home and my first sense of belonging somewhere. I shared my life with a bottle. Now I share it with many other people. When I found a home in Croydon, I could begin my life as I had always dreamed.

First of all – my art. It was a real emotional struggle to buy canvas and acrylic paint. It was so hard that I asked my carer, Jenny, to carry my first canvas from the art shop in Croydon to my home. How to use the new materials was a mystery, but the next day I took the plunge and squirted different colours all over the canvas, using my hands and a palette knife. It's hard to describe my feelings: a mixture of excitement and fear.

I slowly realised that my soul was appearing on the canvas. The child in me came alive in my paintings – and so did Dog! I painted my pain. I paid homage to beautiful Dog. I painted the secrets I had held. It was a journey of discovery.

Now I am able to do something I could never do in my years as a homeless person. I can give back to society. I am able to help as much as I can the people who are now experiencing the same things I had gone through.

I still have a deep sense of bewilderment at the success of my work at exhibitions. I struggle with exhibiting, nervous about hanging my soul on walls. I am sometimes almost in tears, seeing my work there and watching people buy it. It can be difficult to talk to them and believe that their reactions are really for me. But I have been encouraged and supported by remarkable friends.

I feel that through my art, I have grown. I will never be whole, but I am about a half of a proper person.

Painting has pulled me towards an unknown destiny. It has given me self-respect and the strength to keep on going. Each swirl of paint through my fingers, each colour that floats across the canvas, revives my enthusiasm to live my dream. I am able to tell myself that I am good at at least one thing, when as a child I was convinced by abusers that I was useless and good for nothing.

Yes, I still have post-traumatic stress disorder, still have flashbacks and night terrors, but in my heart I realise that I am safe and able to combat these fears by expressing all this on canvas. I have been very lucky to meet special people at the right time.

I've also had some contact with my family, and filled in some of the gaps in my knowledge of the past. I still don't know what happened to my mother and her husband after the police became involved and I was returned to Stoke. I heard Holloway Prison mentioned once. Eventually, their family also moved back to Stoke. I know little about my half-siblings except that the eldest died aged only 42.

I managed to contact my Auntie Opal's family, but found it difficult. There's been too much vodka under the bridge, and too much silence too. It was my family's silence which created the deep belief in me that everything that happened to me must be my own fault. But my cousin Ken, Opal's son, is a lovely man, and the image of his mum. In 2016, he said that he loved me. I had waited 71 years to hear this from a family member. Nowadays I feel that he and his partner, Kath, are my only real family.

Nicky Nicholls

I learned that my mother had died long ago, back in 1967, at the very young age of 42. At the time she died, I was homeless and living in Bradford. She is buried in Stoke, and in 2014 a bout of depression and detachment led me to search for her grave.

This was the person who gave me life. Sometimes I think of what she went through: she ran away from her abusive father while the Second World War was raging. She gave birth at a time when unmarried mothers were put in mental hospitals. She must have been terribly afraid.

I remember, in and out of blankness, that I stood by her grave in Stoke and told her about my friends, about my success as an artist and how I hoped she would be proud of me now. I showed her my paintings on my iPad. Later I was found there by police and carers. After that visit, I painted my mother a picture. Through this image, I showed her that she was a swan, a beautiful swan. I tried very hard to portray myself to her as a proper child, a pretty little girl who might one day be a ballerina. I so wanted to please her.

Having my story written has been a difficult decision. There were a number of reasons: to carry a message of hope to those too afraid to "tell" about their experiences of abuse, and to support my special charities and the work they do.

The last thing I want to say is very painful. When I first entered therapy, my psychiatrists accepted my manslaughter conviction. They explained to me that I had killed the lady in Manchester but that it had been a "proxy killing" – revenge on my abusive mother. Back then, I felt I had to accept what the doctors said. I was so vulnerable, and I knew that they were trying to help me.

Now I feel stronger. Through intensive work, I have recovered some memories of what happened that night. I do not believe that I killed that poor lady. I do not wish to cause further pain to her relatives. But one day I hope, whether I am dead or alive at that time, that my name will be cleared of the crime for which I was sentenced.

At my lowest moments, I feel that my memories have smashed

me into pieces and yet I have managed to glue myself together again. How shattered can one person be? How much more glue is there?

Yet there are also many times when I have a feeling of peace, and an overwhelming sense of gratitude. I achieved a lot when I was homeless, even if I didn't know it. And I achieve more on a daily basis by believing in myself and keeping on saying to myself: Yes! I made it!

Dedications

Dedicated to all survivors who have found the courage to speak and to all those who will.

Elizabeth Sheppard

***

I would like to dedicate this book to the following:

To the Prison Governor, the late and great Joe Whitty. A man who believed in reformation and re-education. He changed my life; he gave me the will to live it.

To my late mother Joyce (1925-1967). You gave me life and it's all that matters. Thank you so much.

To my dearest friend Gwen. A friend of forty years and a lady with a heart full of kindness. You were always there even when I didn't know where I was! You supported me through thick and thin. Thank you so much.

To all my dearest friends, Rene, Mike S. Natwest Bank.

My wonderful mental health carers, JD and JF.

To my blood cousin Ken and partner Kath. You made my family connection right. I love you for that.

To Stoke, where it all began. Thank you to my new family, the Love family. You have made up my own bedroom and given me a key to your home. Just imagine how great that feels! I won't have to be homeless again! Love the Loves!

To Paul Simpson, Tonie, Simone and Tracey and many more, thank you for your kindness and support.

Thank you to Mirror Books and all who have given great support.

Thank you Jon Dollin and all at Southwark Cathedral.

Thank you George Martin and all at The Robes Project.

Thank you the great St Mildreds Church and all of you that put so much care and love into the community.

Thank you Emel. My angel friend, my soulmate.

Thank you to my beautiful Sharma family.

Thank you Elizabeth Sheppard for your patience, your talent.

The final dedication is to a big character in this book.

Dog. My one and only childhood friend. We were abused, starved, but we played together. We had special moments of happiness.

Even after all these years, you are still my hero, and you are so loved by all who see you in my paintings.

You deserve this because you died trying to save me from abuse.

Hugging you Dog.

Nicky Nicholls